LOST MORAY
AND NAIRN

✳

LOST MORAY AND NAIRN

Bruce B. Bishop

BIRLINN

First published in 2010 by
Birlinn Limited
West Newington House
10 Newington Road
Edinburgh
EH9 1QS

www.birlinn.co.uk

ISBN: 978 1 84158 875 9 hardback
ISBN: 978 1 84158 925 1 paperback

British Library Cataloguing-in-Publication Data
A catalogue record for this book is available
from the British Library.

Design: Mark Blackadder

Printed and bound by MPG Books Limited, Bodmin

For Janet

CONTENTS

ACKNOWLEDGEMENTS

Acknowledgements are due to many individuals and organisations. Thanks go to Mr Graeme Wilson and his staff at the Moray Heritage Centre, and to the staff of the Historical Search Room at the National Archives of Scotland in Edinburgh. The Church of Scotland has kindly allowed the transcriptions of extracts from Kirk Session Minutes. Acknowledgements for photographs and other illustrations are due to the Moray Council Libraries and Museums Manager Alistair Campbell for his kindness in granting unlimited access to the Moray Council Library Service photographic collection; Dave Shillabeer of Nairn Museum who provided scanned images from the museum's extensive collection; and Mr and Mrs Gordon Black, Elgin.

INTRODUCTION

Viewed from the hills above Fochabers, or from Fogwatt on the road from Rothes to Elgin, or coming down from the Dava Moor above Lochindorb into Glenferness, the entire landscape of Lowland Moray is spread before us. The purple heather of the windswept and now barren moors and hills is left behind, and we cross the boundary line between the uplands and the coastal plain. The sparkling silver of the Moray Firth is in the distance, the whole scene framed by the distant hills of Caithness.

The earliest people to inhabit this land would have followed the retreating ice sheets northwards after the last great glaciation, a nomadic people who almost certainly came here across the land bridge which stretched from Europe across what is now the North Sea, but they have left us very little evidence of their presence.

As the climate improved the population gradually increased, the nomads settled down and a culture began to arise which laid the foundation for the later civilisation which was to become known as the Pictish people. It took time, generation after generation employed in clearing the great forests of the north and draining the coastal wetlands to provide land for agriculture. They established settlements which were eventually to become our towns and villages, fished the fast-flowing rivers, the Nairn, the Findhorn, the Lossie and the Spey, and even ventured out to sea in their primitive vessels.

The Romans came and went, the Vikings came and went, but the local way of life endured. True, the people incorporated the best of these other cultures, and almost certainly intermarried with them, but the sea to the north and the great arc of mountains to the south and the west preserved the independence of the northern Picts.

Christianity arrived, the missionary monks set up preaching stations, often using the old sites of pagan worship as a means of continuity, and sometimes incorporating and bending to their own use some of the old pagan festivals. People responded better if the change was gradual and not too drastic. Even when the missionaries moved on, these centres of worship were maintained and under their followers eventually became chapels and churches. The towns of Nairn, Forres and Elgin gradually expanded and were granted royal charters, so that they had the rights and privileges of royal burghs. The necklace of villages strung out along the sandy coastline of the Moray Firth provided not only fishing but trade, with other parts of Scotland and also much further afield. Parishes were established, and the Roman Catholic Church became all-powerful.

The common people had their small settlements; fermtouns and small villages, in which they lived and worked under the watchful eyes of the bishops and the priests for their spiritual and moral well-being, and under the firm hand of the landowner for their more everyday necessities such as food, employment and housing. By the late Middle Ages the lands of Moray and Nairn were held by several powerful families: the Inneses and the Gordons in the east; the Dunbars, Grants and Leslies in the centre; and to the west the Earl of Moray with his seat at Darnaway, the Brodies, the Cummings, the Roses of Kilravock and the family of Cawdor. These secular landlords, though, were of little significance when compared with the power of the Church. From the towering cathedral of Elgin, from the abbeys of Kinloss and Pluscarden and from the Priory of Urquhart, to name just some, the Church extended its web of power through the parish churches, the power of the priests and the clerks in holy orders, penetrated into every aspect of people's lives. Until the Reformation of the sixteenth century, the Church was the major landowner and they made certain that everybody knew it.

A microcosm of Scotland, the old Kingdom of Moray, the Province of Moray, whatever name you choose for it, was an independent, and to the southerners, probably a very annoying territory. Times changed though, as they inevitably will, and once the power of the Church was diminished, the landed families were free to impose change on the countryside. It was a gradual change, not really very evident until the second half of the eighteenth century, but, nevertheless, life did change. But perhaps the changes were not always for the better, as with the improvements in agriculture fewer people were needed to work the land, and emigration from Moray and Nairn, whether to other parts of Scotland, further south into England, or often to the new colonies in America and Australia, took many families away from their ancestral homeland.

The towns expanded through the nineteenth century, there were more mouths to feed, agriculture and trade expanded, fishing became a major industry and the coming of the railways revolutionised both travel and commerce.

So what have we now? A 'Province of Moray' – for what better all-inclusive term is there for Moray and Nairn? An area which still prides itself on its independence, for when the main roads to the south and the east are blocked with the winter snow, the airports are closed, and the railway companies find that they can't operate because it is the wrong kind of snow, the sea to the north and that great arc of mountains to the south and the west still preserve the last vestiges of the independence of the people of Moray and Nairn.

In this book we are going to look at 'Lost Moray and Nairn' – to find out what has vanished and what still remains in this proud province – from buildings and architecture to churches and abbeys, from farms and harbours to agriculture and industry. Above all, we will find out about a way of life which has evolved over many centuries but is now rapidly vanishing. Don't walk along the main street of Nairn, or Forres, or Elgin looking down at your feet, the people of Moray and Nairn are much too canny to drop any money! Look up; admire the graceful buildings, the scenery and the hills, and even sometimes the clear blue sky. Feel the wind (and there is plenty of it) on your face, smell the sea and the fields and the heather, and enjoy this beautiful land of Moray and Nairn.

CHAPTER 1

THE PREHISTORIC LANDSCAPE; PICTISH FORTS, ROMAN CAMPS AND 'VIKINGS'

BEFORE THE PICTS

This is an area where we really are delving into 'lost' times. The landscape of Moray and Nairn would originally have been covered by what was known as the Caledonian Forest, sometimes called the Atlantic Forest. Apart from the high summits of the mountains in the south, the whole land lay under the shadow of this endless blanket of trees. Only down on the coast, where the land became marshy, did the forest thin out, but even here the great oak forests extended almost down to the shoreline in some places, especially along the shores of the sea lochs such as the Loch of Spynie. Just looking around carefully we can find evidence of continuous habitation from the Neolithic period right up to the present day in several places. In the upper valley of the River Nairn and in the middle reaches of Strathspey there are the ruins of cairns, there are earthworks such as the henge at Quarrywood to the west of Elgin and there are also various stone circles, or at least their remnants, which seem to occur mainly to the east of Elgin. Cup-marked stones such as those on Roseisle give a good indication of the ritual use of some of these sites.

Some of the early flint-working sites have been identified at various places including Culbin, the Findhorn sands and also in the parish of Urquhart. Some burial mounds have been identified, at Roseisle and near to Fochabers, with several other finds being made of artefacts dating to the Neolithic period. The arrival of the Beaker people from the Rhineland led to a considerable increase in the population during the 500 years leading up to 1500 BC, and the assimilation of these immigrants into the local population gave rise to more ornate burials. These new-fashioned cist graves were often found grouped together, maybe forming a cemetery for a homestead or a group of dwellings. The largest of these cemeteries which has been found so far is the one at Burgie. By about 1000 BC,

OPPOSITE. An earlier civilization – crop marks at Nether Dallachy.

however, this style of burial seems to have gone out of fashion, and there is little evidence of any interments from this date until the early Christian period.

The weather gradually deteriorated during the years 1000 BC to 500 BC; the climate became colder and this must have seriously affected the livelihood of the native population. The tree-line became lower, and those upland areas which had already been cleared of trees were no longer suitable for raising crops of grain. This led to a gradual expansion of stock-rearing in the higher areas, meaning that such a large population was not needed, and probably could not have been sustained anyway. There is still evidence of some of these early field boundaries in the upland areas, however, and of the small cairns of stones which these early farmers had, in milder times, removed from their fields to make cultivation more profitable.

These changes in agriculture meant that the main focus of economic activity, based around arable crops, had now shifted to the lowlands of Moray and Nairn, and this was to provide a sound basis for the Pictish culture which was to follow.

PICTISH MORAY

The lowlands of Moray and Nairn were of vital importance during the time of the Pictish people, being the heartland of one of several self-contained 'kingdoms', which in due course made up a 'Pictish Confederation' embracing the whole of Scotland north of the Forth from about the third century AD until the ninth century. Being isolated from the rest of Scotland by the inhospitable and almost impenetrable arc of mountains to the south and the west, Pictish Moray, 'Fidich' or 'Muref' was, unlike some of the Pictlands further south, easily able to develop its own cultural identity and an economy which was focused to a great extent on the area around what was then the very extensive Loch of Spynie. The fertile lands which had been cleared from the forests provided land for extensive grain production, and this was supplemented by hunting in what remained of the forests, and there was also fishing in the Moray Firth, the Loch of Spynie and the clear fast-flowing rivers.

An example of Pictish engineering is the fort at Burghead, which was probably constructed during the fourth century, during the rise to power of the Pictish people. It used a similar style of construction to the ones at the Doune of Relugas and at Cluny Hill in Forres; and the building techniques for this, and probably many other forts, were probably introduced into Scotland in the Early Iron Age. This fort at Burghead makes use of the two different levels of the headland, which were each enclosed by massive ramparts, with gateways on the south-east sides. A further three parallel earthworks or ramparts stretched across the neck of the peninsula. There are suggestions that the original walls were some 30 feet thick at the base, and about 30 feet high. The face of the wall was set back at intervals in its height, giving something of a step-like appearance, the outer face being of massive undressed boulders while the inner face was made from dressed red sandstone flags. To the people of the time, especially to those who had come to the area with evil intent, it must have provided a forbidding spectacle. There may have been timber buildings within each of the levels of the fort, to serve as dwellings, storerooms and offices, and there is evidence that it was in use until the ninth century. The ruins may have been reoccupied whenever there was a possible Viking threat from the north.

By the sixth and seventh centuries the Pictish peoples of the area had begun to come under the influence of Christianity, as the site of the chapel of St Aethan at Burghead would indicate. This was probably connected with St Aidan or Aeda, a follower of St Columba, c. AD 563. Other later places of Christian worship followed, exemplified in the many small preaching stations such as Kinneddar, Spynie, Birnie, Bellie and also probably at Unthank, Keam and Duffus, many of them around the shores of the old Loch of Spynie. During the following centuries, this Christian presence was to be expanded by missionary preachers such as Gervadius, or St Gerardine, who was known to have been at Kinneddar in AD 934. This period saw Kinneddar become one of the holy places of the north-east, and a castle or fortification, later to become known as the Bishop's Palace, was established there.

The use of place names starting with the Pictish 'pit' – indicative of an area which had been cleared for agriculture and settlement – is quite extensive in Moray, but not so common further west into Nairnshire. Many of the carved stones in the area were probably produced by a Pictish 'school' of masons working from Kinneddar, on the shores of the Loch of Spynie, under the protection of what was possibly another Pictish fort nearby. The portrayal of such well articulated, recognisable animals, of grotesque creatures such as the fish monster on the stone found at Upper Manbeen, and of hunting and battle scenes such as those on Sueno's Stone show a versatility of the mason's work which makes it difficult for us to ascertain the precise purpose of these carved stones. What becomes clear, however, is the impact of the arrival of Christianity in Moray and Nairn, and the symbiosis of Christian and Pre-Christian motifs on the later stones.

The impact of the Romans on the native Pictish society was minimal; their presence at best could be described as transient, which meant that the Pictish society which existed following any contact with the Romans was virtually unchanged from the earlier cultures, and the Pictish masons who used their talents to create the beautiful carved stones were continuing a tradition which dated back long before any Roman feet ever trod the ground of Moray or Nairn.

ROMAN MORAY

The evidence for this Roman 'visitation' – this is probably a better description than 'occupation' – of Moray is somewhat sketchy, but is gradually increasing. The Roman Camp at Bellie was very well defined, until almost all traces of it were obliterated by agriculture and forestry and the building of the airfield at Dallachy. The Roman army on their expeditions through the north-east of Scotland certainly reached the Pass of Grange, and were probably planning to meet up with their naval forces in the estuary of the River Spey, hence the camp at Bellie, but only tentative suggestions have been made as to their actual route north of Grange. They must have reached and crossed the Spey, as indicated by the Roman coins which were found in large numbers at Birnie and other Roman finds in the Sculptor's Cave at Covesea. There are suggestions that the coins found at Birnie were part of a payment or even a bribe to the local Pictish chief, to keep him on side. The camps which the Romans established in Moray were almost certainly the most northerly ones in their exploratory and possibly punitive expeditions into the territories of the northern Picts.

Further west, in Nairnshire, there are suggestions that there was a Roman fort or camp at Easter Galcantray beside the River Nairn. This may indicate that the Roman army also came north by a different route, probably over Drumochter and down the valley of the River Nairn, but whether they met up with the other forces approaching from the east will always be a matter for speculation.

VIKING MORAY

There almost certainly never was a 'Viking' Moray or Nairn. The coastline of Moray and Nairn would have been clearly visible to the Norsemen who settled and ruled the northern Mainland, Orkney and Shetland, and it would have been a very tempting prospect to these people in their search for new lands as they escaped from their overcrowded homelands. Various expeditions would have allowed Jarl Sigurd and other leaders to establish temporary strongholds, probably including one at Burghead, towards the end of the ninth and into the tenth centuries, but the fact that there are so few place names with a Norse derivation would indicate that little or no attempt was made to create permanent settlements. Over the course of the following century, the local rulers gradually regained control of the situation, often by reaching peaceful agreements with the Norsemen, and they were then in a good position to take advantage of the power vacuum following the death of Sigurd the Stout at the Battle of Clontarf in 1014. This allowed the Province of Moray to consolidate under its 'mormaer', or king, that man of such exceptional ability, Macbeth.

CHAPTER 2
SEA AND SAND, THE CHANGING COASTLINE

Although to resident and visitor alike the coastline of the Moray Firth seems to be a picturesque permanence, it has been, and still is, in a state of almost continual change. These changes have not only affected the coast itself, but have also been felt for some distance inland. The lands occupied by the early parishes of Dyke, Moy and more especially Culbin probably bore the brunt of various inundations of the North Sea, as did the coastal marshes surrounding the Loch of Spynie and the other sea lochs in that area, and these events must surely account for much of what is now lost. These inundations were

An early print of Spynie Palace

mentioned in the Red Book of the Priory of Pluscarden as happening *c*.1010, by Boethius *c*.1100 and by Fordun as quoted in Lord Hailes's 'Annals' in 1266. Whether these were three separate events or just reiterations of the one catastrophe we will never know, but it is evident that the geography of the coastline of this part of Morayshire underwent dramatic changes. How this affected the early population is, of course, unrecorded, and the effects on their lives can only be imagined. The vast quantities of sand deposited during this time continued to spread over the land for the next 700 years, overwhelming some parts of Moray and Nairn with a deep cover of dry sand which was to create problems for centuries to come.

CULBIN

Although the Culbin Forest is now a popular place for walkers and for picnics, the sands which have been gradually stabilised by the planting of trees hide a grim secret. This is a story of the possible consequences of a very small change in the climatic conditions which had a devastating effect on the inhabitants of Culbin and the nearby estates.

Back in the seventeenth century passers-by on the King's High Way between Nairn and Forres could not fail to notice the Mavistoun Hills, on the boundary between the parishes of Auldearn and Dyke, and they frequently commented on them. The pure white gleaming sand was a landmark for miles around. They had been formed by the constant westward drift of sand along the coast of the Moray Firth, and many thousands or even millions of tons of this fine dry sand came to rest, forming these sandhills. Beautiful though they may have appeared, they posed a constant threat to the farmers and crofters of the parishes to the east: Dyke, Moy and Culbin. These were areas of rich agricultural land, and when the prevailing winds blew a gale in from the west, the farmers must have kept a wary eye on how much sand was drifting across their lands. Although the hills were an ever-present fact of life, it was only really during the second half of the seventeenth century that they began to become a more serious threat. Whether this was down to climatic change leading to an increase in the prevailing wind speeds, or due to the stripping of the thin turf and bents which had formed on the sandhills, or even whether the quantity of sand had reached some sort of a 'tipping point' we will never know, but move they did, reaching a climax in the autumn of 1694 and the spring of 1695.

The estate of Culbin was centred on the mansion house of the Kinnairds, which according to popular lore was a large square building of dressed stone, situated within a beautiful garden with lawns and orchards, and of course, as with all mansion houses, a doocot. The estate itself was sometimes referred to as the garden and granary of Moray, with some 16 farms and farmhouses in total. To the east of Culbin lay the River Findhorn, with many fishermen's cottages along its western shore to take advantage of the very profitable salmon fishings. Being at one time a parish in its own right, there would also have been a small kirk or a chapel to serve the people of the estate.

On 29 March 1672, the diary of Brodie of Brodie simply states, 'This day Esterbin was buried.' This very ambiguous entry may simply have been a comment on the funeral of the Laird of Easter Bin, or maybe this was a precursor to the burial of the lands of Easter Bin a quarter of a century later beneath the sandhills encroaching from the west? We will never know.

Although there were various small drifts of sand across the fields during that time, it was not until autumn 1694 that the real disaster struck. The great sand drift came out of the west one autumn day; it came suddenly, with little warning. The story goes that reapers in a field of barley had to abandon their crop to the mercy of the sand, and a man ploughing his field had to leave his plough halfway along a furrow. The stinging force of the blowing sand would have been more than man or beast could bear. In a few hours, the whole area was buried beneath the sands as the storm spread eastwards. The dry sand swept in among the thatched turf dwellings of the cottars, and even engulfed the mansion house and its gardens.

The following day the sand had formed such deep drifts that the people had to force a way out of their houses, and in a lull in the storm they were able to rescue their beasts and get them to safety. The storm then began to increase again, and they had to flee for their lives, taking with them only what they could carry. The sand, in its eastward progress, choked the mouth of the River Findhorn, which was to lead to a further disaster for the people of that village (as mentioned in a later chapter). When the storm had eventually abated, the people of Culbin returned to their homes, but were amazed by what they found. No trace of the mansion house, the cottages, the kirk or the doocot was to be seen; the entire estate was buried beneath one vast expanse of sand.

The lack of local stone for building in this area had proved to be a major problem, and little apart from the mansion house and the kirk would have been built of this material. Much of the bent or broom which had formerly consolidated the sandhills would have been pulled to use as a thatch on the turf houses of the cottars, and there is little doubt that this action by the tenants destroyed any natural stabilisation of the dunes which had begun to take place.

The thin turf which had begun to form over the shingle ridges nearer to the beach was also stripped to be used as a building material, or mixed in with the middens to make compost, thereby exacerbating the problem.

These problems were taken very seriously, and led to an Act of Parliament in the late seventeenth century, which may have been intended as a warning to those living in other coastal parishes. Under the Reference K Will III 1 Par 5 Sefs Act XXX, the 'Act for the Preservation of Meadowes, Lands and Pastureages lying adjacent to Sand Hills' stated:

> Considering that the Barony of Cowbin, and house and yards thereof, lying within the Shirriffdom of Elgin, is quite ruined and overspread with sand, the which was occasioned by the foresaid bad practice of pulling the bent and juniper, therefore His Majesty with advice and consent of the estates of Parliament . . . does strictly prohibit and discharge the pulling of bent, broom or juniper off sand hills . . .

Looking back on these events, the minister of the parish of Dyke and Moy, putting pen to paper for his *Statistical Account* of the parish about a century afterwards, noted that 'The gradual encroachments of sand have long continued to affect the neighbouring cultivated land, and a large proportion of the three Mavistoun Hills has been deposited in the north of the parish. The Barony of Culbin was most exposed, and the gradual encroachment led to diminutions of rent and population. It was only at the end of the [seventeenth] century that the mansion house and gardens were overwhelmed, and the mansion house removed to Ernhill, the remaining corner of the Culbin estate.'

Young, in his History of the Parish of Spynie, comments that:

> In the autumn of 1694 and the spring of 1695 Morayshire was visited with a terrible calamity. The coast of the Firth had long been covered with sand, which the currents of the tides carried westwards and threw up into large hills between Nairn and Forres, where it got perfectly dry. Public attention had not been much attracted to that process of nature; but the high winds of these and subsequent years forced the sands eastwards, and dissipated it over the rich Barony of Culbin to its almost total destruction. The River Findhorn was choked up and forced into a new channel. The sand crossed that river and blew eastwards to Burghead, Roseisle, Inverugie and Stotfield, crossed the River Lossie and desolated the country half way to Garmouth.

Over the years, before the sands were stabilised by the planting of the forest, there was a lot of movement of the sandhills. Local tradition has it that a portion of the old mansion house was exposed by the winds about a century after the event, and that when the old kirk and the doocot were exposed some of the stone was taken by the neighbouring farmers for their own buildings. It is even rumoured that at one time the orchard was exposed again, and some of the old trees actually blossomed and bore fruit before the whole area was once more engulfed by the shifting sands.

So the estate of Culbin was lost for ever; the family of Kinnaird, despite a petition to Parliament for an exemption from land tax, were forced to sell out and apply for personal protection against their creditors. Although the laird and his wife, with their son who was aged but a few months and his nurse, had managed to escape the devastation of that night, by 1698 the estate was sold for what little it was now worth, and the laird and his wife died just a few years later. The boy was taken by his nurse to Edinburgh and later enlisted in the army, but died without issue in the 1740s, thereby ending the line of the family of Kinnaird.

THE LOCH OF SPYNIE

The history of much of Moray is inexorably linked with the variations in the extent of the Loch of Spynie and the nearby Loch of Roseisle to the west and the Loch of Cotts to the east, north of where Innes House now stands. In early times the sea entered the lowlands of Moray from the west at what is now Burghead Bay, and extended eastwards through the lands of Roseisle and Kintrae to meet the Moray Firth in a wide area of marshland and salt flats to the south-east of where the town of Lossiemouth now stands. The River Findhorn, originally known as the Erne, probably flowed into this channel of the sea somewhere just to the west of Alves, while the River Lossie had its mouth in the mudflats and marshes in the vicinity of Calcots.

There was probably also a channel to the sea at the western end of Coulardhill, across what is now the golf course, which would have meant that the ridge of land extending eastward from Burghead, through the Hill of Roseisle and Keam, and north of Duffus to Covesea was an island, as was the Coulardhill. There were doubtless many other smaller islands, especially near to the central part of the loch. The appearance of the coastline at that time would have been totally different to the way we know it now.

Even as recently as AD 800–900 the sea channel was still in existence, bordered on either side by marshes, the home to a wide variety of water fowl. These marshlands were backed with woodlands of alder, gradually merging into the remnants of the great oak forests of lowland Moray. There are suggestions that the Vikings were able to sail their longships through the channel from Burghead to Kinneddar as recently as the tenth century, and there is a possibility that the small vessels which were in use at that time were able to negotiate the marshes and reed beds from the sea to the mouth of the River Lossie, near the present farm of Calcots and the Kirk of St Andrew at Kirkhill. They may even have been able to penetrate as far as Elgin itself, as borne out by the Water Yett, or Water Gate of the College of Elgin, which is now better known as the Pans Port. Some writers have hypothesised that the Vikings may have found Burghead useful as a fort, a harbour, and probably a place to build or repair their ships, as the great forests had not, by this time, totally disappeared, but any thoughts of a permanent base must have been quickly abandoned as the incomers were, within a few decades, overwhelmed by the local Picts.

By the eleventh century the islands in the Loch of Spynie and the areas of shallow wetlands were becoming more extensive, as the longshore drift from Spey Bay slowly began to close up the eastern entrance from the sea. Sometime during the last decade of that century, as mentioned earlier, there are suggestions that a great storm, which affected all of eastern Britain, was the trigger which started the closure of the sea passage between Burghead and Lossiemouth. One source comments that in '1092, in the same year, many uncouth things came to pass and were seen in Albion. By the Spring Tides which chances in the Almaine seas (the North Sea) many towns, castells and woods were drowned, as well in Scotland as in England . . . moreover sundrie castels and towns in Murreyland were overthrane by the sea tides.' Boethius, speaking of 'an exundation of the German Ocean' in 1097, says, 'The lands of Moray in Scotland were desolated by the sea, castles subverted from the foundation, some villages destroyed, and the culture of man defeated by a discharge of sand from the sea. Monstrous thunderings came on, roaring so loudly horrible, in such tremendous crashing, that many men in the fields were struck, some cattle were killed, and by their shock also even towers were prostrated.' One wonders whether this could in fact have been a tsunami which affected the Moray Firth at this time. Despite the discrepancy in dates, it is likely that both authors are commenting on the same event. A similar event was described by Fordun in 1266, but whether this is just a reiteration of the earlier event or a later recurrence is unclear.

Maybe these catastrophic events, or possibly a much more gradual process, led to the fact that from the twelfth century onwards the channel between Burghead and Spynie gradually silted up, due in no small part to the quantities of sand which blew across the area from the west. As this happened, the western access to the sea was obstructed first, which then prevented any scouring effect of the tides, eventually resulting in the channels between the various parts of the sea loch becoming impassable.

THE POWER OF THE CHURCH

In early times the bishops of Moray had their seat at Spynie, Birnie or Kinneddar, as they chose, and it was not until 1207 that they decided to fix the 'Cathedral' of Moray at Spynie, later to be transferred to Elgin. The bishops held total authority over the Loch of Spynie, which had now become separated from the Loch of Roseisle in the west by sandbars and from the Loch of Cotts in the east by encroaching shingle banks. The bishops jealously guarded their rights to the navigations on the loch, and maintained a port at Spynie, with access to the sea at the eastern edge of Stotfield Hill where Lossiemouth now stands. There are many well-documented cases of disputes with the burgesses or merchants of Elgin over the following centuries. There are also some indications that there was also a small harbour at Kinneddar, or at least an area suitable for beaching and unloading vessels, but the documentary evidence is fragmentary apart from mentions of a former warehouse there. At a point just to the south of Duffus Castle were the 'Bishop's Steps', a causeway across one of the shallowest parts of the loch to allow the clergy to cross from Spynie to Duffus and other places on the northern shore.

By the year 1480 the shingle bars encroaching from the east had completely cut off the seaward entrance to the loch, and the bishops had, despite their best efforts, now lost the use of their own private port at Spynie. They were now obliged to use either Garmouth or Findhorn, at considerable financial burden as the fees charged by the merchants there were quite high. The other option was to land some of the smaller vessels at the Hythe of Stotfield. As even the Church could not compete with the seas of the Moray Firth, the bishops decided that it would make more economic sense to drain parts of the loch, thus providing more agricultural land which would further enhance their revenues. Good fertile land was reclaimed right up until the time of the Reformation, which in Moray seems to have covered an extended period between 1560 and about 1568. As a consequence of the Reformation, however, the bishops were no longer required to attend to the drainage of the Loch of

Spynie Palace and the old village of Spynie

Spynie, as the lands had fallen into the possession of the Crown who had in turn granted them to favoured landowners. Bishop Patrick Hepburn, who had been Bishop of Moray since 1535, had numerous children by several women, and provided for many of them, both sons and daughters, often giving them lands out of the possessions of the Bishopric and Abbacy. 'He outlived and braved the Reformation, and continued his former mode of life in his Palace and Castle of Spyny, and continued his profuse alienation of church lands till his death, from old age, on 20th June 1573.'

Being cut off from the sea, and with the drainage abandoned, the loch now began to re-establish itself as an attractive inland freshwater lake, probably nowhere more than about 10 feet deep, and in most parts only 4 or 5 feet deep. With its many islands, known as 'holms', it was able to provide sporting facilities for the newly wealthy landowners. Wildfowl were abundant, but with the

River Lossie now having its own channel to the east of the loch, contemporary sources suggest that the only fish in the loch were pike and eels.

A ROYAL VISITOR

In the autumn of 1562 there was a royal visit to Spynie Palace by Mary Queen of Scots. 'Well served of her subjects, and conveyed by great numbers of horse and foot', she arrived there on 17 September and departed two days later. Douglas, in romantic style, comments: 'Down a grassy avenue from Spynie Castle lay the Loch of Spynie. Can we picture Mary Queen of Scots on her famous visit to Moray in 1562 taking a stroll down this green path for a row on the loch . . . and accompanied perhaps by the notorious Bothwell? This fine expanse of inland water in the beauty and quietness of Moray would present opportunities not to be missed.'

Hollinshead, writing a few years after Mary's visit, records that

In this region is a lake named Spiney, wherein is exceeding plenty of swans. The cause of their increase in this place is ascribed to a certain herbe which groweth there in great abundance, and whose seed is verie pleasant unto the said foule in the eating, wherefore they call it Swangirs . . . for albeit that this lake be five miles in length, it was sometime within the remembrance of man verie well stored with samon and other fish, yet after this herbe began to multiplie upon the same, it became so shallow that one may now wade through the greater part thereof.

THE DEMISE OF
THE LOCH OF SPYNIE

Farms and settlements such as Westerfolds, Salterhill, Ballormie and Ardivot graced the northern shore of the loch, and a ferry was in operation between Salterhill and Lochside, near Myreside on the southern shore. In 1783 John Brander of Pitgaveny and other neighbouring landowners proposed plans to follow the example of the early bishops and once again consider the draining of the loch. Although it would have created a lot of new agricultural land, this scheme was looked upon with considerable disfavour by the lairds of Gordonstoun, who were not only anxious about losing the income from their

Gordonstoun House looking south across the Loch of Spynie

ferry service, but probably more importantly their sporting rights on the loch. After much dispute the parties in favour of drainage prevailed, and with the help of a scheme designed by Thomas Telford in the early nineteenth century the water level of the loch was gradually reduced by means of a canal to Lossiemouth, until by the mid nineteenth century only a small corner of the loch remained, just to the north-east of Spynie Palace.

CHAPTER 3

CASTLES AND MANSION HOUSES

HOMES AND RUINS

In a book of 'lost' places, buildings and ways of life, it is quite difficult to decide what to include when it comes to the castles and mansion houses of Moray and Nairn. Some of them, such as Cawdor, Brodie, Lethen, Darnaway and Gordon Castle at Fochabers, while they may in some cases have changed in size, are still very impressive family homes, certainly not 'lost', and indeed a few of them are open to the public. Others have decayed into ruin or disuse, and

Westerton House near Pluscarden, now demolished

Relugas House and gardens, now demolished

several have vanished entirely from the landscape. The castles of Nairn, Forres and Elgin are all discussed in the appropriate chapter on each burgh.

SURVIVING CASTLES AND HOUSES

Let us think about the things which may not be apparent to a visitor to one of the surviving buildings. For example, there are no surviving remains of the former House of Calder, or Old Cawdor as it was also known, which was the family seat of the thanes of Cawdor right up until the middle of the fifteenth century. It would appear from some antiquarian sources, however, that the old 'castle' was a fortified house with a dry ditch and a drawbridge and was on a site which was later levelled for the building of Brackla Airfield during the Second World War. The old 'castle' was replaced in about 1454 by the initial developments of the existing castle, which gradually evolved into its present state.

The seventeenth-century Kilravock Castle was originally built as a quadrilateral keep in the fifteenth century, although some aspects of its design would

Kilravock Castle

have led one to think that it was maybe a century earlier than this. The outline of this old keep was lost to some extent when the castle was enlarged by the common manner of adding a square staircase to the south-west angle with a large rectangular building attached in order to form an imposing south frontage.

Old Lethen House was lost in the winter of 1653–54 when the Royalist forces under the Earl of Glencairn besieged the house. The barns and houses were all set alight, and the mansion house was destroyed. The Brodie family, according to Hugh Miller, met at the ruined house on the last day of January 1654 'in that dreary season amid the blackened and wasted walls, where every streamlet was swollen into a river, and the winds howled amid the roofless and darkened turrets'. Whether the house was rebuilt and lived in once more at that time we may never know, perhaps it just stayed as a mouldering ruin until work on the new Lethen House was started in 1785. The two-storey west wing was completed just five years later but the matching east wing was not completed for almost another century.

Brodie Castle has been the seat of the Brodie family since the eleventh century. Some of the earlier structure may now be lost within the Z-plan tower which was built in 1567. In 1645 Lord Lewis Gordon attacked the castle, burning and plundering, and most of the old family documents were lost. A great part of the sixteenth-century structure has survived, although little of it can be seen now as there have been so many modifications and renovations to the old castle.

Darnaway Castle was built at the instigation of Thomas Randolph, regent to King David II during the king's minority. It was the principal residence of the earls of Moray since the late Middle Ages. The old structure is now lost apart from the imposing great hall, which was built in about 1540, the open timber roof being one of the few surviving examples of such a feature. When the new castle was built in 1810, in front of the old structure, only the great hall was retained, linked to the new mansion, but the walls of the old building were modified to such an extent that all that really remains of the old castle is the timber roof.

The history of the estate of Innes and nearby Leuchars is very closely connected to the rise and fall of the family of Innes. The earliest house to be built at Innes would most likely have been a wooden structure, maybe dating

An early print of Brodie Castle

Darnaway Castle

from just after the grant of the lands by King Malcolm IV to Berowald de Flandrensis in about the year 1157. This was almost certainly situated on the mound or motte to the north-east of the present house, variously referred to as the 'Knights Hillock' or the 'Castle Mound'. At that time the site chosen for this lay on the southern shore of the Loch of Cotts, on an 'innis' or island from which the family took their name. It would only have been accessible to those who had an intimate knowledge of the ways through the mist-shrouded bogs and alder groves. It may also, in early days, have had a limited tidal access to the sea. Apart from the mound, all trace of the old castle of Innes is now gone, and by the fourteenth or fifteenth century the mansion house built nearby would have almost certainly been some kind of fortified tower, which then gradually evolved during the seventeenth and eighteenth centuries into its present form.

The Grant family first acquired lands in Strathspey in about 1346, when Sir John Grant, the great-grandson of Gregory de Grant, Sheriff-Principal of Inverness, Ross, Sutherland and Caithness, received the lands as a royal gift from King David II. Sir Duncan de Grant, the eighth in descent from Gregory, is named in a Charter under the Great Seal dated 1442 as 'Dominus de eodem et de Freuchie', which may well tell us that there was a castle or fortified dwelling house owned by the family of Grant at least a century before Castle Grant came into existence. All traces of the old castle are now lost or are submerged deep within the present castle. The early history of even the second, characteristically L-shaped sixteenth-century castle is unclear, and in many documents from the later part of the seventeenth century the castle was known as 'Bella Chastell'. It is obvious that by the start of the eighteenth century the old Castle of Freuchie, or Castle Grant, was not the most comfortable place to live, and Sir James Grant and Sir Ludovick Grant spent several decades, and no doubt vast amounts of money, completely submerging the last traces of the old buildings in a new construction to bring it up to the standards of the time.

George Gordon, second Earl of Huntly, began building old Gordon Castle at the Bog o' Gight sometime after 1479, and his grandson, George Gordon made considerable extensions and improvements to the castle, which by 1672 had developed into the magnificent moated Renaissance palace as illustrated by John Slezer. The old castle was, in the fashion of the times, probably built to a Z-plan, dominated by a huge six-storey, flat-roofed tower, with a block of buildings linking it to a further tower on the far side. Following the Revolution of 1689, while the Presbyterian Brodies and Roses gave thanks for their delivery from the rule of the 'Papists', the Gordons remained loyal to the Stewarts. The once palatial Huntly Castle had by now been abandoned and allowed to fall into ruin, and the Gordons were now spending heavily on their new home at Gordon Castle.

The old castle is now lost except for the original tower. In 1769 Alexander, fourth Duke of Gordon and eighteenth 'Gudeman o' the Bog' commissioned the

Castle Grant in the eighteenth century

The old Gordon Castle before rebuilding

Gordon Castle after the rebuilding

architect John Baxter to rebuild the castle, specifying only that part of the original tower should be retained. This resulted in a castellated building some 538 feet long, described by McKean as 'a tedious quarter mile of two-storeyed crenalated regularity', which must have involved the servant classes in a great deal of walking. The Reverend Mr Leslie, the minister of Bellie, writing in the early 1790s, takes a more charitable view, suggesting that the frontage was 568 feet long from east to west, 'being however of different depths, the breaks make a variety of light and shade which takes off the appearance of excess in uniformity.'

There are, though, some castles and mansions which are more obviously lost to the public, whether because they are now inaccessible or have just vanished totally from the landscape.

THE LOST OR INACCESSIBLE CASTLES AND MANSION HOUSES

LOCHINDORB

*

The thirteenth-century castle of Lochindorb occupied almost an entire island in that bleak loch, surrounded by inhospitable moorland. There is some archaeological evidence that the island on which the castle stands is not entirely natural, and some parts of the island seem to be man-made additions. This confirms suggestions made in the eighteenth century that the entire island on which the castle stands is an artificial mound.

The castle took the form of an uneven rectangle with round towers at each corner, the walls being about 7 feet thick and some 20 feet high. Edward I stayed for a month at the castle in 1303 on his military progress around the north of Scotland. Catherine de Beaumont, the widow of David de Hastings, Earl of Atholl, lived at Lochindorb in 1335, and the next year it was held under siege by Andrew de Moray, this siege eventually being raised by Edward III. Andrew de Moray then beat a retreat to Darnaway Castle. Lochindorb seems, probably due to its isolated position, to have undertaken the role of a prison by 1342 at which time William Bulloch, a great favourite of King David, died there of cold and hunger. Lochindorb Castle, however, is perhaps better known as the home of Alexander Stewart, the 'Wolf of Badenoch', who lived there from 1372 and used it as a base for his expeditions to burn Elgin, Pluscarden and Forres in 1390.

Following the death of Alexander Stewart, the ownership of the castle is unclear, but by 1455 it was in the hands of Archibald Douglas, the Earl of Moray. The following year, following the earl's death at Arkinholm, the castle which he had fortified against the king was ordered to be destroyed. The work of dismantling it was entrusted to the Thane of Cawdor, who seems to have done just enough to make the building unusable. Many of the walls, however, still stand to their full original height. There are traces of buildings along the south wall of the main enclosure, the most westerly one being known as 'The Chapel'.

ASLEISK

*

MacFarlane, writing in about 1720, comments that 'The next to the house of Monaughty is the House of Asleisk. It is a strong fencible house and hath a large heath hill and good pasture bounding to the south-east with the parish of Elgin, and to the south-west with the parish of Raffuird. Near to the house there is a physick well called the Rees Well and is very much used by such as are gravellish, of which house and lands and the toun of Monaughty the Laird of Brodie is proprietor. The house of Asleisk was built by the Dunbars'. It would seem from these comments that although Asleisk was called a castle, it was in fact a fortified mansion house built in a very typical fourteenth-or fifteenth-century style. Virtually no trace of the old castle now remains.

EARNSIDE
*

Nothing is known about the old Castle of Earnside except that it was built by the Cumings of Altyre in about 1450. It probably had a relatively short useful life as castles go, as the desire for greater comfort, and the diminishing need for a defensive structure meant that it would soon have been replaced by a more comfortable mansion house. No trace of the castle now remains.

BLERVIE
*

The castle of Blervie, which dates from the twelfth century, was formerly known as Ulerin. At this time it was a royal residence held for the king by Alexander Comyn, the Earl of Buchan. There is evidence in the Exchequer Rolls of an account by Comyn to repair and garrison the castle in anticipation of an invasion by Haco or Hacon, king of Norway, in 1263. The original castle was built as a Z-plan structure with a tower, possibly circular, at the south-eastern corner.

In the sixteenth century the castle and lands of Blery or Blervie passed into the hands of the powerful Dunbar family, who added to the original structure. The square tower at the south-western corner was five storeys high, with a room on each floor and a flat roof. It was built for defence, with a raised parapet, bartizans at the corners, and gun loops and shot-holes. The first-floor fireplace which was exposed in the ruins carried a mantel with heraldic carvings and the date 1598.

In 1684 Patrick Dunbar, designated 'younger of Blervie', was the proprietor of the estate of Blervie. From 1712 to 1735 Alexander Mackintosh was Laird of Blervie, and also there were James Mackintosh from 1712 to 1733, William Mackintosh from 1729 to 1737 and Ludovick Mackintosh at the time of his father Alexander's death in 1735. No documentary records appear to have survived from the period when Blervie was owned by the Mackintosh family, and by the time the estate was purchased in the middle of the eighteenth century by William, Earl of Fife, the castle was derelict and the estate probably consisted of a mansion house and associated farms which now came under the ownership of the Seafield Estates. In 1776 Major Lewis Duff, the son of William, Earl of Fife, demolished much of the old castle to make use of the stones for the building of the present House of Blervie, but the tower resisted all attempts at demolition, and was left to stand until it gradually began to decay of old age. A mere fragment now exists but an etching of the castle is given in Rhind's 'Sketches of Moray' showing the building as it stood in 1839.

BURGIE

*

The old house of Burgie was almost certainly erected by the monks of Kinloss at some time prior to the Reformation, and most probably in the late twelfth or early thirteenth centuries. By 1602 this house was neither large nor imposing enough for the new proprietor, Robert Dunbar of Burgie, and the building of the 'old' castle was begun in 1602. In one of the walls a carved stone bears the initials AD and KR, for Alexander Dunbar and his wife Katherine Reid, and also the initials RD for Robert Dunbar. As Alexander had died in 1593, this stone was either a relic of the previous building or had been placed in the wall after his death by his wife or his son Robert.

In 1640 Robert Dunbar Jnr was served heir to his father Robert. The service was 'of the lands of Burgie', dated 20 November 1640, and 'of the lands of Bishopmill, Pittenkirk and Colliescruiks' dated obviously erroneously on 31 June 1643, with confirmation of titles of the lands of Over and Nether Hempriggs. Robert Dunbar had originally favoured the Covenanting cause during the Civil War, but by 1646 he had embraced the Royalist doctrines. By 1650, the time of his repentances for his actions during the Civil War, his fortunes were at a very low ebb, the estates mortgaged to the hilt. Just some examples of the pressures he was under become evident when in July 1650 his estates were 'attached' at the instance of Mary Davidson, the widow of an Edinburgh Writer to the Signet, and in November 1652 when they were 'attached' at the request of Sir John Baird of Cowbairdie as security for a loan of £5,000 Scots. They were 'attached' again in 1653 by Patrick Dunbar of Westerton. It seems as though everyone was chasing Robert Dunbar for money.

By 1660 he was beginning to sink under the pressure from his creditors, and three years later he was threatened with arrest for non-payment of his debts. He garrisoned himself in the house of Burgie, but by the decision of the Lords he was ordered to give up the house and appear for trial, which he refused to do. On 14 May 1663, John Spens, the Rothesay Herald, arrived at Burgie with all the pomp and paraphernalia of his office and summoned the occupants to surrender. The laird had already fled, and his wife Isobel Leslie surrendered the house by handing the keys to the Rothesay Herald. Robert Dunbar made his way to Edinburgh and sought refuge in the Abbey of Holyrude, availing himself of the right of sanctuary, but eventually he had to come out and was arrested. In 1665 he was freed, and was 'granted licence to eat flesh in the forbidden time of Lent'. Immediately after Lent he was imprisoned once more in the tolbooth of Elgin, and was forced for the next

The remains of the tower of Burgie Castle

month to endure the 'noisesome smell' of this foul and unsanitary building. He was freed by force by some of his friends, but did not enjoy his liberty for very long. By the following year his creditors were pursuing him with even more vigour, and he was unable to pay either the capital or the interest on his debts. He was eventually saved from prison and bankruptcy by Thomas Dunbar of West Grange, who purchased the 'Mains of Burgie, tower and lands thereof, Colliscruikis, Bogharberie, Berriemuiris, Craighead, Burnend of Tarras, Easter and Wester Lawrencetoun' on 10 April 1668, no doubt all at a knock-down price, but it was enough to save Robert Dunbar.

About a month after the sale, on 16 May, Thomas Dunbar, the new owner, had not yet taken up residence at Burgie, although his furniture and posses-sions were already there. Despite the fact that the former proprietor had directed that Thomas should be put 'in peaceable possession' this did not suit Robert, the son of the former owner. The problems are best described in Thomas Dunbar's own words in his complaint:

> Young Robert Dunbar, with a number of loose and dissolute persons, Alexander Petrie, Alexander Russell and other their accomplices, came upon 16th May last to the said house of Burgie armed with swords, guns, pistols, dirks and other weapons invasive, and did violently eject his uncle and his whole servants furth thereof, and seized upon his trunks, papers, jewels, gold and silver and furniture within the said house, planted themselves in form of a garrison therein, and made provisions for keeping out a siege.

The Earl of Moray, as a member of the Privy Council and Sheriff of Inverness, wrote to Robert Dunbar Jnr, ordering him to lay down his arms immediately and leave the house forthwith. When John Innes, messenger-at-arms, went to Burgie the following day with the letter, he was met with a display of force, and Robert Dunbar Jnr told the messenger that he would reply to the letter in his own good time. When the messenger reported this, the Privy Council arrested Robert Dunbar Snr yet again, and also Alexander Petrie, and they were imprisoned in Edinburgh. Events then moved rapidly, and under the threat of force of arms against them, the occupiers of Burgie surrendered at the end of July. Although Robert Dunbar had disponed the estate of Burgie to Thomas, he and his descendants continued to be known by the designation 'of Burgie', while Thomas and his descendants were designated 'of Grange' or 'of West Grange' until the end of the eighteenth century. Robert Dunbar Snr died in 1679, his wife Isobel Leslie died at Bishopmill on 10 January 1688, and was buried in Spynie Churchyard. In about 1680, after the new laird of Burgie had run deeply in debt to his cousin, Grange got possession of Burgie by adjudication, and made it his seat.

In 1722 Ludovick Dunbar of Grange and Burgie conveyed the lands to his four-year-old son Joseph Dunbar. Ludovick died on 1 November 1725, and in his will he nominated Joseph Brodie of Milntoun, John Dunbar of Burgie, James Dunbar of Kilnflat and Patrick Dunbar of Bowermadden as the curators of his young son. Their irresponsible handling of the estate seems to have gradually led young Joseph Dunbar into a financial crisis. He put all of these financial problems down to the mismanagement of his father's executry and the reluctance of his tenants to pay their dues, either in money or in kind. This may have been a result of the primitive runrig methods of agriculture being used at the time. He also lays some of the blame on the 'prodigious quantities of grain' now being imported. The pressure from his creditors caused many headaches, and by August 1741, at the age of just 23, Joseph had decided to personally take control of the accounts and finances of the Dunbar estates of Burgie and West Grange. By October of that year his credit standing in Forres and Elgin was in such a precarious state that he, being down to his last pair of stockings, was unable to purchase more; none of the merchants were willing to give him credit and he had no ready money. All of these events were noted in his diary, but throughout the remainder of 'Joseph Dunbar – His Book', the writing gets smaller and more illegible, the ink-blots more numerous, and there seems to be no light at the end of the tunnel.

It must have taken a long time to pay off debts of £31,000 Scots, but little further detail of the fortunes of Joseph Dunbar is recorded during the following four decades, so things must ultimately have got better. Joseph Dunbar of Burgie and Grange, having, in 1788, expressed his intention to sell the lands, died on 7 October 1794, at the age of 79, and was buried in Rafford Churchyard.

In the *Old Statistical Account*, written in the same year, the minister comments that 'The house of Burgee is the seat of Dunbar of Grange'. He describes it as a large and beautiful fabric, a square tower of six storeys built in 1602 and an adjoining mansion founded about a century later. The gardens occupy several acres, contain a variety of fruit trees and are skirted with double rows of fine spreading beech trees. 'In approaching this place, which is very conspicuous, the mind is powerfully impressed with an idea of ancient magnificence.'

In November 1801, Lewis Dunbar put forward specifications for a new house to be built at Burgie and specified that 'In general the whole of the work to be executed in a plain and substantial manner . . .' The greater part of the old building was demolished in the process of building the new house, and all that now remains of the old castle is a square tower, part of what was originally a typical Z-plan building, and a small portion of the main block with the coat of arms above the fireplace as mentioned earlier.

MILTONDUFF HOUSE

*

The old Mansion House of Miltonduff was built in about the year 1640, and has been described as 'an ancient and picturesque building'. The grey walls are said to have been of immense thickness, and mostly covered by pear trees. The theory that these pear trees were originally planted by the monks of Pluscarden is most unlikely, as, by 1640, some 80 years after the Reformation, the last monk ever to be recorded as living at the abbey until recent times had been dead for nearly half a century.

The house was described as being 'one of the most interesting and curious dwellings ever visited', and there are also extensive references to its pleasure gardens and fruit gardens.

The earliest references to Milton are found in a Charter of Excambion dated 23 March 1309, at which time it is apparent that all of these lands were under the ownership of Adam, son of Stephen, Burgess of Elgin. (This was in the days before surnames were in common usage.)

What happened to the lands following the Reformation of 1560 is unclear, but eventually, in about 1640 or 1650, the lands of Milton and Inverlochty were purchased by Francis Brodie, the sixth son of David Brodie of Brodie, and it was probably at his instigation that the 'Mansion House of Milton Brodie' was built. In 1673 Francis Brodie left the estate to his son, probably the man identified in 1685 as Francis Brodie, 'an Elder of the Kirk of Elgin'.

On 5 June 1730 Joseph Brodie of Milnetoun was declared heir to the deceased Francis Brodie of Innerlochtie, but later that year the lands and estates were sold to William Lord Braco. It seems to have been some time before the Brodies relinquished their hold on the estate of Milton Brodie, and on General Roy's Map of the area in 1747 the house is still referred to as Milton Brodie House, the map showing the house and its gardens very clearly.

It must have been about 1750 when a branch of the Duff family finally took up residence at the Mansion House of Miltonduff, the first resident probably being the Right Honourable George Duff, the third son of William Lord Braco, by now designated the Earl of Fife.

So the name of the estate, and of the neighbouring community, was changed from Milton Brodie to Milton Duff, a common event when such valuable lands changed hands. George Duff, however, did not seem to want to stay at Miltonduff, probably having a much more palatial dwelling elsewhere among the vast estates of the Duff family, or maybe preferring his town house in Elgin. So on 29 May 1769 he placed an advertisement in the *Aberdeen Journal* for the lease of the house:

> That upon Wednesday the fifteenth day of June next at three o'clock afternoon there is to be let by tack in public roup within the house of Robert Gordon, vintner in Elgin, for nineteen years after Whitsunday last – All and haill the Mains, Mills, Mansionhouse and Gardens of Milltown belonging to the Honourable George Duff Esq. The farm is of considerable extent pleasantly situated within two short miles of Elgin having a good house, an office houses, and well accommodated in moss [peat]. For particulars enquire at the proprietor at his house in Elgin or at Archibald Duff, Sheriff-Clerk of Elgin, his factor.

On the lands of Miltonduff House stood the doocot, which remains to this day, and was carefully conserved by the proprietors of the Miltonduff Distillery in 1970.

In 1798 the estate of the Honourable George Duff centred on the 'Mansion House of Milltown of Duff' was valued at £1189 9s 0d. During his time as landowner of Miltonduff, George Duff was responsible for the planting of a great deal of woodland on what had previously just been barren moorland, including the woods to the north of Miltonduff House and also towards Manbeen.

In the mid nineteenth century, the Honourable George Skene Duff, sold the Mansion House and estate to Alexander William George, Viscount MacDuff, the only son of the Earl of Fife. The house had for many years been let out to tenants, including Andrew Pearey, one of the founders of the Miltonduff Distillery, and by the 1870s it was owned by William Stuart of Aldroughty, a proprietor of the distillery.

Thomas Yool had been purchasing parts of the estate of Auchtertyre from the Earl of Fife, including part of Miltonduff, Pluscarden and Kellas. In 1897, after the death of William Stuart two years earlier, Thomas Yool bought the remainder of the Miltonduff Estate, including Muiryhall and the Distillery, from the executors of William Stuart, and the amalgamated properties in due course became known as the Auchtertyre Estate.

At one time about the turn of the century the Yool family had plans drawn to erect a new house on the site of the Mansion House, but this never came to fruition.

The Mansion House had by now been reduced to the status of little more than a farmhouse, but the layout of the buildings as shown on the 1905 OS Map still gives some idea of its former glory, despite all the more recent farm buildings surrounding this once beautiful mansion house.

It deteriorated gradually through the years, until it became virtually uninhabitable by the middle of the twentieth century and was demolished in the 1970s. All that remain now are a few of the old trees which once marked the boundary of the gardens, and of course, the doocot.

DUFFUS

*

Duffus Castle, standing prominently above the former Loch of Spynie, dates from about 1151, when King David I undermined the northern resistance by his introduction of Norman noblemen to the north of Scotland. The castle comprised a large outer bailey, with a surrounding moat, with a walled and ditched inner bailey, surrounding a great stone keep on top of the motte. The moat may well have originally only been on the northern side of the castle, which was built on an artificial promontory extending into what was then the loch. Hugo de Freskyn from Strabock in West Lothian was transplanted to Moray from which he drew his title 'de Moravia'. In the late thirteenth century it was held by Sir Reginald le Cheyne for Edward I.

Originally the castle would have had a wooden palisade protecting the bailey. This proved little defence in 1297 when the castle was burned by the Scottish patriots under Andrew de Moray. Moray led a rising in the north contemporary with that led by William Wallace in the south of Scotland, and on 11 September 1297 a joint force of the troops of Wallace and Moray routed the Earl of Surrey's English army at the battle of Stirling Bridge. Andrew de Moray was later to die of the wounds he received in that battle.

The central three-storey keep of the castle dates from the rebuilding following the events of 1297, as did the stone-built curtain wall, but it was sacked again in 1452. Following this, various new buildings, including a great hall, were built against the north curtain wall. With the draining of the Loch of Spynie which had once surrounded it, and the changes in the social life of Moray during the sixteenth and seventeenth centuries, the castle, which in its later years was sometimes described as being the 'summer residence' of Alexander Lord Duffus, was finally abandoned in the late seventeenth century. The enormous weight of the masonry on top of the artificial mound on which it was built eventually proved too much, and parts of the castle gradually began to slip down the slope. Duffus House, a 'gentleman's residence' was built to the north of the old castle and next door to the estate of Gordonstoun. This 'gentleman's residence' was much more in keeping with the fashions of the times.

COXTON TOWER
*

The estate of Coxton is mentioned as early as 1529, when James Stewart, the Earl of Moray, received a charter of the lands from his father King James IV. Later in that century the Innes family became proprietors of Coxton. Coxton Tower is one of the more unusual buildings in Moray and Nairn, and is very similar to one of the old Borders towers in that it was built entirely of stone. The tower was built in the early years of the seventeenth century, certainly

Coxton Tower near Lhanbryde

before 1644, and some sources suggest that it may actually date back to the
sixteenth century. Sir Alexander Innes of Innermarkie seems to have feared
fire as much as foe, and the horrors resulting from the burning down of
Fendraught Castle in 1630 may account for the style of building, and of course
may indirectly help with the dating of the structure.

Apart from the two external doors, no wood was used anywhere in the
building, with each floor being stone vaulted. The vaulting is at opposite angles
on each floor, to help to balance the structural loads and to do away with any
need for external buttresses. The gable-ends of the tower are crow-stepped,
and the whole building is roofed with stone slabs. A removable ladder originally gave access to the main door on the first floor, but in about 1846 this was
replaced with a stone staircase. Over the entrance is a large armorial tablet,
bearing the initials R.A and A.I at the top and J.R and K.G at the base, with
the date 1644. There are few windows in the tower, the only ones being on the
south and west sides of the building. Some of these have shot-holes underneath for arrows and musketry, and, to quote McKean, the building is 'grossly
anachronistic for that date'.

ROTHES

*

The earliest mentions of Rothes are in the twelfth century, when the superiors
of Rothes, the de Polloc family, were recorded as having their residence in 'The
House of Rothayes', later described as the castle. This castle guarded an
important highway along the valley of the River Spey in the Middle Ages. The
de Polloc family had been introduced into Moray about 1160 by King William
the Lion in an attempt to curb the lawlessness of the Highlanders. Petrus or
Peter de Polloc who was described as the 'Lord of Rothayes', was witness to
Charters dated between 1189 and 1198. There was a thirteenth-century chapel
just to the south or south-west of the castle, said to have been situated 'within
the enclosure of the Castle Ground' and dedicated to 'Our Lady of Grace'. This
chapel is known to have had its own burial ground either within or just outside
the castle grounds. The hamlet of Rothes stood at the base of the castle hill but
some sources suggest that there was an even earlier settlement on the heights
of Ardcanny.

The great-granddaughter of Peter de Polloc married Sir Norman Lesly of
Lesly in 1286, and it must have been soon after this that this branch of the
Leslie family came to Rothes from the Garioch in Aberdeenshire, their
ancestral homeland.

Following his visit to the north of Scotland, and having held court in Elgin on 28 and 29 July 1296, King Edward and his 1,000-strong army decided to travel south by a different route to that which they had come north a few days earlier, and, leaving Elgin by the South Port and passing through the Moss of Strathcant (now called The Wards), they entered the forest of Longmorn, passing the old church and churchyard which now lie below the distillery there. This great forest had a keeper and, like the forests of the Enzie to the east and Darnaway to the west, it was carefully preserved and managed for the benefit of the king and other notables when they visited to hunt. Going by way of the Glen of Rothes, the royal party took up residence at Sir Norman Lesly's Castle of Rothes. Having earlier acknowledged the supremacy of the English king at Aberdeen, it was Sir Norman Lesly himself who managed to get back to his home in time to welcome the king to his 'manner house of Rothays' overlooking the River Spey.

On reaching Rothes on that summer Sunday afternoon in 1296, the king was arriving at the edge of a country where he was less popular. One of the first tasks was to send out detachments of troops to scour the neighbouring countryside, especially to search the lands of Badenoch, and they set up a garrison at Ruthven. Another force, made up of the Bishop of Durham's squadron of horse, was sent south over the mountains as a diversionary tactic – the mountains were still not under the control of anyone except for the local chiefs. After receiving submissions from other nobles, Edward and his troops crossed the Spey at the Ford of Ardentol, now Arndilly, and passing the old church there they left Moray at Mortlach, now known as Dufftown, on their way to the Cabrach and the Mearns. The enormous number of men involved in an expedition of this nature must have almost exhausted the resources of the entire countryside, and for the following few months the people of Moray probably suffered serious food shortages and all of the hardships which this would have generated.

The first Leslie who actually bore the name 'of Rothes' was Sir George, described a 'Dominus de Rothes' in a contract of marriage dated 26 April 1392. In 1457 or 1458 the Leslies were made earls of Rothes. They continued for almost two centuries to live at Rothes, but their main interests lay further south, and by 1620 the Leslies finally abandoned the Castle of Rothes and moved to Fife. This is how the village of Glenrothes in Fife derived its name, eventually becoming the new town which it is today.

The castle gradually fell into disrepair, and in 1662 the local villagers burned and destroyed the remains of the building, which had become a refuge for thieves and vagabonds. The area was by no means immune to the raids by the Highlanders out of Badenoch, and the old castle was said to have given them a good hiding place. The following apology is said to have been subscribed by one of the villagers and is dated 17 March 1662. 'Whereas the Right Noble Earl of Rothes is highly irritated for burning the "House of Rothayes" therefore I, John Innes, testify my submission and repentance for the same'. Whether the Earl of Rothes cared a jot whether his old castle had been burned down or not is never recorded, he was now well away from the scene.

CHAPTER 4

ABBEYS, PRIORIES AND MONASTERIES

The counties of Moray and Nairn were favoured by several of the monastic orders as an area where they could safely and profitably establish monasteries and also be of benefit to the local community. There is no doubt that they would also have received the support and encouragement of the king beyond the mountains as one more weapon in his royal armoury against the 'wild northern men'. The remains of Kinloss Abbey, and the restored Convent of Greyfriars in Elgin are evidence of this faith, and the rebuilt Abbey of Pluscarden continues to provide a haven of peace in the Vale of St Andrew to the west of Elgin.

KINLOSS

The foundation of St Mary's Cistercian Abbey of Kinloss was begun by King David I in about 1150, with a group of his favourite Cistercian monks being brought to Kinloss from Melrose Abbey. King David reputedly stayed at the nearby Castle of Duffus while the plans for the building of the abbey were finalised. In the abbey church were also eventually erected 11 chapels, these being the Chapels of the Holy Rood, St Mary, St Anne, St John the Evangelist, St Peter, St Andrew, St Magdeline, St Jerome, St Lawrence, St Bernard and St Thomas the Martyr. The marches or boundaries of the abbey lands were reputedly fixed by King David himself as including 'The brook falls into Massat (The Mosset Burn), the marsh down to the wood, the land on which the Scotch Mill stood, with the fishings and the lands of Eth, as possessed by Twethel (a landowner, possibly an early form of the name Tulloch) a net in the water of Eren (the River Erne or Findhorn), and the wood of Inchdamin.' Later additions included a mill on the Massat, and a ploughgate of Burgin or Burgie. These were all very profitable and would have provided a good income to the abbey.

The formal date of the foundation of the abbey is recorded as 20 June 1151, and the Royal Endowment was confirmed to Reinerius, the second abbot, by a bull of Pope Alexander III in 1174.

In the autumn of 1303 Edward I, having made Moray his ultimate target in his endeavours to force the Province of Moray and the far north of Scotland into submission, stayed at the Abbey for six weeks, and a detachment of his army remained there after his departure. He also seized Lochindorb, making this Comyn stronghold his base for about a month while he consolidated his position in the north-east. Kinloss Abbey was burnt by Edward III in 1336.

The monks were 'granted licence in that in the common brewery founded of old in the neighbourhood of their monastery they might also bake cakes in the oven . . . and furnish them to travellers and others at their own charge'. One isolated source suggests that, in common with many other monasteries in Scotland, the monks at Kinloss also provided a hospital there. The fifteenth abbot, Adam de Teras, who died in 1401, had been responsible for the completion of the Abbot's Hall in 1391. He was recorded as having 'lived lewdly and had issue in concubinage'.

Although the abbots of some of the smaller houses in Scotland were obliged at times to dispose of some of the assets of the religious houses due to shortage of money, the powerful mitred abbots of Kinloss had few such difficulties, but despite this Abbot James Guthry sold off many of the assets of the abbey in 1470, including the organ, a silver basin and a ewer, and had to be prevented from resetting the painting above the altar. William Galbraith, the twentieth abbot, was also the Subchanter of Moray, and probably spent much of his time at the College of Elgin, in the precincts surrounding the cathedral there. The valuable salmon fishing rights on the Findhorn were within the gift of the abbot, and it is recorded that in 1488 he granted certain of these rights to Urquhart of Burdsyards. He died in 1491 and is buried in the Chapel of St Peter in Kinloss Abbey. His successor, William Culross died in 1504, and his body was laid in the Chapel of St Thomas. Thomas Crystall, the twenty-second abbot, is referred to in many documents which relate to his disputes with the people of Forres over the rights to the fishing, mainly for salmon, at the mouth of the Findhorn. The abbot invariably seemed to have been successful in these disputes.

An inventory of the abbey was taken by Ferrerius in 1520, which showed that Kinloss had '150 feather beds, 28 arras coverings, 2 silk beds, and pewter vessels. The library was very well stocked and the church was ornamented with paintings, statues, organs and altars.' The lay brothers who served the Cistercian monks tilled land that was renowned for its fertility, and in the

sixteenth century the cultivation of fruit trees was one of the Kinloss special-
ities. In 1526 the records suggest that Abbot Robert Reid employed an expert
French gardener to supervise the care of the lands of the precinct. Reid, who
had become the administrative head of the abbey at that time, improved the
library and employed a celebrated artist to paint new altar-pieces for the three
chapels in the abbey kirk. In 1530 the Abbey lands were erected into a burgh of
barony at the instigation of Robert Reid.

On 12 August 1535 King James V wrote a letter to Francis, King of France,
advising him that he had appointed Robert, Abbot of Kinloss, as one of his
ambassadors to the French court. By 1540, however, it was becoming apparent
that Catholic power in Scotland would soon be facing a crisis, and the once
extensive library of the abbey had been reduced to only 20 books. In 1561, the
year following the Reformation, the revenues of the Abbey of Kinloss were
recorded as £1,152 1s 0d Scots, 47 chalders, 11 bolls, 1 firlot and 2 pecks of bear
and meal, 10 bolls, 3 firlots of oats, 34 wedders, 41 geese, 60 capons and 125
various poultry. This fairly modest income would indicate that the abbey was
already now in terminal decline.

Walter Reid, the Abbot of Kinloss who had supervised this period of the
Reformation, granted a charter of the lands in 1565 to Edward Bruce. In 1574
the bailiary of Kinloss was sold to Robert Colleas of Balnamoon and his son,
and the same year a marginal note on one of the pages of the manuscripts of

The ruins of Kinloss Abbey

Ferrerius in the Advocates Library records that 'the stepell of Kynlos fell the fyft day . . . . 1574'. It is interesting to note that the decay of the structure had already begun so soon after the Reformation.

By 1576 the abbey lands had fallen into the possession of Archibald Douglas of Pittendreich (near Elgin), the natural son to the regent, James, Earl of Morton. A Confirmation of the Bailies of Kinloss was granted by King James in favour of Archibald Douglas the following year. This process of redistribution of the church lands was later complicated by the revival of the monarchy from 1584 onwards, under James VI, who used his power to control the distribution of church lands in order to build up a Royalist interest among the remains of the feudal aristocracy. Abbot Walter Reid was dead by 1589, following which Edward Bruce is identified as 'Commendator of Kinloss' during disputes with other local landowners regarding fishing rights in the Bay of Findhorn. The Bruces were a lowland family associated with the crown. Much of the land was feued to local landowners or substantial tenant farmers, but they were often outbid for these feus by incomers prepared to pay a higher rental.

In 1650 Alexander Brodie of Lethen observed that 'the buildings were far more extensive than were requisite for a kirk, and the stones were excellently squared, large, and well-calculated for buildings of strength. Brodie agreed to provide a new place of worship for the parish, "with which they were well pleased" and then "had full liberty to pull the abbey to pieces" and with barbarous haste he did so, making traffic of the stones, many of which were bought (by Cromwell's soldiers) for the building of the Castle of Inverness.' The demolition of the abbey is well documented in correspondence between Joseph Brodie, Robert Innes of Muirtown, James Spence of Woodhead and others in November 1651:

> Whereas that part of the Abbacy of Kinlofs called the Chapter is and hath been since the Reformation of Religion in this Kingdome a public place for the preaching of the word, administration of the sacraments and marriage, and now by reasons of a Condecendance betwixt the Laird of Lethen and the English Garrison at Inverness the fabric of the Abbacie of Kinloss is taken down . . . it is agreed (between the Presbyteries of Elgin and Forres) . . . that there shall be a church and a particular congregation erected for Kinlofse and the people thereabout who are now almost without the means of the Gospel . . . and that we may have the happinefse be a Law to have a settled minister there as hath been agreed upon.

The names appended to the various documents at this time included Sir Robert Dunbar of Grangehill, James Spence of Woodhead, David Duncan in Kinloss, Moses Hill in Findhorn and John Brodie in Langcot, all of whom participated in the decisions regarding the proposed boundaries of the new parish.

Only a small part of the abbey was in use as a place of worship by the local population, and it was noted that 'The Laird of Lethen has offered an indefinite sum of money for building of a kirk and purchasing of a glebe and manse to a minister at Kinloss.'

Old engravings confirm the eighteenth-century descriptions of 'specimens of the most beautiful Gothic architecture'. Two rib-vaulted chambers, one converted into a chapel, part of the cloister walls and ruins of the abbots lodging were all that remained by the late eighteenth century.

During 1802 and 1803 part of the lands of the Barony of Kinloss was sold by Miss Anne Brodie to Mr William Forbes, and by about 1840, with only the side and gable walls of the abbey standing intact, the local people soon set about levelling them and using the abbey as a quarry for stone for building dykes and other farm offices. 'Had not the trustee of the estate, a gentleman of antiquarian tastes and attainments, interdicted the spoilation, and caused the east gable, which narrowly escaped destruction, to be propped by a buttress of mason work, not one stone would now remain of the abbey'.

Kinloss main street

PLUSCARDEN

The Abbey of Pluscarden was supposedly built in 1232, during the reign of King Alexander II, and in the Chartulary of the abbey one of the documents reads 'Anno MCCXLJ obiit Rex Alexander, qui fundavit Monasterium de Pluscardyne, et regnavit xxxij annis'. The decision of the king to establish an abbey on this site may have been motivated as much by the need to maintain good order in the area as by any religious motives. The wildness of the area at this time is borne out by the fact that in the years just after the foundation of the abbey the monks were allowed to set traps to catch the local wolves. Within the precincts of the abbey the monks had a corn mill, turned by a millwheel in a lade extending from the River Lochty, now known as the Black Burn.

Alexander Stewart, 'The Wolf of Badenoch', visited the abbey in 1390, probably while on his way to burn down the cathedral in Elgin. He seems to have raised fires at the abbey, but there is no contemporary record of the damage which he inflicted.

By about 1440 the prior and the Cistercian monks at Pluscarden were becoming very licentious, and were quite content to sit back and let the local hired servants do all the work. Although this arrangement was probably quite agreeable to the local population, providing a useful source of income, it was in direct contravention of the rules of the Cistercian order, and the monks were all expelled from the monastery. This took place at the time when John Flutere was the abbot, and when the Cistercians were banished from Pluscarden the Benedictines were introduced in their place.

Prior Robert Hawor was a very energetic leader, and landlord of the Pluscarden estates from 1487 until 1509, and just three years before the end of his term of office King James IV paid a visit to the abbey, at which time he made a gift 'to the Masons of Pluscardy xiiij shillings'. These new monks, however, seem to have been little better than their predecessors, and the Prior of Pluscarden in the years leading up to the Reformation of 1560, one Alexander Dunbar, was noted for his licentious habits. He had various relationships with the local women, and made provision for several of his brood of illegitimate children out of the lands of the abbey.

The period of the Reformation during the decade or more following 1560 must have created quite a change for the residents of this peaceful Glen of Pluscarden, or the Vale of St Andrew, as it was sometimes known. This change was not for the better; the local population had lived under the shadow of the great abbey for nearly 350 years and had been protected from any external

Pluscarden Abbey before partial restoration

violence or profiteering by the strong arm of the Catholic Church. Whatever had been the faults of the Popish clergy, they had at least been famed for their hospitality and kindness to the poor.

The author of the *Old Statistical Account* of 1793 summed it up very well:

The valley of Pluscarden is the only district in the country which seems to have suffered by the substitution of the Reformed for the Roman Catholic religion, by which they enjoyed the pompous establishment of the priory in the midst of this sequestered vale. The minds of the people were cheered throughout the day, and soothed even during the stillness of the midnight hour, by the solemn sound of the consecrated bells, calling the venerable inmates to their statutory devotions; and they had access to the consolations of sixteen Holy Men, in every season of distress, with the free and easy accommodation of the most splendid social worship; they had the means also of educating in the most commodious manner their little ones, in a share of the literature of the times. Now all is cold and silent, forlorn and melancholy desolation, no national establishment nor any private institution for their assistance in civil or religious erudiation within a distance of ten miles.

Maybe this author was right, but was there not a little shade of rose tinting on his spectacles?

Although the local people had been served by the occasional visiting preacher, who had maybe held services in the now ruined abbey, it was not until 1760 that they built a church just to the east of the monastery, on the low marshy lands of Netherbyre. By the 1830s this too had become a ruin, and was demolished. By now the abbey was owned by the Earl of Fife, and in about 1835 he allowed the congregation to fit up the old arched kitchen on the ground floor of the old abbey as a place of worship. This arrangement continued until the building of the new church in 1898.

BLACKFRIARS

The monastery or Friary of Blackfriars in Elgin really is a 'lost' building, and no plan or illustration of it exists. Sometimes also referred to as the Dominican Friary, it was situated just to the north of the castle, at the foot of Ladyhill. It was founded in 1233 or 1234 by Alexander II, and was dedicated to St James. It was in decline by the time of the Reformation, and all of the brethren had left before 1570. There are unsubstantiated reports that workmen on the site in the eighteenth or early nineteenth century found bones which may have been associated with a burial ground at the monastery, and Pococke commented in 1887 that some traces of the foundations were still visible, but there is now no trace of the site, overshadowed by the Elgin Leisure Centre, to be found.

GREYFRIARS

The Observantine House of the Franciscan Friars was founded in Elgin by Alexander II, and in 1479 it was moved to the site now occupied by the Convent of Mercy, or Greyfriars Church. At the time of the Reformation it fell out of ecclesiastical use and into the possession of the Burgh Council, and it was used as the Elgin Court of Justice by 1563. It was devastated by the Earl of Huntly at this time, and gradually fell into ruin, although it was later owned by the King family of Lesmurdie. By 1843 the whole site was a ruin, but half a century later the third Marquess of Bute provided funds for its restoration for use by the Sisters of Mercy.

The restoration work was planned by the architect John Kinross, and during the work the conventual buildings grouped around the courtyard to the south of the church were rebuilt on the old foundations, incorporating some fragments of the old structure. The original stone well still survives in the centre of the courtyard, and on some of the rafters in the refectory one can still see traces of the old medieval paintings.

The restored church contains some of the grave slabs and monuments of the King family of Lesmurdie, and is still in use as a place of worship. To the east of the buildings is the burial ground for the community of the Sisters of Mercy.

FRANCISCAN FRIARY OF ELGIN

In about 1821 the Franciscan Friars Minor Conventual received lands for the upkeep of those members of their order who 'for a time or in the future may be in occupation of their house in Elgin beside the Cathedral', but this must have been very temporary as the lands they had been gifted were soon used for other purposes. The order then moved to a site on the south side of the east end of the High Street, later the site of Dunfermline Cottage. This may well have included some of the lands of the Greyfriars Church as mentioned above. There is now no trace of this earlier establishment as the whole area around Dunfermline House was cleared to make way for a supermarket, which itself now lies derelict.

URQUHART

The Priory of Urquhart was a cell of the Benedictine Abbey of Dunfermline, and was founded by King David I in about the year 1125, in honour of the Blessed Trinity. In 1150–53, the king gave a grant to the Priory of Urquhart of the patronage of the Kirk of Bellie. This was at the time of the subjugation of Moray by the Scottish Crown following the defeat of the last of the line of the mormaers, or rulers, of Moray, and the foundation of this and other ecclesiastical sites in Moray are almost certainly another aspect of this subjugation.

A Papal Commission in 1394 narrates the rights, among those of other places, of the priories of Urquhart and Pluscarden, and another document reproduced in the Chartulary of Moray, reiterates an ancient charter in favour of Urquhart, which shows that at the time of the foundation of the priory it was granted the lands of Urqwhard, the two Finfans, the place of Fochober, with pasturage, a fishing in the Spey, an annual income of 20 shillings from the

Burgh of Elgin for clothes to the monks, and rights over all the lands in Moray which were held by the monks of Dunfermline. The lands immediately surrounding the priory may well be the 2 acres of the 'Holy Rood' as mentioned in a charter of 1545.

In the Constitution of Elgin Cathedral written sometime after 1224 there is no mention of a church at Urquhart, which may indicate that the priory was the only place of worship in the fledgling parish. Some other sources, however, indicate that the church was there before the priory. In the rentals of the churches or chapels c.1350 the priory is identified as 'Capellani de Urchard five Rethis de Spee'.

To quote from Cramond:

Little is known of the inner life of the priory. For long, no doubt, it had a fair and useful record, but in 1429 rumours of misdeeds reached the ears of the Abbot of Dunfermline, and in that year the Bishop of Moray addressed a letter to the Abbot granting his approval, as Bishop of the diocese in which the priory lay, of a visitation and inquiry regarding certain charges brought against the priory and Andrew Raeburn, the prior. At the same time the prior was summoned to appear before the Bishop, or Sir John Shaw, procurator of Dunfermline, within the priory chapel, to answer certain 'crimina, scelera et falgicia, defectus et deformitates'. The result of this inquiry is unknown.

Urquhart main street in the late nineteenth century

It is unlikely that at any one time, however, there were more than just the prior and four or five monks at Urquhart.

As already mentioned, the Priory of Pluscarden was undergoing a similarly troubled time, and after an existence of over 300 years the separate histories of the two priories came to an end. In 1453 a Papal Bull was issued by Pope Nicolas V, which incorporated Urquhart with the Priory of Pluscarden. The reason given was that there were only two monks at Urquhart and six at Pluscarden, and a union was desirable owing to the troubles of the time and the reduced revenues of the priories. After its incorporation with Pluscarden the Priory of Urquhart was allowed to fall into ruin, and in the rentals of 1565 there is no mention of it. In 1654 it is recorded that the remaining stones were carried off and used for the building of a granary at Garmouth.

The *Survey of the Province of Moray* in the 1790s comments that the ruins of the building are to be discovered with difficulty, in a hollow north-east of the present church of Urquhart. The current site known as 'Abbey Well' is the only memorial to the priory still remaining. Cramond gives directions as to how to find the site of the priory, to the north-east of the old church and burial ground, in the lands of Wester Clockeasy farm:

> Leaving the village of Urquhart, when just past the village 'arms', you find the main road leading to the railway station, but turn into another old road on the right, and, passing down it you observe traces of its windings ahead, even in the corn. In the hollow is now a ditch, and after passing from one field to another, but before crossing the ditch, you reach the site of the Abbey Well, now drained into the ditch. The site of the well is a few paces from the ditch at the angle formed by the ditch and the fence between the two fields. The site is within the field that reaches to the railway. Crossing the ditch and continuing in the same direction we then cross the railway, and find ourselves on a level piece of ground lying well to the sun, and nearly surrounded by a ditch. The uncultivated braes on the south side of the railway between the railway and the village are called the Abbey Bank. The priory site is east of the railway bridge, and in the course of ploughing the stones of the building are sometimes met with. Here also was found a bronze pot of uncertain age . . .

A carved wheel cross, built into the church hall, is the only surviving relic of the priory.

CHAPTER 5

SOME OF THE OLD PARISH CHURCHES

Moray and Nairn, in common with the rest of Scotland, was divided by the Church into parishes in the twelfth and thirteenth centuries. Due to the overriding power of the Church, the boundaries of these parishes then became the most important administrative delineations of the country from the point of view of the general population. The parishioners knew which church they must attend on Holy Days, and where they were going to be punished for their frequent misdemeanours, but also who they could turn to in times of need. The major landowners were sometimes in dispute about who had the rights to install a new minister in a parish, and held on to their rights of patronage with a fierce determination.

The parish structure survived unchanged for many centuries, and it was not until the early twentieth century that the parishes lost much of their significance to the local residents. Even to this day, however, the parishes are still a serious factor in the life of the congregations of the Church of Scotland.

So how was a parish structured? Before the Reformation the priest would have been chosen by the patron, who was usually a local laird, the nearest monastery or in some cases the diocesan bishop, but in any case the appointment would have to be approved by the bishop. After the Reformation, patronage was briefly abolished then reintroduced by Parliament after the Act of Union, but with the kirk session having right of veto. The patron in these post-Reformation times was usually the major landowner, with rights to install a minister of his choice, but sometimes, it seems, especially in the early days of the Established Church, that these appointments were made out of nepotism or even for financial considerations. This minister, once installed, was responsible for his kirk session, a body of gentlemen, sometimes elected, sometimes appointed, almost always quite prominent in local affairs, which effectively ran the life of the parish. The kirk session appointed a treasurer, responsible for the financial affairs of the parish, and a kirk officer, who was responsible for the more material affairs, such as the maintenance and cleaning of the kirk and the

Ardclach Bell Tower, the church being in a deep valley the belltower was built on the hill above

care of the churchyard, and who also often acted as gravedigger. The session was also responsible for discipline in the parish, and a glance through any set of Kirk Session Minutes will reveal the variety of cases which appeared before them.

The parish church was the focus of life for the community, but sadly many of the old churches have been replaced, and are crumbling into decay. Although the remains of the structure may still be standing, they have lost their place in the lives of the people around them. Some have been sold off and have been converted into houses and even pubs.

Some, such as Altyre, Dundurcas and Duffus, still show traces of their former glory, but at other places such as Spynie, Essil and Urquhart no trace of the old church remains. In some places part of the old church may have been converted into a burial aisle for a prominent local family, such as the Leslie Aisle at Rothes. The site of the old Kirk of Drainie now lies in the middle of the very active airfield at Lossiemouth, with only the outlines of the foundation of the church still being visible, and all of the surrounding tombstones have been laid flat in case an aircraft should veer off the runway.

Many of these old sites are well worth a visit, but some such as Altyre, on a private estate, and, of course, Drainie on RAF Lossiemouth, are not accessible.

DUNDURCAS

The old Kirk of Dundurcas dates back to the thirteenth century, if not earlier, and during the following centuries the kirk would have been surrounded to the north and the west by the Kirktown or village of Dundurcas itself, with a small mill. The original church is long gone, and the ruins of its replacement can be found on a promontory overlooking the valley of the River Spey. A small burn trickles past the churchyard, and it is difficult now to imagine how such an insignificant water supply could have powered the local mill, but there are traces still of the stonework which may have been linked with the water supply. The church was of an almost standard post-Reformation design, but the thatch on the roof must at some time have been replaced with slates, probably after 1760, as there is no mention of it in the Kirk Session Minutes.

In 1782 the parish was suppressed by order of the Boundaries Commission. The greater part of it was annexed to Rothes and the remainder to Boharm, and the parish church was closed at this time.

It is recorded that after the closure of the kirk two slaters came to remove the roof from the old church, as a means of ending the activities of an 'insane preacher' who continued to hold services there after the union of the parish with Rothes and Boharm. 'The women of the parish swooped down upon the slaters and stoned them from the churchyard. They tried to escape by wading across the Spey, in order to return to Keith, but one was drowned in the get-away.'

The journey down the track from the road above the kirk is well worth it if only for the peace and tranquillity of this delightfully mouldering churchyard and the rapidly decaying church.

DUFFUS (ST PETER'S)

The original village of Duffus was situated immediately to the north of Duffus House. St Peter's Kirk, which was physically, religiously and economically the focus of village and parish life, lay in the centre of the village. The houses surrounding the churchyard in earlier times, the Kirktoun of Duffus, are now all long gone, but they would have been little more than single-storey stone and daub structures with thatched roofs. Each cottage would have had a small area of garden on which to grow vegetables, and to keep a pig, maybe a cow, and some chickens. Each cottager would have also held strips of land in the runrig system, on which to grow bere (an early type of barley), corn or oats.

The old church, dedicated to St Peter, was in existence as early as 1226, and one of the oldest portions still to survive is the basement of what was once a western tower. In 1290 the name of the village and the parish was spelt 'Dufhus', later evolving through 'Duffous' into its present form. A Gothic porch was added by the rector Alexander Sutherland in 1524. The medieval mercat cross is situated in the churchyard, to the south of the ruined church, and this is a reminder that right up to the late seventeenth century this would have been the venue for the village markets. The table stones marking the last resting places of many of the better-off parishioners made excellent stalls for the display of wares. The churchyard has some exceptional examples of early tombstones, including a beautifully carved Calvary cross in a burial aisle to the east of the kirk. A cobbled roadway was laid around the outer perimeter of the churchyard by Cromwell's soldiers, who were garrisoned at Duffus in the aftermath of the Civil War. There is now no evidence of this roadway.

The medieval church was replaced by a new building in the eighteenth century, but the base of the western tower and Alexander Sutherland's porch were retained. The outside stairs on the north and east walls gave access to the timber lofts, and the sockets in the walls for the supports for these lofts can be clearly seen inside the building. It is well worth seeking out the key to have a look around inside the ruined, roofless remains of the old kirk.

Within the churchyard, especially to the south of the church, there are many excellent table stones and recumbent tombstones, with emblems of mortality and other carvings, many of which are Masonic emblems reflecting the local quarrying industry on the coast of the parish. There are also carvings of a maritime interest, a reminder of the rich fishing and merchant trades of the harbours of Burghead, Hopeman and Covesea. These stones have all recently been cleaned, recorded, drawn and photographed for posterity by the local Moray Burial Ground Research Group, but it is amazing how quickly they are recolonised by the all invasive green moss.

ALVES

Records suggest that the original church was stone-walled with a 'thack' or thatched roof, and on 17 March 1642 'The roofe and the thack of the queir being found ruinous therefore the sessione was appointed to see to the repairing of it.' The Presbytery agreed to these repairs on 8 November 1649, and various stents or taxes were imposed on the people of the parish. Many repairs were carried out between 1650 and 1663, resulting in the demolition of the 'queir' at the east end of the kirk, the building of a new east wall and the erection of lofts in the kirk to accommodate the increasing congregation. The seating in the kirk consisted of wooden planks supported on stones, and some private 'dasks' and pews. The congregation was segregated by sex, at least in the poorer classes, and the scholars were confined to one part of the kirk. On 31 May 1663, John Alves in Windiehills 'presented a desire to enlarge his dask, and the session considering that the Alves are ane honest and auncient family in the parish grant this desire'. By 1666 the planks and stones were becoming unsightly, and not in keeping with the newly restored church, and the owners were given until the autumn to 'put up decent seats'. In 1670 the wooden stair to the loft fell down, and was replaced by a 'handsome stone stair'. A loft was built in the east end of the church by John Russell in Easter Alves in 1684 for the use of his family and servants.

In 1769 the new Church of Alves was completed, with its belfry at the east end. It stood alongside and to the north of the earlier church. It had windows on the south side only, and was 75 feet by 25 feet. The pulpit was in the centre of the south wall, and a stone staircase on the outside of the south wall led to west and east galleries and a common loft on the north side. The church building went through many modifications during the course of the next century, but, although now derelict, it remains 'a model of Presbyterian severity, yet not without a simple dignity'.

ROTHES

The old kirk on the Burnside had been in use by the parish since the closure of the chapel at the castle. The last Catholic priest of Rothes, George Thomson, had left his chapel on the Chapel Hill and moved to the new church on the Burnside in 1555, no doubt in anticipation of the events which were to occur just five years later. Following the Reformation of 1560, he remained as the parish priest until the appointment of a Protestant minister in 1563. By the 1770s the church on the Burnside was falling into disrepair and, although during 1779 John Duncan had put in a new pillar to support the kirk loft and had also mended the stairs, this had not remedied the problems with the building, and it was still not considered safe enough for public worship. In November the Session Minutes record 'the kirk being quite out of repair'.

The following year we find 'the old kirk being now pulled down and materials gathering for building a new one beside the New Town . . .', and a footnote in the Session Minutes reveals that 'the New Kirk of Rothes was built in the year 1780 by Lord Findlater at [his] sole expence . . .' The new church, the one which still stands in the square, was built to a T-plan, of random rubble with tooled granite ashlar dressings. Although work on the new church may have been started in 1780, it was not completed for over a year.

There is now little evidence of the old Kirk of Rothes on the Burnside, but if you look down from the new cemetery on an autumn morning when the dew is heavy, you can still make out the outlines of the foundations of this lost church, just around the now rapidly decaying Leslie Aisle at the eastern side of the old churchyard. The black-coated tombstones surrounding it bear witness to the effects of the local distilleries.

ESSIL

The old church which served the parish of Essil was dedicated to St Peter the Apostle, and is mentioned in the early thirteenth century as the seat of the Sub-Treasurer of Elgin Cathedral. It served the parish for some five centuries, but there is little record of the history of the building itself.

The parishes of Essil and Dipple were amalgamated into the new parish of Speymouth in 1731, and after this the old church was allowed to fall into ruin. What few stones were useful from the ruin were 'quarried' by the local farmers for their walls and buildings, and the kirk was left to decay in the middle of its graveyard. Only two isolated fragments of the walls still survive, and these are now used to display memorial tablets, but although there is some doubt as to whether these are still in their original positions, excavations at the site suggest that these are in fact part of the outline of the old kirk of Essil.

BELLIE

The kirk at Bellie dates back to the twelfth century, although unlike the neighbouring churches of Dipple and Essil there is little documentation to verify this. Due to its location on what was at that time the east bank of the estuary of the River Spey, it may well have been built on the site of an early Christian preaching site, and originally have been little more than a simple cross near to a dwelling for an anchorite, or holy man. The first church would have been built of wood, or of boulders and clay, with a thatched roof. This would very soon have been replaced by a stone-built structure, probably in the form of a simple oblong, or less likely it may have been of a cruciform shape as at

Kinneddar. The divot-thatched roof would probably have remained throughout most of its life, although there is some evidence that the post-1730 building had a slated roof.

The church was dedicated to St Peter, and sometime between 1150 and 1153, during the reign of King David, the Priory of Urquhart was granted patronage of the Kirk of Bellie, and also the lands which included Finfenn (Finfan), to the west of the Spey, and Fochoper (Fochabers) to the east. The site of the church is shown on Pont's map of the late sixteenth century, and again on Gordon's map of 1640, showing that the church continued to be of importance at these dates.

It was during the incumbency of William Sanders that, on 15 September 1632, the Earl of Angus 'was mareit at the Kirk of Bellie with Lady Mary Gordon (third) dochter to the Marquess (of Huntly) be Maister Robert Douglass, minister at Glenbervie, whome the Erll of Angous brocht with him of purpoiss'. On 28 November following, the Master of Abercorn and Huntly's youngest daughter were married there by 'ane Irish minister' (at that time the word 'Irish' was used to signify anyone who spoke Gaelic). 'The corpis of the first Marquis of Huntly (who died at Dundee in 1636) was convoyit with sum freindis to the kirk of Belly' where it was kept overnight while on its way to the family tomb at Elgin.

In the seventeenth century, Spalding also informs us that Lord Graham, Montrose's eldest son, had come with his father 'with the bodie of his armie', from Elgin on 4 March 1645 to the Bog o' Gight (now Gordon Castle). While there, the son, 'a proper youth about 16 yeiris old, and of singular expectatioune, takis seiknes, deis in the Bog in a few dayis, and is bureit in the kirk of Bellie, to his fatheris gryt grief'. Despite many attempts to locate it, including a search of all stones now buried beneath the surface, no stone marks the spot of his burial.

The tombstone of William Sanders was lost for many years, being buried beneath some 6 inches of topsoil, and has since been relocated. The inscription reads 'Hic jacent cineres Magistri Gulielmi Alexander qui primus post reformatam ab errore oribus ecclesie Romane religio nem 77 annos huic ecclesie be Bellie pastor obiit AD 1663 ætatis sus 107', which freely translated reads as 'Here lie the ashes of Mr William Saunders, Pastor of the Church of Bellie for 77 years, the first Pastor after the reform of religion from the error of the Church of Rome, who died in the year of the Lord 1663 in the 107th year of his age'. The name Saunders is synonymous with the Alexander inscribed on the tombstone. There are obvious discrepancies regarding his age and length of ministry, and the 77 years of his ministry must relate to the whole of his period of ministry, as he was only at Bellie from 1607 to 1663 (56 years).

In 1711 there is evidence that the kirk did actually have a belfry, when on 17 June, 'The officer did acquaint the Session that the bell is loose in the stock and in danger to fall, and also that severall people in his absence ring the bell double when they come with ther children's and friend's corpses to bury them. The Session appoints a man of skill to look to the bell and mend what is necessare, and desires that none hereafter ring the bel double at Buriels, because it is undecent and looks not otherways than as heathenish.'

The repairs to the church made slow progress. In 1730 the Presbytery were urging the heritors, in the shape of the Duchess of Gordon, to repair the building without delay. It was said that the church would be repaired by the following spring, 1731, but nothing appears to have been done, for in November 1732 the minister complained that his church was 'without doors and otherwise insufficient'. Things were put right by the next summer, the total expenses coming to £1,121 Scots. The windows of the church had been glazed by 1733.

By 1740 improvements had been carried out, and in 1741 the minutes suggest that 'the church fabric is in good repair, but the dykes are ruinous'. There seem to have been no further problems with the buildings during the next 40 years or more, maybe the minister had given up complaining. In 1750 there is evidence that the windows of the kirk were glazed.

The proposals for the removal of the kirk and manse to the town of Fochabers were under consideration in 1785, but in March 1787 the factor was asking that, although work had been planned to commence in the summer of that year, the erection of the kirk and manse might be delayed for a year, for financial reasons. The delay was obviously longer than this, as in the *Statistical Account* of 1795 the Revd James Gordon wrote '. . . the church of Bellie, upon the old bank of the Spey, (is) soon to be translated to Fochabers . . .' It was not until 1797 that the new church in Fochabers was finally completed.

Following the move of the church to Fochabers the old kirk and its manse were allowed to quietly fall into disrepair and decay, any useful surviving stones being 'quarried' by the local people for the building of dykes and other structures. As with many other churches, such as Kinneddar, Essil, Dipple and Lhanbryde, it was only a very short time until no trace of the original structure remained visible above ground.

There is however, one fragment of the church wall remaining, which contains a memorial tablet to William Annand. Some sources consider it unclear as to whether this is in its original position, or was rebuilt later from some of the rubble of the old church. Excavations carried out during July 2003, however, have revealed evidence of the probable line of a wall extending westwards from this monument for at least 10 metres, which would, had the tablet been located on the inside wall of the church as would be expected, identify this as being part of the south wall of the kirk. J. di Folco comments 'A heavily damaged wall monument set in a fragment of the ruined church commemorates GULIELMUS ANNAND, minister, who died in November 1699. A matrimonial achievement of an Annand and a Hamilton is surmounted by a helmet and mantling. Only a few isolated letters of the inscription remain.'

The burial ground continued to be used following the transplantation of the kirk to Fochabers, and to this day it is still the main burying ground for the parish.

GEDDES

The old chapel of St Mary at Geddes was said to have been built in 1220, but the first documentary evidence of it is in a Charter of 1473. Until the middle of the nineteenth century the churchyard was the site of a fair held on or about 5 April each year. The chapel stood within a circular churchyard, which may be evidence of the pre-Christian or very early Christian use of the site.

The more recent building on the site is not an antiquity, but was built as a private burial place for the Roses of Geddes and Kilravock, and probably sits on the site of the earlier chapel. Some evidence of the earlier chapel was found by gravediggers while digging a grave against the north wall of the existing building.

NAIRN

The original Holy Rood Kirk of Nairn is mentioned in the following chapter, but the church which replaced it in 1765 was itself rebuilt in 1811. This old Riverside Parish Church is now itself a ruin, with the surviving walls barely extending to 6 feet in height, although a large part of the south wall extends to the former roof level. The surrounding graveyard contains about 200 tombstones. The absence of any early church records makes it impossible for us to find out any other details of the history of the kirk.

CHAPTER 6
THE ROYAL
BURGH OF NAIRN

NAIRN IN EARLY TIMES

Although it may not be too obvious to the modern visitor, the town of Nairn is a very ancient settlement at the mouth of the river from which it takes its name. The old town at the river mouth was probably situated about half a mile west of the present harbour, but the encroachment of the sea, and the changing coastline have all but destroyed any evidence of the old place. Some of the inhabitants of Nairn in the eighteenth century claimed to have seen the foundations of a castle at very low tide, but it is more likely that these were in fact the remains of a former anchorage or harbour. The castle was actually situated at what are now the Constabulary Gardens, near to the High Street. The castle, according to Bain, had a central keep, the east side being protected by the river and the north and the west by ramparts and ditches, the entrance being by a drawbridge. The castle ground extended as far as what is now Bridge Street, probably near to the old ford at Brochar's Brae. The whole castle grounds, it is suggested, were enclosed by a strong wooden palisade. There was a mill, known as the Mill of Invernairn, mentioned in documentary sources from the time of King Alexander II in the first half of the thirteenth century.

Nairn, a typical royal burgh, a burgess town, with its long riggs running back from the High Street as burgage plots, has almost certainly stood in its present location since the twelfth century. The earliest extant royal charter dates from 1589, granted by King James VI of Scotland as a replacement for a much earlier charter which it is surmised must have been granted by King Alexander I. The old name of the town was Invernarne, the mouth of the River Nairn, the water of alders. Even into the nineteenth century a dense thicket of alders extended up the river for several miles, and regenerated quickly when they were cleared.

Nairn took as its patron St Ninian, and the church was dedicated to him. Standing as it does, to this day, on the dividing line between the Highlands with their Gaelic culture, and the Lowlands with their Saxon influences, it was in many ways quite different in culture from the other royal burghs in the north. There is an old story, probably apocryphal, that James I referred to Nairn as a town so long that the inhabitants of one end of its then single street did not understand the language of those at the other. In actual fact it is likely that the lower classes spoke Gaelic, and as in most other major towns, the merchants and the better-off spoke lowland Scots. The lairds in their castles may even have used French as their everyday means of communication within the family, and the church services would, before the Reformation, have been conducted in Latin.

The church that served the parish and the burgh of Nairn was originally a mensal church attached to the Deanery of Auldearn. The old church, the Holy Rood Kirk of Nairn, was dedicated to St Thomas à Becket and stood near the

Nairn Tolbooth

Constabulary Gardens and the castle, and whatever remain of the foundations of the old church now probably lie beneath the garden of 79 High Street.

The tolbooth of Nairn is mentioned in the late sixteenth century, but was burned by Royalist troops in 1716. This may well indicate that, like in many burghs, it was originally a wooden structure. The tolbooth was the centre of administration for any royal burgh, serving as a place where the taxes could be collected, where the council could meet, and usually also containing the town jail. The Nairn tolbooth was rebuilt as a stone structure in 1750.

The original bridge across the River Nairn was built in 1631 or 1632, but suffered repeatedly from the frequent floods which swept down the river. The town house of the Roses of Kilravock, which stood in the High Street, was renovated in 1722, and the carved stone to commemorate this, with its Latin inscription, is on the front of the house which still stands at 36 High Street.

NAIRN IN THE EIGHTEENTH CENTURY

A new parish church was built in 1729 or 1730, as shown by a plan in the National Archives of Scotland. Whether or not the building was completed at that time is unclear, as other sources suggest that a church was built in 1765, on or near to the site of the earlier church, and again rebuilt in 1811. The Market Cross was moved from its site in the centre of the High Street in 1757 and was rebuilt at the north-east corner of the manse wall. In the twentieth century it was again moved, this time to a position against the wall of the County Buildings. The cross, in its original form, was 1 foot in diameter and stood 7 feet high, on a base of circular stone about 4 feet in diameter. At the top were sundials, probably the old Horloge Stone. The base has undergone many changes during the past years. The town gallows stood at the west end of the town, and the road leading to it was then known as the Gallowgate, and is now Lodgehill Road.

In 1746 the Duke of Cumberland's troops entered Nairn in pursuit of Prince Charles Edward Stuart and his rebel forces. The little town was totally unable to accommodate or provide for the 7,000 foot soldiers, 2,000 cavalry and the train of artillery which had descended on them from the east. Some of the troops, mainly the officers, were lodged in the tolbooth, and others in various buildings in the town, but most of the soldiers and the horses passed through Nairn and camped about a mile further west at Balblair. The Duke of Cumberland himself was accommodated at Rose of Kilravock's town house in the High Street; and this house, the manse and the homes of other prominent townspeople were each allocated their quota of welcome, or sometimes unwelcome, guests.

Cumberland had learned from his spies that although the rebels were preparing for battle on Drumossie Moor at Culloden, some miles to the west, an attack on the camp near Nairn was expected, and possibly also an attack on the town itself. The fears of the townsfolk were, however, soon dispelled when Cumberland's army marched away westwards to the final decisive battle at Culloden.

According to Dr Samuel Johnston at the time of his visit there in 1773, the Royal Burgh of Nairn was in a state of miserable decay, and things did not improve greatly during the next 10 years, in 1782 nearly half of the bridge was swept away by a spate on the river. It was only because the magistrates funded a temporary repair, made of timber, that passage was again possible. The constant complaint was that unlike the Findhorn and the Spey, there was no passage boat or ferry across the River Nairn, the old bridge having to carry all of the traffic on the High Road. Things could only get better, though, and by the time of the *Old Statistical Account* in the early 1790s the herring and salmon fisheries at Nairn, as with many of the other coastal towns, were prospering, under the watchful eye of the landowners. Nairn had a flourishing, one may almost say famous, grammar school, and the schoolmaster there was so well thought of that 'gentlemen from all quarters of the country, and some from England, send their children to be educated here'. There was also a school for girls in the town, with a house for the schoolmistress, who received a salary of £10 a year.

The town was by now also becoming well known as a watering place, and in 1793, in addition to being 'remarkably well calculated for sea bathing' it also possessed two very good inns, one of which, under the proprietorship of Mr James Brander, even in these early days of the tourist trade, could offer the hire of a bathing machine. There were, besides the inns, so many alehouses and whisky shops in the town that the minister thought that mention of them all might, to strangers, perhaps appear incredible. He expressed the wish that these 'tippling houses' should be entirely abolished, as they were 'a nuisance in any place and highly detrimental to the health and morals of the people'. The minister also lamented the 'unbelievable' rise in prices, and his comments suggest that during the previous 30 years prices of most things had risen by 300 per cent.

Improvements to the harbour of Nairn were mooted in the 1790s, and the changing of the course of the River Nairn at its mouth to facilitate the building

Daniel's view of Nairn 1821

of a new harbour pier was considered. But this all came to nothing, as a result of which Nairn was later bypassed by the steamer services sailing between Leith, Lossiemouth, Inverness and Cromarty.

NAIRN IN THE
NINETEENTH CENTURY

The new bridge over the River Nairn was first mooted in 1800, probably to a design by George Burn. It was completed some three years later, but even this new three-span stone bridge suffered damage in the floods of 1829 and 1868. It has undergone many reconstructions since it was originally built, as the traffic on the A96 has increased both in size and in volume.

The tolbooth was apparently rebuilt again in 1811, with further improvements in 1870. Although local people consider that it originally stood on the site of what is now the Town and County Building and the Sheriff Court, there is no documentary evidence for this.

Widening of Nairn Bridge to accommodate the main A96 road

Research into the history of the Burgh of Nairn is considerably hampered by the fact that there are no surviving Kirk Session Minutes before 1819, which means that many of the lives and misdemeanours of the population in the early days of the Burgh are a mystery to us.

THE BOOMING
FISHING INDUSTRY

By the time of the second or *'New' Statistical Account* in 1842 the new harbour was in use and fishing was really booming in Nairn. The Fishertown had expanded considerably, although it still remained separate from the main part of the burgh. In the summertime the entire male population of the Fishertown, anything up to 200 men and boys, would set sail for the Caithness coast, where they would spend about six weeks, mainly in Wick, and would then return with a considerable amount of money, which greatly benefited not only the town's merchants but probably also the various inns.

In 1842 it was noted that Nairn had seven vessels based there, amounting to some 370 tons of shipping, which would indicate that they were all small

LEFT. Fisherman at Nairn, early twentieth century

BELOW. Nairn fisher girls at Great Yarmouth

BOTTOM. Fishermen sorting lines

Nairn Harbour in 1890

coastal vessels. These were, of course, in addition to the fishing fleet. A good deal of trade was carried on through the harbour by vessels from other ports, importing coal, lime and bone-dust, and exporting wood, which was the principal export, and, when there was a surplus, also exporting corn. The small pier, which had been erected in the early nineteenth century at the mouth of the river, had been so badly damaged by floods in the river and by sand deposited by the sea that it was now of little use except for mooring some of the fishing boats and other smaller vessels.

EXPANSION AND IMPROVEMENT
✳

An academy, probably replacing the grammar school mentioned half a century earlier, occupied a neat building at the west end of the town on land gifted by the late Captain James Rose RN. The educational provisions of Nairn were completed by a sessional or church school, and also by what was known as a 'monitory school', both of which were built by public subscription. The National Bank, British Linen Company Bank and Caledonian Bank all had branches in the town at this time, the National Bank having built a handsome new building as their banking house. Gas had been introduced into the town by 1842, and was proving to be a great benefit not only for lighting the streets, but also to bring better illumination to the shops and homes of the people. The

Nairn High Street in 1895

main street, which was formerly a rough cobblestone road, had, according to the minister, been 'Macadamized and much leveled, but in dry weather was inconvenient as there was an increase in the quantity of dust on the street'. Three coaches each day stopped at the 'excellent well kept hotel', while in the eyes of the minister the new Temperance Society 'promises to be productive of good'.

The coming of the railway to Nairn in the 1850s not only gave the people of Nairn easier access to Inverness and Aberdeen, but opened up a through route to the south across the Dava Moor. It was not only the ability to travel away from Nairn that was a benefit, though. Even in the late eighteenth century medical practitioners had started to send their upper-class patients to the resorts which were springing up around the Scottish coast, and Nairn was no exception. The bathing machine mentioned earlier was of great benefit to those 'who require the benefit of the salt bath', and the coming of the railways meant that these 'medical tourists' had a much more comfortable journey. It was not only the wealthy who were able to take advantage of the sea, the country people from further inland would visit Nairn and board with the fisherfolk of the Fishertown. They usually came in August, and, like Blackpool, this set the foundations for a summer visit to the seaside which continued for many generations, and, among many families, continues to this day.

Nairn had been made popular by the writings and the connections of

Nairn bathing machines in 1880, the 'Brighton of the North'

Changing fashions, bathing beauties at Nairn

Nairn Jubilee Fountain

Dr John Grigor, an eminent physician, backed by a Town Council which was intent to make the most of the tourist trade. By the 1880s at least half of the people who visited Nairn each summer were from London and the south of England, and as it became better-known to the London physicians who were acquainted with Dr Grigor, the number of visitors to this self-styled 'Brighton of the North' rapidly increased. The kind climate of the Moray Firth also attracted more permanent settlers; many of them were former military gentlemen and ex-colonials, who made their homes along the coast, in Forres as well as in Nairn. Even in the winter the climate was reputed to be so beneficial to health that the number of visitors continued to be a good source of income for the shops and hotels of Nairn.

It was at this time that Nairn became not just two but three distinct settlements. Around the harbour there still clustered the cottages of the Fishertown, home to the fishermen who were taking full advantage of the thriving fishing industry. Inland was the Burgh of Nairn, the business and commercial part of the town, where the merchants and the businessmen had established good livings and fine houses. To the west, and up towards the beach, was the 'new' part of Nairn: the hotels to accommodate the tourists and the houses of the

Nairn town crier,
Mr Thomas Manson

wealthy families who had decided to make Nairn their home. The late nineteenth century was a time of expansion and prosperity for the town.

The Nairn Golf Club was founded in 1887, but at this time the game was subject to serious class distinction. Only the wealthy played on the Nairn Golf Club's course, but the interest in the game extended to other strata of society as well, and by 1899 a separate course, the Nairn Dunbar links, was designed for 'the artisan class', and was laid out on land donated by Sir Alexander Dunbar. Maybe this stratification of society in the golfing world was also very representative of the class distinctions between the three separate parts of Nairn.

Between 1841 and 1911 the population of Nairn had increased from 2,672 to 4,661, a rise of 70 per cent. New villas were built not only near to the beach, but also adjacent to the new golf courses, and the rate of building in the town meant that virtually all of the old town of Nairn was destroyed in the process. Sadly, the proposal to build an amusement pier at Nairn, adjacent to the promenade, never came to fruition.

Rampini, writing in 1897, commented that the fishing population, both in the family names and customs, still showed some evidence of what he called their 'Scandinavian' origin, and occupied the village next to the harbour at the mouth of the river. This idea of a 'Scandinavian' origin has now been almost totally disproved by DNA testing. The rest of the citizens, some of whom maybe classed themselves as Highlanders and others as Lowlanders, lived in the area which now forms the main section of the town of Nairn.

NAIRN IN THE TWENTIETH CENTURY

The new century brought many changes to Nairn. The old thatched cottages of the Fishertown were gradually refurbished, some with slate roofs, but many with roofs made from corrugated iron. Although many of the old wooden sheds were removed, a good number of them still remain in the yards of the cottages. The lanes of the Fishertown were surfaced, and the access to the harbour was improved as horse-drawn carts gave way to motor vehicles.

Any lingering remains of the original old town were by now totally lost as the western end of Nairn was developed even further for the tourist trade, a process which was to continue well into the second half of the twentieth century. The town of Nairn itself was subject to a facelift as the buildings in the old closes were gradually demolished, and new structures took their place. The

Collector's Close, a typical town close in Nairn

shops and other buildings along the main street were, in the main, retained in their nineteenth-century glory but were gradually defaced by new 'modern' shop fronts and signs. Very few of the older buildings in Nairn have been demolished, but it is fascinating to look beyond the frontages, and venture down the closes and alleys at the sides of the buildings, to see just what does remain of the old town, and consider what is now lost for ever.

CHAPTER 7

THE ROYAL
BURGH OF AULDEARN

THE RISE AND FALL
OF AULDEARN

To the motorist travelling along the A96 as it bypasses Auldearn, the village may seem to be of little importance. In the twelfth century, though, it was a much more significant place, briefly outranking nearby Nairn, Auldearn was in fact a royal burgh. The castle at the western end, the parish church in the middle and the single main street straddling the King's High Way from Inverness to Banff and Aberdeen, are all typical of such an embryonic burgh.

The Royal Castle of Auldearn, or Auld Eren, was supposedly built during the reign of William the Lion sometime before 1180, and is mentioned when he signed the second Charter of Inverness at the castle there. The town, having a castle, would then have almost automatically received a charter, which would have granted it the status of a royal burgh, but its claim to prominence was not to last. In 1308 the Earl of Ross submitted to Robert the Bruce at the castle, but this seems to be the last act in the history of the burgh. Auldearn was soon eclipsed by neighbouring Nairn with its more prominent and probably more easily defended castle, and its easy access to the sea.

With the demise of the castle, the Burgh of Auldearn quite quickly fell out of royal favour, charters were not renewed or updated and a gradual decline set in. The town, now reduced in status to little more than a village, was never to achieve the burgess rights and the 'lang riggs' or burgage plots which became such a feature of the later royal burghs. The wealthy people and the merchants turned their attention, and their money, to Nairn, with its expanding economy.

COVENANTERS

It was not until three centuries later that the name of Auldearn was again to come into public prominence. During the Wars of the Three Kingdoms, as they became known, the commander of the Covenanting forces, Colonel Hurry, had been ravaging the countryside of the Gordons, but was being hotly pursued by the forces of Lord Montrose. Hurry, having been camped in the vicinity of what is now Buckie, received news of the enemy's approach, crossed the Spey and proceeded westwards. Drawing Montrose and his troops into lands which were in general hostile to the Royalists, he made for the area around Nairn, confident of the Covenanter sympathies of the local people there. Hurry was also joined by three other regiments, Campbell of Lawers, who had recently returned from a campaign in Ireland, and also Buchanan's and Loudon's, giving his army a strength of 4,000 foot soldiers and some 300 horsemen.

On the evening of 8 May 1645, Hurry discovered that the Royalist troops were camped near the village of Auldearn, in a hollow above Boath House, hidden from sight by the ridge of land on which the village stood. According to contemporary sources, it was one of those nights when the rain fell unabated. The Covenanter soldiers sought cover in the cottages of Auldearn itself, others in the surrounding area. Montrose, probably due to the weather, did not even bother to send out scouts.

The battle started just after first light on 9 May, with the rain continuing to fall, and the ground underfoot becoming sodden and treacherous. The Royalist onslaught soon stopped the advance of the Covenanters, who were pushed back into the village by sheer weight of numbers, although in actual fact the Royalist forces were not as numerous as the Covenanters. A stand was made in the gardens and the yards at the back of the houses, and the fight seems to have flowed back and forth through the village for some time, and Royalist reinforcements were beginning to arrive on the very chaotic battle scene. The Covenanter forces became confused, the horses getting mixed up with the infantry, and it was not long before the Royalist attack from the north of the village was driving the Covenanters from the field of battle. In the annihilation which followed, and in the inevitable pursuit, some 1,500 Covenanters died, the village must have been a scene of carnage by the end of the day.

Little is heard of Auldearn following the battle. No doubt the villagers cleaned up the bloodstained mess, buried the corpses, kept quiet, at least for some time, about where their political sympathies lay and gradually reverted to a normal way of life.

From that time onwards, the village has been little more than watering place on the road between Nairn and Forres, one of its two inns still named in remembrance of the bloody events of 1645.

CHAPTER 8

THE ROYAL
BURGH OF FORRES

FORRES IN EARLY TIMES

The town of Forres has a long and chequered history. In the sixth century there are suggestions that Forres, lying at the mouth of the River Erne, later to become known as the River Findhorn, was the most important town in the north. It had a strong merchant base and considerable trade with other ports around the coast, and possibly even across the North Sea to Norway, Denmark and the Baltic ports. At this time the river would have lapped against the base of the Castle Hill. The mouth of the river was in a rather vague area of wetlands covering what is now Findhorn Bay and extending eastwards to meet with the Loch of Spynie somewhere between Kinloss and Alves, probably in the vicinity of the later Earnside Castle. The small trading vessels of this time did not need very much in the way of harbour facilities, as it was possible to load and unload them in small inlets such as the mouth of the Mosset Burn or on the banks of the river itself.

In 535, Toncet, the King's Chancellor, 'causit divers merchantis of the Towne of Fores in Murayland, as then the chiefest towne of all that countrie, to be accused of treason. Efter sundrie wrangles and oppressions done to him, the Chancellor of King Coranus, in the king's auctoritie callit afore him certane merchantis of Forres in Murray and for small or wane causis put them to deith as misdooris. Syne confiscat thair guddis to the kings behwffe.' How much faith can be put in these early writings by Boece we will never know, but they certainly represent the earliest documentary sources referring to the merchants of Forres.

CASTLES AND MORMAERS

Following this one brief mention the town retreats again into the vagueness of undocumented history. It is another 400 years before we hear any more of it, but it almost certainly continued to be a small, wood-built, heather-thatched town whose merchants had trading links with many other ports. The castle was built during this time as a wooden palisaded enclosure into which the townspeople could have retreated in times of trouble, whether actual or perceived. It may be that the first castle was burned to the ground by the Vikings, in about the year 850, as suggested by some sources, but it was certainly then rebuilt.

The tenth century saw an increase in the importance of this Castle of Forres in the political affairs of the north of Scotland. At this time, of course, the castle would have improved much beyond the wooden structure on the hill at the western end of the town. In 908 King Donald, the son of Constantine, died suddenly at Forres, probably from poisoning. King Malcolm I, obviously undeterred by Donald's death, was a frequent visitor to the castle in the years leading up to his death in 959. Some sources allege that there were in fact two Malcolms in Forres at this time, in conflict with each other, one being the king and the other being Malcolm, Mormaer of Moray. Other sources suggest that King Malcolm was in fact himself also the Mormaer of Moray. At this time Forres was considered to be a much more important town than Inverness, Nairn or Elgin.

Forres continued to be quite a risky place for any king to visit. In about 965 or maybe a couple of years later, King Duff or Duffus was supposedly murdered by the governor of the Castle of Forres, whose name is not revealed, 'on the classic ground of Forres'. There is a curious story that his body was hidden under the bridge at Kinloss, and until it was found the sun did not shine again. This may not have been all that far from the truth, as the later years of the tenth century seem to have been affected by a general decline in climatic conditions. In 976 it was noted that snow fell at midsummer and no grass or crops grew anywhere in the Province of Moray in that year, the year of the 'Muckle Hunger'.

By this time the power of the mormaers, or chieftains, of Moray extended from the River Spey in the east to Lochaber in the west, and northwards to the Viking territories of Sutherland. Many pacts and even marriages seem to have been made with these northern Vikings to avoid conflict wherever it was possible to do so without any impression of subjugation by the northern neighbours. The mountains to the south seem to have prevented any major disputes with the Scots beyond the Grampians, and to all intents and purposes Moray was an independent country.

The castle at Forres was burned by the Danes in 1008, but again rebuilt, and there is mention in 1032 of the death of Gilcomgan Maolbrige, Mormaer of Mureve or Moray, who lived at the castle. He is said to have been the great-grandfather of Angus, an ancestor of Hugo Freskyn de Moravia. In 1085 there is a record of the death of Maclonechtan MacLulach, a later Mormaer of Moray, which also probably took place at or near to the Castle of Forres. By this time the power of the independent mormaers was waning, as was the power of the Vikings in the north, and Scotland was becoming united under the kings beyond the mountains.

THE DEVELOPMENT OF A
MORE STRUCTURED SOCIETY

The twelfth century saw three innovations which proved vital to the establishment of a stable society. The first of these was the gradual introduction of 'family names', sirenames or 'surnames', which would aid clarity of identification and documentation of the now increasing population. Secondly, there was the concept of 'parishes', which went a long way to the formalisation of the structure and power base of the Catholic Church. The third innovation was the establishment of 'sheriffdoms' to give structure to the power of the barons and ultimately to the Crown.

The parish structure began to be established during the reign of Alexander I (1107–24), together with the installation of monasteries and abbeys such as Kinloss and Pluscarden. During the reign of David I (1124–53) this process was continued, as was the establishment of the sheriffdoms to conduct the legal processes which were now becoming more defined. By about 1150 Forres, with its parish church and castle, was erected into a royal burgh. One person initially held the position of sheriff of both Forres and Elgin, the latter probably being a much smaller town than Forres, although Elgin too had its own castle on the Ladyhill at the western end of the town.

During the reign of David I a trading union or 'Hanse' which had been formed some 50 years earlier by the coastal towns of Aberdeen, Banff, Elgin, Forres, Nairn, Inverness and probably also Cromarty and Dornoch, was given the king's full approval and recognition. This allowed free trade and possibly free movement of tradesmen and craftsmen between the burghs. This may have been a further formalisation of the trading links that had existed for maybe the past five or six centuries. By the twelfth century, it was probably becoming associated with the fledgling 'Hanseatic League', which was eventually, as vessels grew larger, to see trade links with Bergen in Norway, the Danish and North German ports, the Baltic, and ultimately much of northern Europe. Such trading links would have led to the eventual expansion of Findhorn, the port for Forres, into one of the principal ports of the Moray Firth.

The later years of that century saw the first documentary mention of the Greishop or Greeschip lands as a part of the lands held by the Sheriff of Forres. In 1184, 1189 and again in 1198, William the Lion was in residence at the Castle of Forres where he signed various charters.

THE POWER OF FORRES

The early years of the thirteenth century saw an increase in the power of the town of Forres when in 1214 Alexander II (1214–29) established a Royal Mint there. By now the name of the town had various spellings, such as Forais or Fforeys, according to either the whim or the educational status of the scribe or cleric preparing the document. Moray was not quite the stable province that this implied, however, and there were rebellions in the area in 1212, 1215 and 1229. Following the building of the Cathedral of Elgin in 1224, and the foundation of a firm base for the Bishopric of Moray, Elgin gradually began to attain a more prominent status in Moray, and Forres, for long the major town in the area, gradually began to fall into decline.

The earliest Charters are now lost, but were replaced by one granted by King James IV on 23 June 1496 which narrates:

> that the ancient charters have been destroyed in time of war, or by the violence of fire, and grants of new in free burgage with the lands formerly belonging to the community, particularly the lands called Griveship, Bailie-Lands, Meikle Bog, with the King's Meadow, Lobranstoun with Crealties and Ramflat, and common pasturage in the forest of Drumondside and Tulloch, with power annually to elect a Provost, Bailies and other Magistrates and Officers necessary, and to constitute the Provost and Bailies Sheriffs within the Burgh and its liberties, and discharge the Sheriff of the shire of Elgin and Forres, to exercise his office within the said burgh or its liberties, with power to have a Cross, a weekly market, and an annual fair to continue for eight days, with all and sundry other privileges and immunities of a free burgh . . .

There is still a building in the same place, a little more modern now, but the tolbooth, in the centre of the town near the market cross, has always been a focus of town life. The early tolbooth was a wooden thatched building which had been erected for the use of the Collector of Petty Customs. The adjacent town cross was the site for the proclamation of statutes and ordinances, which did not become law until they had been formally proclaimed at the tolbooth by the bellman. The tolbooth was also the place where the provost, magistrates and council would convene their meetings, and was the site of the town jail. This part of the town was also to become the location for the markets when they were banned from the churchyards at the end of the next century.

FORRES IN THE SIXTEENTH CENTURY

The town was by now typical of many of the smaller Scottish burghs. The High Street, also known as the King's High Gait or the Common Street, ran through the centre of the town and the North and South Back Streets enclosed the town outside the ends of the burgess plots. These were probably protected by a peat or mud wall, which also served in a small way to delineate the boundaries of the burgh at that time. The Tolbooth Wynd and the Bullet Loan both ran south-wards from the High Street and formed the main routes out of the town in that direction. To the north, the Kirk Vennel provided the main route to the north and west, crossing the Burn of Altyre or the Mosset Burn at the Lee Bridge and ford, and continuing to the crossing of the River Findhorn at Waterford, and also to Tannachy. The road to Findhorn and the Abbey of Kinloss branched away to the north at the Little Cross at the east end of the High Street.

The original feus of the town were 18½ feet wide where they fronted on to the High Street, and the burgesses to whom these 'burgess plots' were origi-nally allocated were required to build a property on them within two years. The houses were built with their gable-end to the street, and the doors opened off the close or lane adjacent to the property. The land beyond the house was used to keep a cow, pigs, poultry and, for the better off, there was a stable for a horse. The burgess plots also provided garden ground for the house. The boundaries of the feus were delineated by stone markers, and the boundaries were inspected annually by the 'line-masters'. Outside the Back Streets the town's lands were allocated and farmed in runrig, but with all the townspeople having access to the grazing of the common pasture.

FORRES LIFE IN
THE SIXTEENTH CENTURY

*

Like most of the burghs of barony, the town of Forres for many years retained
the power of 'pit and gallow' and employed its own hangman. The hangman
preferred to be known by the title 'locksman' as he was paid in locks of meal,
and it also kept his occupation a little more anonymous. His wife had the duty
of bringing up any orphaned children in the town, even when they had been
reduced to this state by her husband's activities, a sure recipe for resentment.
Apart from caring for the orphans of the town, under an act passed by King
James II in the middle of the previous century the nearest relative was deemed
to be responsible for any person in the town who was unable to support him
or herself, for whatever reason.

There was of course no police force in these early times, and the discipline
of the town at the end of the sixteenth century was maintained by four of the
bailies, each of them given the task of maintaining peace and order in his own
district. An example from 1586 shows that:

James Vaus – was to take charge 'from the Castle to the house of
James Urquhart snr.'

James Urquhart – 'from his own house to the Smyddie'

James Urquhart Snr – 'from John Robb's house to Gilbert Anderson's
house anent The Cross'

John Dunbar – 'from the Yat Wa's to the Castle'.

One aspect of life which is now 'lost', and a hazard we fortunately no longer
need to beware of, are the dung-heaps at the entrance to every close. One of
the consequences of these foul-smelling heaps was that the rather primitive
town drains were regularly getting blocked. An act recorded in the Burgh
Court minutes of 24 October 1586 ordained that:

Borrow Curt in Tolboyt – Presiding Provost and Bailies. Quhilk day
it is statute and ordenit yt all mydings be tane of ye calsay and the
gutters clengit and red yat ye watter may gett ane fre passiage, and
this to be done betwixt this and Halloevin under ye pane of aucht
shillings of inlaw of averie person.

Beggars and vagrants were always a source of irritation to the town during the summer and autumn months, and, typical of many years, in October 1587 an inquest was held by the Burgh Council 'to see who are lawful neighbours or not, and who have thair kailyard and pettistack'. Pearson's Well seems to have been one of the main sources of water for the townspeople at this time and, being located somewhere near the centre of the town, it was to remain in use for almost three centuries after this date.

Some sort of defensive measures for the protection of the town were obviously needed, as there were continual threats to the townsfolk from the Highlanders and the 'Outlanders'. In 1588, James Urquhart Snr in Baillifields was instructed by the town to build a 'dyk' around the town to 'keip out Owtland's men', and he was to instruct the neighbours 'to big thair heid yairds suffuciently with mudd or feall'. In addition to the defences provided by the 'dyk' around the town, there were also town gates, or 'ports', and it is mentioned that the East Port of the town was adjacent to Mr Fridge's house at the eastern end of the High Street.

The church roof, which was thatched, was obviously deteriorating quite seriously by now, and it was ordained that 'The south side of the kirk of Forres shall be thekit wi sclaitt'. The church at this time was described as a Gothic building with side walls 20 feet high and a very high roof. There were side aisles with stone pillars ranged along the inside, and about 20 feet from the side walls, to support the roof. There was also a transept, which was converted into a porch following the Reformation. The choir was at the east end. Lofts were added at either end in the late sixteenth century, with access by means of external stone staircases. The church, with its pre-Reformation origins, was considered to be overly long for Presbyterian worship, and part of the west end of the church was used as a schoolroom and a meeting room. The plans to re-roof the church with slate do not seem to have materialised, and some five years later John Andersoune, wright, replaced the thatch on the whole building, including the schoolroom. This work also included repairs to the buttresses of the church, and a few years after this the east gable was rebuilt.

A watch or a clock was not usually a possession of the working people of the town, and as a wake-up call the town drummer walked around the town beating his drum at 5 a.m., and there was also an evening drum. In 1589 a bell was fitted to the clock in the tolbooth so that everyone had access to the correct Forres time. This would not, of course, have corresponded to any sort of national time as each burgh would set its own time corresponding with its longitude. The Little Cross, which marked the east end of the burgh, was mentioned in documents of this time, but had probably already been in existence for many years previously.

On 11 October 1595 it was decided that the town markets, which had previously always been held in the churchyard on the Sabbath, should be discontinued. 'That day it is statute and ordainit yt na mercatt sall be holden on Sunday under ye paine of escheitting ye guiddis, geir quatsomevir and ye samen to be publisit at ye Mercatt Croce.' This put an end to a long tradition of Sunday markets, but paved the way for a more regular weekday market to be held in the burgh, probably initially on a Monday, at the head of Tolbooth Street or on the Market Green.

The country was not at peace even at the end of the sixteenth century, and the town's burgesses were still required to maintain arms, which they could be called upon to use at any time on the king's behalf. This was in addition to their many other privileges and duties. A traveller had the right to graze his horse in any royal burgh as long as it did not eat the crops, a useful facility in those days when the horse was the main form of transport. Royal permission was required before anyone could open a brew house or a bakery, and this included permission for the barn for fermenting bread and ale.

Two of the burgesses were appointed as constables, generally on a half-yearly rotation. Anyone who was instituted as a bailie had to accept the obligations of 'scottyn and lottyn' (the assessment and collection of taxes) and of 'wakyn and wardyn' (the policing and general control of the burgh), which they could be called upon at any time to undertake.

As their businesses expanded, the merchants not only lacked the time to cultivate the long riggs behind their properties along the 'Kings High Gait', but as a consequence of their increasing trade they needed to house an expanding work force. They built houses or cottages along their feus, and thus the characteristic 'closes' were formed.

A few of the building which we now see in Forres are probably built on the footprint of these earlier houses, and it is well worth a venture into some of the closes.

The houses were small, usually of two rooms, but as the merchants prospered they would add an upper storey, and make use of the ground floor for their business premises. As their families grew, a third or even a fourth floor would be added, and space in the roof would be used for the servants' quarters. Each household had to grow and produce much of its own food and, in addition to the land in their feus, all were entitled to a share in the town's lands, in a runrig system, and also to the town's grazing for their cows, sheep and horses.

FORRES IN THE SEVENTEENTH CENTURY

In 1603 it was recorded that the close at what is now No. 96 High Street extended back to the lands known as the Hainings, which were let on a three-year tack at this time. 'Hainings' was originally a term used to describe a well-watered meadow, but later became specifically reserved as a title for the lands where the king's horses were grazed when he visited his burghs to collect revenues and judge serious criminal cases. These visits became important dates in the calendar of the town.

The appearance of Forres until the middle of the seventeenth century was totally different to what it is now; the houses were almost wholly built of wood, with a thatch of turf, heather or bracken. Straw could not be used for roofing as it was such a valuable animal feed during the winter. Fire was a constant hazard, and the curfew or 'couvre-feu' was sounded by the town drummer along the street each evening to warn the townspeople to cover their fires. Usually this meant covering the peat fires with ashes for the night, the ashes being removed in the morning and the fires rekindled on the still-glowing embers of the peats.

In 1625, the town of Forres consisted of little more than the High Street, with the tolbooth at its centre, and closes and lanes running off at right angles to the main street. The lanes of Kirk Wynd, leading to the Lee Bridge, and Tolbooth Wynd and the Bullet Loan, the road to Rafford, seem to have been the only other significant streets in the town. It is possible now to be more definite about the location of the town ports, the West Port being near to the kirk, probably somewhere down the Kirk Vennel, which would also have served as the North Port, being on the main road into the town from the north-west, in the vicinity of the old archdeacon's manse. The East Port was near to what is now Grant Park, and the south port would have been at the foot of Tolbooth Wynd. The kirk was by now being described as 'a mean structure thackit with turf or heather', and was no doubt falling into ruin, although still usable for services. This year brought the start of the troubled times of the Covenanters, doubtless the very problems that had been anticipated for the past five years. Meetings of any kind, even council meetings, were looked upon with suspicion, and the keeping of any kind of documentary record was considered dangerous as it might implicate those involved in future proceedings.

The years from 1638 until 1650 were a time of trouble during which Charles I attempted to force Episcopacy on Scotland, and in 1642 there was Civil War in England. Montrose was in the north, and there were Covenanter garrisons at Aberdeen and Inverness. The area in between, especially the burghs of Elgin, Forres and Nairn, was in a constant state of turmoil, with soldiers being garrisoned in Forres, and frequent columns of troops passing through the town.

The funds of the burgh were totally exhausted by 1648, mainly due to the expense they had borne in paying for the soldiers who were stationed in the town. Now that the upkeep of these soldiers by the Burgh Council was not possible they were quartered on the inhabitants, who then became personally liable for the feeding and care of the soldiers billeted on them. On 17 and 18 February 1649, it was noted that 'There was quarterit upon the said Burgh 23 horse sojers of Captain Smith's Company under command of Col John Innes', and 10 days later, '19 foot sojers were quartered there'. On 5 March, 'The haill troops under the command of the said Lieutenant General . . . quarterit upon the Burgh . . . and the quartering of the said troops for their ordinary amounted to above £100.'

By this time it had become obvious to the military that the Burgh of Forres had been drained dry, and Army Orders of 5 March 1649 read that 'In respect this town and parish thereof has been overrun by the quartering of all the troops already advanced and cannot but be much damnified thereby. The [orders] are to desyre you to advance the troops over the water [the River Findhorn] to the wester parts of parishes next adjacent thereto and that you quarter them now upon them [Forres] not at all. This you are to do as you will be answerable'. A letter to the officers commanding the troops advancing towards Inverness: 'Major McDonald – Let none under your command trouble the town of Forres upon any pretext soever'.

In 1655 the tolbooth is still described as a 'thackit' building, with the walls 'crackit to the very top', and although it was in need of a new roof the old walls could not bear the weight of the thatch. It was not until 1671 that George and John Balmanno started work on a new stone-built tolbooth.

The records of the town during the second half of the seventeenth century are quite vague, maybe due to the continuing troubles, but there are suggestions that the first Castle Bridge was built during this period, so that the main road to the west may have crossed the Mosset Burn near to the castle as well as at the Lee Bridge.

FORRES IN THE EIGHTEENTH CENTURY

On 23 January 1700, the Town Guards were to be called out so as to give them an opportunity of becoming acquainted with their captains. They were to remain on duty from 9 p.m. until 3 a.m., while all 'vagabonds and whores' were to be removed from the town by tuck of drum. The Kirk Session, being the main force of discipline in the town, instructed that 'The said day it being represented that because of the desolation of this place the Lord's Day is woefully profaned, and it was agreed upon that whither there be a sermon or not in the town, there being no minister at this time, some of the Elders should goe through the same, and bring in there report to the nixt session on who shall be in Breach of Sabbath or who shall fall from ordinances'.

Despite this edict from the church, the breaches of the peace continued to be a major cause of concern to both the Magistrates and the Kirk Session. Forres must have been quite a rough place to live, but it was probably no worse than many other towns at this time. On 6 April 1702, the Town Clerk was ordered to advertise at the public market, by tuck of drum, that 'if any of them be found swearing or drunken within this Burgh, that for each oath and for each drunkenness they shall pay 2 shillings Scots toties quoties'. Some time after this, it was enacted that 'the Bailies purge the town of idle persons who have no way of livelihood' and that a day be appointed for their expulsion.

It was probably not very pleasant to be arrested and imprisoned as the tolbooth and the jail seem to have been very damp and dismal places. Although the welfare of the prisoners didn't seem to matter greatly, in 1702 it was proposed that the Town's Charter Chest should be removed to the third floor of the building as the cellar had become very damp, and the documents were at risk of damage.

The streets of Forres were becoming very polluted by 1704, and it was decreed that 'the muck upon the streets without a channel and the muck of the vennals from time to time be given to Robert Taylior, he keeping the street vennals and the close heads clean'. Robert Taylior seems to have been the first road sweeper in the town, but this arrangement did not prove entirely satis-factory. After this the dung-heaps and middens in the High Street and Closes were rouped every year, the highest bidder being required to remove them at regular intervals, either for his own use or to sell off to local farmers.

In about 1737 William Warden, a glover burgess, started to build the block of shops and private dwellings later to become known as 'Warden's Buildings'. This land had always been an open space between the western end of the burgh and the castle, and in the days before the High Street was extended westward to the Castle Bridge it probably formed a southward extension of the church lands. These early buildings were replaced by more modern structures about a century later.

By the middle of the eighteenth century, the Burgh of Forres was slowly beginning to recover from the dire financial consequences of the 1745 Jacobite Rebellion. The town was continuing to lose influence in the affairs of Moray, and Elgin had now become the major town in the area. A garrison of soldiers continued to be based at Forres through 1750, and the local ladies continued to enjoy their company, some of these women being described as 'Lewd women in the Town', one of them identified as a 'Base woman in Pye's Close'. As their fraternisation with the soldiers continued, little seemed to escape the attention of the kirk elders.

Planning laws came to Forres in 1750. When John Robertson, a merchant in the town, built a house which created problems for his neighbours, the council were forced to act. The complainants noted that 'whereby he carries the front of his house quite out of the venal, and even upon a part of the venal, whereby his house is lyable to do damage in case of rain and speats to his neighbours. It is an apparent eyesore and deformity to the town, and yet it is the duty of the town to preserve the policy, ornament and beauty of the town as well as the property of the Burgh'. The council enacted that 'all inhabitants shall not for the future begin the building of any house without previously calling for the Magistrates and Dean of Guild to know the same, and have their consent and approbation'.

The town seems to have been quite hospitable to visitors, though, and when the Duke of Gordon and his entourage stayed at 'The Crown Hotel' in

Forres Old Parish Church

Forres on 21 October 1774 his hotel bill included £1 11s 5d for corn and £1 4s od for hay for the horses. In addition to this, he paid the blacksmith 2s, the hostler 7s 6d, and also paid 1s 6d for drinks for the servants. Some four years later, 'The Crown Tavern' was described as having '16 fine rooms, garrets, barn, stables, brew house and a garden of 1 acre 2 roods and 5 falls, with a quantity of large growing trees, ash, etc, and possessed by William Tulloch, vintner'.

In the same year, the Town Council eventually gave up on their attempts to patch up the old church and reached the decision that a new church should be built. It was completed the following year, but at 72 feet in length and 36 feet in breadth, the council, who had contributed half of the cost of the building, were obliged to express their disappointment with the smallness of the structure. They said that the building had 'no pretension of elegant architecture' and was not befitting of a royal burgh such as Forres.

There were about 60 merchants and shopkeepers in the town at this time, who had 'formerly principally been supported by travelling and vending their goods in all the villages and market towns to the west and north, particularly Sutherland, Caithness and Ross, and even as far as Orkney'. This trade had now largely gone as these areas now had their own shopkeepers. The spinning of linen yarn, a major source of employment in Forres for the previous 20 years, was now in decline due to mechanisation. As a way of improving the economy of the town, it was suggested in the council that a canal should be cut along the course of the Mosset Burn so that vessels could sail from Findhorn Bay right up to Forres, but the idea never came to fruition.

At the Grammar School, Latin, Greek, French and various branches of mathematics were taught, and 'a young gentleman may have board and education for £20 a year'. The school for reading, writing and arithmetic was co-joined to the Grammar School under the same master 'assisted by an usher'. The master received a salary of £35 sterling a year for his work, together with the fees of generally more than 100 scholars. The girls who attended studied at a separate hour of the day. There was also a boarding school for young ladies in the town 'where the various branches of needlework, music and other parts of the female education are taught'. The schoolmistress received a salary of £16 a year and 'a young lady may have every requisite accommodation for £15 a year'. The lessons in music cost 2 guineas, in gum flowers 4 guineas, tambour was £1 and plain needlework was 10s. In all of the schools in Forres particular attention was paid to morals, honour and discretion, 'and there is not anywhere perhaps a more eligible place for the education of youth'. There were also several private teachers in the town for both boys and girls, and a pianoforte teacher for the girls.

FORRES IN THE NINETEENTH CENTURY

Elizabeth Grant of Rothiemurchus, on her travels around the Highlands and the north at the start of the nineteenth century commented that '. . . we travelled to Forres, one of the prettiest of village towns . . .', but several other visitors at about this time were not quite so complimentary about the untidy streets and closes.

The high taxation of the latter decades of the eighteenth century, to finance the wars with France and in America, had meant that there had been little money to spare for the improvement of the town and few new buildings and very little industry had been introduced to Forres over the past years. The layout of the town had changed little over the last two centuries. The coming half-century, however, was to see a massive explosion of building and regeneration in the town. Many of these improvements were funded by the recent changes in agricultural methods, which had brought increased wealth to the local landowners, and by the return of several gentlemen from India and the West Indies, who were prepared to invest their fortunes in the town. A good example of this is the building at the west end of the High Street of an 'extensive range of substantial and elegant shops and houses with an open space in the centre'. This was done in 1808 by Robert Warden on the site of his ancestor's earlier buildings, and it was, by and large, all financed from the fortune he made in India. Several of the buildings along Tolbooth Street date from this time, with many of them continuing to be built gable-end to the

Forres Tolbooth in the nineteenth century

street, but the Red Lion Hotel is an exception to this.

Colonel T. Thornton, in his 'Sporting Tour' of 1804, notes that 'The inn I put up at was the Falcon, kept by Barnes. I requested the favour of Baillie Forsyth's (my wine merchant) company, I ordered supper and he passed the evening with me. A very well served one it was and I never slept in a more comfortable plain bedchamber. In the great street is a town-house with a handsome cupola, and at the end an arched gateway which has a good effect.'

In 1806 it was proclaimed that a monument should be erected to commemorate Nelson's recent victory at Trafalgar. The document records that 'it is proposed to erect, by subscription, on the summit of the Cluny Hills near Forres, a tower, of which a plan furnished gratuitously by Mr Charles Stuart, architect at Darnaway, is herewith laid before the publick'. The subscription list was opened and the site was chosen, and it was stated that 'it will form a most agreeable object to every traveller and the country at large, a useful sea beacon, and a commanding alarm post in the event of an enemy's approach by sea or land'. Obviously, despite Nelson's victory, the threat of invasion was still lingering in the minds of many people. It was estimated that a total subscription of 700 guineas would be required for the completion of the building. The foundation stone of the Trafalgar Monument, later to be known as Nelson's Tower, was laid by Brodie of Brodie on 26 August 1806, and the building work commenced. The three-storey structure was 66 feet high and contained panels inscribed 'In memory of Admiral Lord Nelson. Nile 1st August 1798, Copenhagen 2nd April 1801, Trafalger 21st August 1805'. Just seven years later, however, additional subscriptions were being sought to pay for repairs to the roof and other parts of the tower.

Improvements proceeded apace, and street lighting was introduced into the High Street in 1813, when the council authorised the purchase of 25 oil lamps. The Goosehill was levelled and fenced in 1814, and was later to become the site of the Cholera Hospital.

On 8 April 1814, a Forres Police Force was formed, 'The council, considering that in some respects the police of the Burgh has relaxed for want of proper police officers and town officers, they therefore authorise the Magistrates, upon getting a fitt, truly and attentive person to act as town constable and police officer within the Royalty, and to look after and take care of the Town's lands, mosses, plantations and moors, to allow him an annual salary of ten or twelve pounds, and also to give a yearly allowance of two pounds to any person capable of conducting the office of Procurator Fiscal within the Burgh, and who would be active in carrying out the duties of that station to effect'.

On 14 May 1820, it was noted that the churchyard dyke fronting on to the High Street was in a ruinous state, and plans were made to demolish and rebuild it. As part of this general improvement of the town, many of the old cottages in Urquhart Street were demolished and several new ones were built at about this time, although the old ideas still remained, with some of them still being erected gable-end to the street. Tosh's Bar in Urquhart Street is one of the few remaining eighteenth-century buildings.

Despite all these improvements, it was thought that the introduction of a piped water supply, which had been mooted by the council, would be too heavy a burden on the council finances in these difficult times of high unemployment and low living standards following the Napoleonic Wars. This decision not to implement a supply of piped water to the town led to a rent reduction of 15 per cent to the tenants of the Burgh, but there was still enough money to pave the north side of the High Street. It was suggested that four or five new wells should be provided in the town, but whether these ever all came into use we may never know.

The new building for Jonathan Anderson's Institution, a Grecian structure at the east end of the town, was completed two years later, to a plan by William Robertson. The Freemason's Hall, the St Lawrence Lodge, was also built at the same time and was extended by Archibald Simpson some six years later.

It is obvious that in the preceding years, grave-robbery had become quite common in the north, and the churchyard of Forres was no exception. 'In almost every town and village in the north nightly watches are appointed over the churchyard. In Forres, where a short time ago a regular system of disinterment was carried on, a handsome little building has been erected in the churchyard for the purpose of protection, which is furnished with windows looking out in all directions, and is nightly tenanted with guards.'

Despite the new Anderson's School having been built, it was still thought that there had been a gradual decline in educational standards in Forres over the previous 15 years or so, and in 1829 the magistrates decided to take matters in hand. The two earlier schools were replaced with the Forres Academical Institution. The various other teaching establishments in the town were amalgamated into a new school under a headmaster and two assistant teachers. Duncan Robertson was appointed headmaster, the second master was Mr Longmuir and the third master was Alexander Forsyth. Shortly afterwards James Watson was also added to the staff.

Following an unprecedented heatwave throughout May and June 1829 which was accompanied by severe drought, and then heavy showers, rapid fluctuations of the barometer and even sightings of the Aurora Borealis during

July, the 'Great Moray Flood' of 3 and 4 August 1829 was the result of an estimated 6 inches of rain, probably more, falling on the Monadliath Mountains and the northern Cairngorms in a very short period. The rivers Nairn, Findhorn and Lossie were very seriously affected by the flood, and the bridge over the River Findhorn at Mundole was destroyed.

The plain of Forres was totally inundated, a sheet of water extending from the Findhorn across the lands of Tannachy and as far as the Bay of Findhorn itself. The River Findhorn and the Altyre Burn or the Mosset Burn met under the Castle Hill at the west end of Forres, and the bridge at that end of town was partially washed away. 'The inundation spread over the rich and variously cropped fields and over hedges, gardens, orchards and plantations.' Boats from the port of Findhorn sailed over the fields of Tannachy and Edgehill and were effective in rescuing many people. The ground immediately around the house of Tannachy remained dry, and the house itself was only flooded in its cellars. The houses of Moy on the west bank of the Findhorn and Tannachy on the east provided hospitality for many people who had been driven out of their homes by the flood. The flood, and a subsequent smaller flood on 27 August, left no fewer than 188 cases of utter destitution in the parish of Forres. The farmers at Greishop, Balnageith, Waterford and Edgefield suffered severe losses, their crops being totally ruined by the flood waters.

Feeing markets were introduced to Forres in the 1830s to allow the new consolidated farms a steady supply of labour controlled by the farmers. These feeing markets were condemned by Robert Grant, a Forres advocate, for lowering the moral standards 'of our labouring classes, both male and female', possibly because of the excesses of alcohol consumed on these occasions, but despite these reservations they provided a useful, one may even say vital service to the agricultural labourers of the time.

Although not actually in the town, the Findhorn Bridge was vital to the economy, and work on the new suspension bridge at Mundole had been initiated in the previous year with the architect Alexander Mitchell making a site visit in July 1831, and providing estimates. There were delays in the supply of the timbers and the chains for the bridge, and it was not until 24 September 1832 that the first chains were in place. On 14 October the first passage across the river was effected, the width of a single plank! The work was delayed further by the weather, the contractors complaining that it was either too wet, too windy, or both. However, despite this, on 7 November Alexander Mitchell was able to write 'A week will finish the whole, the painters are at work, but the weather is against their operations'.

On 1 December 1832 Alexander Mitchell wrote 'Yesterday the bridge was opened by a procession of the Trustees, Subscribers and inhabitants of Forres to the number of about 2000 persons. Everything went off well and all seemed highly delighted – it was very gratifying to me to see the pleasure everyone felt in their bridge'. The cost of the bridge was some £30,000, which was recouped by means of 'pontage fees', which were charged until 1881 at the small toll cottage adjacent to the bridge.

The south entrance to the churchyard from the High Street was re-opened in 1831, the access previously being by way of the Kirk Vennel, also known now as the Burn Vennel. The pavements which had been constructed at the south-west end of the High Street some two years earlier were now extended so that the whole of the south side of the High Street had pavements to separate the pedestrians from the ever-increasing traffic on the turnpike road through the town. Tolbooth Wynd was repaired and upgraded the following year. As befitted the new thriving town, the National Bank of Scotland opened its premises in 1833 under the management of Alexander Watson.

In 1834 the two mail coaches through the town were the 'Defiance' and the 'Star'. The morning mail arrived at Forres from the west at 5 a.m., followed by the 'Defiance' from the same direction at 9 a.m. From the east came the 'Star' at 8.30 a.m., and the 'Defiance', on its return journey from Elgin, reached Forres at 2.30 p.m. The mail arrived in the town from the east at 4.30 p.m., and the 'Star' passed through the town on its return journey from the west at 7 p.m. The coaches stopped at Fraser's Hotel, the main hotel in town, formerly known as Louden's Hotel. It was later renamed the Commercial Hotel.

In 1834 the property which had begun life as a Lint Mill became the Forres brewery and, having its own mill lade taking water from the Mosset Burn, it was ideally situated for this purpose as it had the possibility of a direct outlet for waste back into the burn. The new brewery was equipped by Mr MacDonald and Mr George Urquhart, but although they were named as the tenants of the property the 'delicious Forres beverages' were actually brewed by Donald Munro, who lived in one of the former mill cottages. The buildings were owned by the Fraser Tytler family, and lately by Captain Fraser Tytler. The original road entrance to the mill would have been near the foot of the Castle Hill at Castle Bridge, running alongside the Mosset Burn. Once the building had been converted the entrance near Castle Hill would have been inconvenient for the large number of wagons needing access, and the building of the new 'Brewery Bridge' in the same year gave easier access to the site. The mill cottages which had been built some six years earlier provided useful accommodation for the brewery workers.

The behaviour of teenage boys has obviously changed little over the last

Forres Brewery, later the Aerated Water plant

two centuries, and in 1835 it was reported to the council that the boys selling pies in the town, obviously a popular 'fast food' of the nineteenth century, were inclined to be disorderly. As the complaints increased the council brought in the following regulations:

1. Names and ages of boys employed to sell pies were to be given to the council,
2. Boys must not go along the pavements or stand at the shop doors or windows,
3. Boys are not to importune people passing, nor shriek, nor scream, nor cluster together. They must behave properly and go singly along the street.
4. The boys must find security to the extent of £5 for their good behaviour.

New Buildings, New Ideas
*

The old tolbooth had consisted of a great rectangular three-storey tower with battlements, which was attached to the courthouse with access from the first floor of the tolbooth. In 1837 an Act for the building of a new Court House and Public Offices was passed, and the Town Council later decided that the new court house and jail should be combined using a design by William Robertson. The site of the St John's Masonic Lodge, which was adjacent to the tolbooth, was chosen as the site for the new jail, and the whole site, tolbooth, court house and jail, was opened in 1849. The replacement followed a similar layout to the old building, and the cupola was not dissimilar to the one on the old structure. The similarity in design was said to have been made in response to 'the wishes of many gentlemen of undoubted taste who, at the same time, take a warm interest in the prosperity and ornament of the good town'. The Town Council continued to meet in the building until the demise of the council during the reorganisations of 1976.

The year 1837 also saw the opening of the new gas works, which meant that the old oil lamps along the streets of Forres were now replaced with gas lights. Mr R. Weir became the minister of the Independent Church and served for the following seven years. Although there had been a nurse and a midwife operating in a private capacity in the town for some years, a qualified district nurse was now appointed and Isabella Anderson, the widow of John McIntyre, builder, was installed in this post. A dispensary was also founded in the town, with opening hours from 9 a.m. to 10 a.m. on two days each week, but in addition to this home visits were also arranged. The doctors in the town are identified as James Bell, John Grant, George Adams, Archibald D. Brands and James MacKenzie. Smallpox struck Forres in 1838 and in August alone no fewer than 38 cases were admitted to the Cholera Hospital, which was now also being used as the town jail. Free vaccination against the disease was offered to the people of Forres, but only a few accepted the offer. The Plough Inn, later to become the Moray Arms Hotel, was run by one A.C. Audley at this time.

In 1839 the Forres National Security Savings Bank opened. The duties of Mawlin Thomson, the town Police Officer, seem to have been becoming more hazardous, and Forres got its first 'police dog' when he was given one for his own protection. The church was modified at this time, with several of the windows being enlarged and a new gallery added. The church now had four large arched windows on the south side, a main entrance in the east gable and a quadrangular belfry containing two bells at the west end. The British Linen Company Bank opened its premises in this year, on the corner of the High Street and Gordon Street.

St John's Episcopal Church was built in 1841, a small but handsome building in the Italianate style, with nave, aisles, transept and chancel. It was, unusually, orientated north to south on a site on the northern side of the eastern end of the High Street, almost opposite Forres House. The following year, 1842, was one of serious food shortages, and a temporary meal house was set up in the jailer's house to distribute meal to those in need. It was agreed by the council that street name signs should be put in place where they did not already exist, and that houses and other properties in the town should be numbered.

In 1844 the proposal for a new market place, which had been originally mooted some three years earlier, was finally put into practice. To make room for the market place some properties in Tolbooth Lane were purchased from William Smith and from the Mathieson family for the total sum of £330, these buildings then being demolished on the authority of the council. A new market cross was erected at this time, to a design by Thomas Mackenzie, but the base of the original cross still lies hidden within the base of this more modern structure.

On 1 August of that year, in a memorial to the Provost, Magistrates and Town Council of the Burgh of Forres, it was noted that:

The churchyard is becoming overcrowded, the inconveniences being
(i) a want of room for providing graves in which to deposit the bodies of the dead,
(ii) the health of the lieges from the Nephritic Gas, an offensive effluvia which at all times arise from this burying ground.

Under these 'alarming circumstances', a particular spot on the north-west corner of the Cluny Hills with a southern exposure was suggested for the new burying ground, but this idea was not immediately taken up.

The new main railway route to the north was being planned in 1845, and the Forres Town Council added their weight to a petition for the line to be routed from Aviemore, across the Dava Moor to Forres and then onward to Inverness. There was to be a branch to Elgin to join with the new railway coming from Aberdeen.

On 7 April 1845 an inventory was taken of the musical instruments of the Rechabite Band, the town band of the time. This list included 3 trombones, 8 flutes, 7 clarinets, 2 French horns and 1 carnopian. The financial restraints of 20 years earlier now seem to have been overcome, and the 'Forres Water Company' was formed with the eventual intention of providing a piped water supply to the houses in the town.

On 11 March 1847, a meeting of the Kirk Session, the Heritors and the Magistrates was held 'to consider a statement made regarding the necessity of providing an additional Burying Ground for the parish of Forres . . .', a matter which had originally been raised before council some three or four years earlier. The town also finally got rid of the dung-heaps in the streets. The 'Proclamation of Sanitary Reform' prohibited accumulations of 'dung, fulzie or other matter pernicious to the health of the lieges . . .'

On 7 October 1847, a meeting was held in Forres to consider the establishment of a Mechanics Institute and Library. The first subscriptions towards this were received during the week following the meeting, and the plans were finalised some seven years later, with the old Freemasons Hall or St Lawrence Lodge being acquired at the end of 1854. There were various improvements and extensions to the building during the early 1880s, with the new façade being proposed during the last year of the nineteenth century.

The Post Office in Forres had occupied a building in Caroline Street, and the postmaster was a Mr Gill, but in the early 1880s it was moved to the west end of the High Street. In 1910 the new Post Office was built at the Castle Hill, just below where James Anderson would continue to graze his cows. Nearby was the shop of the wine merchant Mr Fraser. The Post Office still stands on that site, now as part of a convenience store.

Just below the Castle Bridge was the cottage where Lord Strathcona was

Lord Strathcona's birthplace near the Castle Bridge in Forres

born, but by the later years of the nineteenth century it was known as 'The College'. This was a school run by James Fraser, the children often playing on and around the Castle Bridge, and maybe watching Mr Jenkins herding his ducks and geese on the banks of the Mosset Burn. Where the rose garden now lies was 'Cowie's Hole', the house and workshop of Mr Cowie the cabinet-maker. Lord Strathcona's birthplace is long since demolished, the cabinet-maker's house and workshop a distant memory, but the ducks and even a few geese still waddle around their ancestral haunts on the banks of the burn.

In the 1890s venturing east along the High Street took the visitor past the shops of Mr McGarrow, a small man known for his sales of snuff and 'Brig o' Turk' whisky, James Grant the bookseller and John Helenzon, a dapper and self-important man who was the town's tobacconist, hairdresser and tooth extractor. The shops where they served their customers are mostly still standing, as are the ones going further east towards the tolbooth. Two of these shops were the premises of Mr D.K. Stewart, the bookseller, and his neighbour George Cutler, the draper.

At the tolbooth, with its jail, and looking very little different to the way the modern visitor sees it in the twenty-first century, were often to be found the two local policemen, William Lyon and John Campbell, keeping some kind of law and order among the Forres 'loons'. The eastern half of the High Street was home to many more shops, including that of Robbie Oustie, antique dealer, musician and seller of pies and lemonade. 'Dean' Wight, the ironmonger, was close by, and Mrs Morrison's shop, at the end of Batchen's Wynd, was a popular place with the children from the school across the road to spend their pennies on sweeties. No need for a lollipop lady to get them across the High Street in those days!

A row of old thatched cottages lined the north side of the High Street at its eastern end, and opposite was the forbidding 9-foot-high wall which surrounded the grounds of Forres House, the home of Sir Alexander Grant. The thatched cottages, the wall and the mansion house are now long gone.

FORRES IN THE
TWENTIETH CENTURY

The early years of the twentieth century saw little change in Forres apart from a gradual improvement in the roads as the horse-drawn vehicles of earlier times gave way to motor cars, lorries and buses. Some of the older buildings saw changes of use as shopfronts were developed, and former dwelling houses were sold off as offices for solicitors and other businesses. Most prominent of all, however, was the building of the new Church of St Laurence.

On the site of the old typically Presbyterian Church arose a beautiful Neo-Gothic building, designed by Inverness architect John Robertson, its tower and spire soaring 120 feet towards the heavens. The old churchyard was almost totally destroyed during the building of the new church, most of the old tombstones being taken away and broken up to be used as rubble for the new road building schemes. The foundation stone of the new St Laurence Church was laid on 17 August 1904, and the first service was held on 28 February 1906. The stone for the new church came from the Newton Quarries, and is probably one of the last examples of the traditional stonemason's craft in this area.

During the First World War, the Mechanics Institute and Library were used as a hospital for the war wounded, and the Library and Reading Room were closed in 1915. After the war, the managers of the local Red Cross organisation handed the building back to the directors of the Institute.

Although Forres House was bought by the Town Council in 1919 and subsequently let out, it was not until the 1920s that it eventually became of benefit to the people of the town. There were suggestions that part of the

Forres House and Grant Park

Forres, North of Scotland Bank, c.1940

Victoria Hotel Forres

building could be used as a house for the Provost, but in 1925 the huge wall surrounding the house was removed, opening up panoramic views of Cluny Hill and the Nelson Tower. The mansion house was converted into bathrooms, recreation rooms and other facilities for the benefit of the townspeople. The grounds were laid out as ornamental gardens, a cricket ground, and bowling and putting greens.

Times changed, and by 1969 the public baths and the other facilities were closed, and the house became derelict, only to be destroyed by a fire in November of the following year. The gardens and the grounds still remain as Grant Park, a reminder of this once-beautiful estate.

The buildings along the High Street remain a symbol of the wealth of the town in the nineteenth century. Many of the houses along St Leonard's Road to the south of the town speak of a period of prosperity, of wealthy nabobs and merchants returning from abroad, and a general feeling of self-satisfaction in the town.

But much of old Forres is now lost, not just the buildings and the old closes, but a way of life which would be almost foreign to the modern resident or visitor. The dung-heaps are gone, one thing for the better; the pie-boys have gone and we will never know what those Forres pies tasted like. The inns remain, but the Forres brew is a thing of the past, and the soldiers marching back and forth through the town are now replaced by the very welcome airmen from nearby Kinloss.

CHAPTER 9
THE ROYAL
BURGH OF ELGIN

ELGIN IN EARLY TIMES

There is no real evidence for the existence of the town of Elgin before the twelfth century, although it is probably safe to consider that there was some form of settlement here, at a crossing point of the River Lossie, from a much earlier time, probably contemporaneous with Forres. Originally it was probably little more than a collection of closely situated crofts or small farms along a 'street' on the ridge of land lying to the south of the River Lossie. The river originally flowed much closer to the edge of the 'town', but it must have been at about this time it changed its course a little further northwards to flow against the foot of the ridge of Bishopmill, leaving a wide area of marshland and bog, later to be known as the 'Borough Briggs', through which the river meandered, often flooding, and leaving behind a very fertile and very necessary flood plain.

The early traders of the area, shoemakers, weavers and other artisans, would have had workshops attached to, or even inside their homes, and derived a living from their trades, and also from the land they had around their cottage. Any sort of retail market economy was still in the future, and it is doubtful whether any tradesman could have survived without the food and the few beasts which he and his family were able to produce.

CASTLES AND ROYAL POWER

Times were beginning to change, however, and the twelfth century was to see the beginning of a different way of life for the people of Elgin, and indeed for much of Scotland. In 1109 King Alexander I began a reign which was to last for 15 years, to be succeeded by David I in 1124. King David had been educated at the English Court and was greatly influenced by the Normans. He sought to 'civilise' Scotland, and in many aspects of this he was very successful. He created a 'New Order' very much like that which evolved in England after the Norman Invasion of 1066, and through this means he was able, at least for a short time, to undermine the resistance to the monarchy in the north. It was at this time that the burghs of Scotland were being established, and Elgin, along with Forres and Nairn, was no exception. The king encouraged the growth of these burghs to expand the economy of the country, and the towns were granted charters to trade. Hereditary sheriffdoms were created, and castles were built to act as centres for the enforcement of the laws of the land. The earliest mention of Elgin as a burgh is in 1151, when King David granted to the Priory of Urquhart an annual payment out of the rentals of his 'Burgh and Water of Elgin'.

The castle of Elgin was built on what would seem to be a modified natural hill adjacent to the river. At first it would have been a wooden structure, probably just a palisade on the hilltop surrounding a cluster of wooden buildings, a place of refuge for the townspeople if needed. In later years, a stone structure would replace the earlier castle, and the king was able to put his own men in charge of the castle both to enforce the rule of law and to provide protection for the townspeople.

There was a continuing influx of Normans, Saxons and Flemings into the north at this time, and the town underwent a rapid expansion along the single street which ran between the castle at its west end and the parish church at the east end. King William, who had succeeded to the throne in 1165, visited Elgin several times during his reign accompanied by many of the leading nobles and clergy of the time. Elgin by now must have been of considerable status to have the accommodation for the royal visitor and his retinue. The king appears to have viewed Elgin as an important centre of government, and during the course of his 49-year reign he granted no fewer than fourteen charters to the Burgh of Elgin, as compared with one to Inverness and six to Aberdeen. He may even have used Elgin as a base for his military expeditions into Ross-shire and the far north.

ELGIN IN THE
THIRTEENTH CENTURY

Despite repeated attempts to bring it under the control of the 'establishment', Moray continued to maintain some semblance of its former independence. Its eventual success was probably due to the efforts of Kings Alexander II and III, who, with the help of the Church, brought about the beginning of a 'Golden Age' for Scotland. This may well also have been helped by the steady improvement in the climate, which allowed a much more varied form of agriculture, and even the establishment of vineyards in some of the more sheltered glens occupied by the newly founded monasteries.

The houses in Elgin were, in general, built with a timber frame, infilled with wattle and daub, and with a thatched roof, the floors in most cases being of clay or beaten earth. The few larger houses in the town may have been built of stone, with stone flagged floors. Under the protection of the Church, the landowners, and ultimately the monarchy, the Burgh of Elgin and the other burghs in the north began to expand not only in terms of the population but also in their economy. The building of the cathedral was started in 1224, on the lands of the Holy Trinity to the east of the town (see Chapter 10). Close by was the monastery of Blackfriars, on the north side of the town by the river under the shelter of the hill on which the castle stood. To the east lay Greyfriars, situated on the south side of the High Street, and the hospital of Maisondieu where there was also a leper hospital.

In 1242 Alexander II was in Elgin with his queen Mary de Couci, one of several reputed visits he made, but his successor, Alexander III, possibly only

The site of the old Castle of Elgin on Ladyhill and the Gordon Memorial

made one visit to Elgin in 1263. The middle of the thirteenth century was a time of peace, and during this expansion of the arts and of industry, the climax of the 'Golden Age', the burgh attracted great wealth and importance, eclipsing neighbouring Forres, which in earlier times was the principal settlement in the area. Since Elgin was the seat of the Bishop of Moray with his glorious new cathedral, much of the land in the area was under the power of the Church. This power base in the north no doubt attracted many nobles and barons to live in the town or at least to build their residences close by. The establishment of the religious houses saw the monks becoming schoolmasters, architects, tradesmen and farmers, generally boosting the local economy 'into a civilized state of peaceful industry'. The burgh now had its provost, town clerk and burgesses, but the good times were not to last.

THE DEMISE OF THE 'GOLDEN AGE'

✳

The later years of the thirteenth century were to see a return of troubled times. The demise of Alexander III in 1285 sounded the death knell of the 'Golden Age' and led to a time of Scottish revolt and punitive attacks by King Edward. Henry de Rye, one of Edward's men, was in charge of the castle at Elgin in 1291 and 1292, and on Thursday 26 July 1296 the king himself was in Elgin, where he found what he described as 'a good castle and a good town'. He stayed in Elgin for two days, and according to some contemporary reports he had with him 5,000 armed horsemen and 30,000 foot soldiers. How accurate these figures are we will never know, but in any event his visit must have been a logistical nightmare, his troops outnumbering by far the population of Elgin, and almost certainly devastating the economy of the town which had to provide for all these men and no doubt many camp-followers. The visit, however, resulted in no structural damage to the town, at least not on this occasion.

ELGIN IN THE
FOURTEENTH CENTURY

In 1302 King Edward resolved to humble the Scots and marched northwards, eventually reaching the northernmost point of his expedition at Elgin, where he stayed from 10 to 13 September. Apart from the documentation about his visit, the records at this time are strangely silent, and it is difficult for us to envisage what went on in these troubled times during the Wars of

Independence. Elgin continued to develop as a typical medieval Scottish burgh, lying as an elongated oval between the castle to the west and the parish church of St Giles at its eastern end. Small lanes ran off to the north and the south at either end of the burgh, and the whole was bounded by the North and the South Back Gaits, sometimes known as the 'Back Passages'. The North Back Gait ran along the line of what are now Blackfriars Road and North Lane, while the South Back Gait followed the line of the present South Street.

Within these rather tight confines lay the burgess plots or riggs of the townspeople, stretching back from the High Street out to the Back Gaits, some of them well over 100 metres long. Access from the High Street to each of the burgess plots was through the gaps between the houses, which were later to develop into the pends, wynds and closes so characteristic of a medieval burgh. Even at this time buildings such as barns and stables were being erected along the sides of the burgage lands to accommodate the beasts kept by the townsfolk, and of course they also grew their own foodstuffs not only in these burgage plots, but also in the runrig lands which many of them held in the lands beyond the Back Gaits.

The High Street widened at what was then its eastern end to accommodate the church of St Giles and its churchyard, and also to provide a market area for the burgh. The market cross, which was mentioned as early as 1365, stood within the churchyard. Whether it is this cross which now stands in the cathedral churchyard we will never know. In addition to the church and churchyard, this area was home to the town tolbooth, where the Burgh Council met and the taxes were collected, and also the jail. Like the majority of Scottish burghs at this time, Elgin had no town walls, but protection was provided by the boundary walls at the foot of the riggs, these almost certainly being substantial enough to ensure that the only way into the town was through one of the four town 'ports' or gates. The precise location of these town ports at this time is unclear, but it is likely that the West Port was just to the south of the castle and the East Port was near to the entrance to the College of Elgin and the Cathedral Lands, somewhere near to the Little Cross. The North Port, which has now been removed to a position at the rear of the museum, was in Lossie Wynd, and the South Port was at the top of School Wynd, now Commerce Street.

Later in the fourteenth century, Elgin began to fall into an economic decline. Although as late as 1400 it is suggested by Young that 'The Loch of Spynie being an arm of the sea . . . it is probable that vessels entered the estuary (of the River Lossie) and delivered goods to the Bishop's Port of Spynie', there must have already been many problems with navigation into the loch, and the silting up of the loch, together with the increasing size and draught of the ships, must have eventually rendered the 'Bishop's Port of Spynie' almost unusable. Together with the strict controls and taxes which were now being imposed by the church over the goods which passed through the port, this led to many protests by the burgesses of Elgin, and was a primary factor in their decision to make more use of the port of Garmouth.

This decision was made easier for the burgesses when, in 1393, the Earl of Moray granted them freedom from customs on their goods, such as wool and cloth, which were exported through his 'haven' or harbour of the River Spey, the port of Garmouth. Although it was maybe not quite so convenient as the old harbour at Spynie, at least the burgesses were guaranteed a good harbour which was, unlike Spynie, right on the coast, and also freedom from the crippling taxes imposed by the Church. The fate of the harbour at Spynie was finally sealed.

Attackers and Raiders

*

The various incursions into the north of Scotland by the English monarchs and their forces in the closing years of the fourteenth century, combined with what appear to have been three events of 'pestilence', probably the plague, weakened the status of Elgin and the other burghs. According to the local historian William Cramond, on 1 May 1390, the Earl of Moray 'remitted the assize (tax) of ale formerly paid to the Earl's Castle of Elgin, or in lieu thereof 100 shillings out of the fermes of the burgh yearly, in consideration of the damage occasioned to the burgh by three pestilences and various attacks made by different persons'.

In May of the same year, Alexander Stewart, the 'Wolf of Badenoch', in protest against his excommunication, attacked and burned much of the Burgh of Forres, and the following month he rose again from his lair at the Castle of Lochindorb to attack Elgin, probably calling in at Pluscarden Abbey on the way, as it is known that he also inflicted damage there at about the same time. He burnt much of Elgin, its wooden buildings succumbing readily to the torch, and also set light to the Church of St Giles, the cathedral, the houses of the canons in the College of Elgin, and the hospital of Maisondieu. Before his death some four years later Alexander Stewart was absolved of his crimes and accepted back into the church, on condition that he should make recompense to the Bishop and the Church of Moray. Whether he was also required to recompense the burgesses of the town is never recorded, but the cathedral was rebuilt by 1397.

ELGIN IN THE FIFTEENTH CENTURY

On 3 July 1402, Alexander, the third son of the Lord of the Isles, attacked Elgin, burning much of the town which was only recently rebuilt following the earlier attacks. He plundered the cathedral, but on a subsequent visit some four months later he was absolved by the Bishop of Moray. As a token of his contrition he is thought to have erected a cross and a bell at the boundary between the Burgh of Elgin and the walled lands of the Cathedral and College of Elgin, probably at the point where the Little Cross now stands.

With the crowning of James I in 1406, royal authority was finally established over almost the whole of mainland Scotland, and despite arguments and quarrels between families such as the Douglasses and the Gordons, this became a time of relative peace. The threat of attack from the Vikings to the north and the English to the south was a thing of the past, but the Highlanders still remained in the west. The Castle of Elgin had been maintained in some degree of order by the earls of Moray since the time of David I, but it was now falling into ruin, being of little further use. Finally only a chapel, dedicated to the Blessed Virgin Mary, survived in use, and in time the hill became known not as Castle Hill but as Chapel Hill or Lady Hill.

The peaceful times gave a sense of security and well-being to the people, and this was a period of expansion not only of the burghs but also of the surrounding villages and fermtouns. Some of the strongholds of former times began to become more comfortable residences, evolving into fortified houses. The Church continued to exercise its influence over the population, and although the people were becoming increasingly disenchanted with the cathedrals and monasteries, the parish churches, although often quite insignificant buildings in their own right, were now beginning to benefit from the endowments made by the more wealthy parishioners. The parish church was, by now, becoming more central to the life of the whole community.

When the Earl of Huntly went south to fight at the Battle of Brechin in 1452, the Earl of Moray took advantage of the power vacuum and invaded the lands of Strathbogie and burned down the Castle of Huntly. On his return the somewhat displeased Earl of Huntly pursued Moray as far as Elgin, and finding out that part of the town, particularly the west end, was not entirely favourable to his cause, proceeded, in what seemed to be the custom of the time, to set light to the houses there. Some people have suggested that as a consequence of this much of the western part of Elgin, around the castle, was abandoned, and new development took place to the east, finally linking the Burgh of Elgin with the walled cathedral city.

The Burgh of Elgin was first represented at the Scottish Parliament in 1469, but by the end of the century there was a joint representative for both Elgin and Forres. Many of the houses in Elgin had by now been rebuilt several times, and the fashion was for two storeys, but still, in general, with a thatched roof. Some stone town houses were now being built by the major landowners, such as Huntly's house near the Little Cross and Cumming of Lochtervandich's house, also at the east end of the High Street, which almost certainly would have had a slated or stone-slabbed roof.

ELGIN IN THE SIXTEENTH CENTURY

For many people this new century represented the beginning of the decline of the ignorant and superstitious Middle Ages. The clergy were becoming all-powerful, maybe too powerful, and the Church was, at least in the first decades of the century, continuing its ruthless acquisition of lands. The Burgh of Elgin continued to expand and the population to increase. The affairs of the burgh were still conducted in the old, mostly wooden, thatched tolbooth, which functioned not only as a tax collection point, but as the seat of local government, increasingly a symbol of the power of the Town Council and magistrates. It was also a court, a prison and sometimes probably a place of execution. The jail was not always very secure, and in 1541 one of the prisoners

The old town jail in the town centre

made his escape by simply removing the whole lock, intact, from what was probably a very old and rotten prison door.

THE DEVELOPMENT OF ELGIN
*

More and more of the buildings were being constructed of stone, in some cases now reaching up to three storeys and extending out over the roadway. The characteristic closes of the town were appearing, as cottages and workshops were built on what would in earlier times have been the gardens or toft lands of the merchant's houses. Many of the closes took the names of the merchant or burgess who owned the land. Shops or 'booths', something like modern market stalls, were appearing along the High Street, displaying the wares of a growing number of tradesmen and merchants. The trade guilds continued to expand their powers as well, giving some sort of protection to the livings of the tradesmen and artisans and also providing security for them in times of need. Later in the century market days were set as Wednesday and Saturday, and the selling of meat was forbidden at all other times.

Education in the town was becoming well-established and in addition to the Cathedral School, which had been in existence for almost three centuries, there was also the Grammar School, which came under the control of the Burgh Council. The 'Sang Schule' or 'Musick Schule' was founded in 1550, and in 1594 it was granted a royal charter.

THE EARLIEST RECORDS
*

The earliest surviving Burgh Records date from 1540, and one of the first entries refers to David Hardy being created a freeman of the Burgh on payment of 'ane stane wax'. In the same document, Agnes Baldon was convicted of 'casting ane staine and breking of Katherine Falconeris heid and drawing bluid of the samyn'. The minutes go on to give a very interesting picture of life in Elgin throughout the century, and mention many people from all ranks of society in the creation of freemen, disputes over land, arguments over horses and the frequent 'dingings', or fights, too numerous to mention here. John Bell alias Stuart was censured for 'noise pollution' by playing his bagpipes in the town, maybe not a very favourable comment on his standard of performance.

The Burgh Council was, however, imposing much stricter regulation on the lives of the townspeople, probably due to the ever-increasing number of people living there. They were prohibited from winnowing corn in the High

Braco's Banking House, Elgin High Street

Street, but the dung-heaps at the mouth of each close were still a constant source of smells, dirty water and probably also of disease. Regulations about the weight and size of a loaf, of a candle and also of the cost of ale, together with the movement of horses and cattle, were all announced from the tolbooth, and probably just as quickly ignored by the people.

Elgin was now prominent among the burghs of Scotland and now ranked superior to Forres and Nairn in the Stent Rolls, the league tables of the time. The chapel on Lady Hill was never mentioned again after 1557 and had almost certainly fallen out of use at the time of the Reformation.

CHURCH AND STATE

✳

Although 1560 saw the start of the Reformation in Scotland, it took several years before its impact was finally felt by people all across the country, and it may have been another five years or more before the new ideas of worship were accepted in the north. Elgin appears to have been one of the principal Episcopal towns in Scotland, and the Church was a major part of the economy, so there was little appetite for change among either the people or the clergy. But, inevitably, change did come, and within eight years of the start of the Reformation in Edinburgh the magnificent cathedral (the 'Lantern of the North'), the monasteries of Greyfriars and Blackfriars, and the Preceptory and Hospital of Maisondieu were all to be abandoned in favour of the Protestant Church. The town house of the bishop and the manses of the canons in the College of Elgin were all to fall into decline, and many of the nobles and landed gentry who had built houses in Elgin in order to be able to resort to the Catholic bishops now had second thoughts and retreated to their country estates, leaving the economy of Elgin to decline still further.

The Catholic clergy were replaced by the new Protestant ministers, and the old ecclesiastical buildings were being used as 'quarries' to supply stone for the new buildings in the town. This was now the main building material, and the High Street was soon lined with new houses and shops, some of them with ground floor arcades such as that still seen on Braco's Banking House at the east end of the High Street. Just seven years after the start of the Reformation the lead was removed from the roof of the cathedral, destined to be sold to pay for victuals for the troops, but, whether through divine intervention or retribution we will never know, the ship carrying the lead sank and all was lost. This started the decay of the building and allowed the weather to exert its destructive forces on the now unclad roof and beams.

The tolbooth was repaired and re-thatched in 1572, during which time the

Braco's Close, Elgin

Burgh Court, and probably also the council, met in the nearby parish church of St Giles. It soon became obvious that the repairs to the tolbooth were little more than a convenient stop-gap and could not be a permanent solution, and a burgh such as Elgin needed a more substantial and impressive building. Moving with a speed which would have impressed any modern town council, it only took another 30 years for this idea to be realised. The mercat cross survived to perform its secular function in the old churchyard of St Giles, and the markets were still held in the churchyard.

The carrying of arms without a licence, either openly or concealed, was banned in Elgin in 1580. The statute ruled that 'Siclyk it is statut that nadir freman nor onfreman within this burgh in na tymes cuming sall beir or weir jak, pleit slewis, culvering, dag, pistol nor suord upon tham . . .' Whether this made the town a more peaceful place or not is never recorded.

The foul smell of plague was in the air again by 1585, with cases having been reported from Aberdeen and also on board a ship moored off Findhorn. All of the inhabitants of the town were made responsible for the guarding of the town ports, probably on a rota basis. The back walls of the burgess plots were built up and strengthened, the wynds and the North and South Ports were closed off with turf walls and the defences of the town at the East and West Ports were strengthened. Obviously these latter two could not be closed completely as they guarded the 'King's High Way', the main route between Inverness and Aberdeen, but for a year or two Elgin was a virtual fortress against the spread of infection.

Superstition was not yet dead in Elgin and the other burghs in the last decade of the sixteenth century. Trials for witchcraft were again beginning to come before the Kirk Session and the flames of the bonfires at the old pagan celebrations of Beltane, celebrating the onset of summer, of Midsummer and of Hallow's e'en still lit the skies over the town. The Catholic Church was not yet dead either, despite the Reformation. Many of the followers of the 'auld faith' in Elgin were censured for visiting holy wells and shrines in various parts of the district, in some cases facing banishment from the town if they repeated the offence. Christmas and New Year 1599–1600 must have been a really cheerful time, as the Kirk Session passed an act against people either within the Burgh or the College of Elgin 'futballing through the town, snaw balling, singing of carellis or other prophane sangis, guysing, pyping, violing and dansing', and these were even more expressly forbidden in the old cathedral churchyard, except, for some reason, the playing of football there. All women and 'lassis' were also expressly forbidden to go to the old cathedral. This act was in force from 25 December until the last day of January. A merry Christmas indeed!

ELGIN IN THE
SEVENTEENTH CENTURY

William Rhind, writing in 1834, gives us his own ideas of how Elgin must have appeared at the start of the seventeenth century. While he gives no sources or proof for any of his statements, and is possibly exaggerating the antiquity of the buildings, many of his ideas fit in very well with contemporary documents.

> The houses on each side were of a venerable antiquity, with high roofs covered with great slabs, and piazzas or forestairs in front, consisting of a series of arches supported by pillars and containing a

paved court within. Diverging from the main street were alleys or closes, occupied on each side by houses of an inferior grade. The business of the town consisted of the usual trades and crafts for the supply of home consumpt, and of the burgesses, who were generally shop-keepers, for the retail of the necessaries and luxuries of life to the surrounding country . . . A mass of miscellaneous articles were huddled together in a small dark shop or cellar, of various qualities for various purposes. A country purchaser did not always pay hard cash, but a species of barter added still more to the heterogeneous compounds of the warehouse. A shopman, trusting to the perfect honesty of the place, thought nothing of leaving his half door 'on the bar' while he went for an hour or so for breakfast or dinner, or perhaps took a stroll with a neighbour on a summer's afternoon. The street was paved with an ancient causeway . . . it rose high in the middle and 'the crown o' the causey' was distinguished by a row of huge stones, while those of lesser dimensions occupied the sides. The drains ran along the street, and the common gutter crossed it at right angles. After heavy rains this gutter not infrequently swelled into an impassable torrent.

And so on in a similar vein. Rhind may present a somewhat rose-tinted view of life in Elgin at that time, never making a mention of the stinking dung-heaps that lined the High Street at the mouth of every close, and the poor from the country who had come into the town to seek a means of survival. The common gutter was there, flowing down the brae from the South Back Gait and crossing the High Street just underneath where the Marks and Spencer Food Hall stands today, discharging its putrid waste as a filthy stream into the River Lossie at the Borough Briggs.

The threat of plague and pestilence was still never far away, and the inhabitants were warned to receive no strangers into their houses, and to ensure that the back dyke walls and the town ports were in good repair. It is obvious from the Kirk Session Minutes for the first decade of the new century that there were cases of the plague nearby, maybe in the ports of Garmouth and Findhorn. The cases of witchcraft continued unabated, and Papism and idolatry were still causing concern to the Protestant minister. Fast days were being ignored and church attendance was falling, but this may have been as much due to a lack of faith as to the incumbency of a rather uninspiring minister, Alexander Douglas. His failings towards his flock, however, did not prevent him being promoted to become Bishop of Moray in 1606.

CIVIL POWER AND CHURCH AID

*

The tolbooth, repaired just 30 years earlier, was again falling down around the ears of the burgesses, magistrates and prisoners. In 1602 William Dunbar and James Ross, indwellers in Elgin, were awarded a contract to 'big (build) ane sufficient tolbeith within the said burgh quhair (where) the auld tolbeith thereof presently stands, of threescore (60) feet length, twentie futtis of braid and wydness (breadth)'. It was to be built using stones from the now almost redundant kirkyard dyke, and sclaited (slated) with 'stanes frae Dollas (Dallas)'. The new building contained a prison house, a council room and other accommodation, and it was finished three years later at a cost of 513 merks. At this period in time a merk was worth 1s 1½d sterling, giving a total cost of just under £29, which probably represented at least a quarter of the town's total tax income for a year. For the time, this was an expensive project. The completion of the new tolbooth coincided with the end of burials in the church and churchyard of St Giles, probably in no small part due to the destruction of the kirkyard dyke to provide the stone for the building work. Some burials may have continued to take place within the church itself.

The Bede House, near to the East Port, was built in 1624 with the purpose of providing a home for four Bede Men, generally burgesses of the town who, through age or infirmity, had fallen on hard times. They were issued with a uniform, a small amount of land on which to grow food and a small pension. In return for this, they were obliged to attend the kirk every day for morning and evening prayers, failing which they would lose their rights to the Bede House.

An invaluable, but probably not always very popular member of the community was the town drummer. Every morning at 4 a.m. he would make his rounds of the town beating his drum to awaken the inhabitants. This was usually followed by a further round at 5 a.m. and the ringing of the church bell at 6 a.m. The evening or curfew bell was rung at 8 p.m., and at 9 p.m. the town drummer made his final rounds. This curfew bell was not an instruction to the people that they must be off the streets, but, deriving from the French, was an instruction to 'cover or curb the fire'. Although many buildings were now being constructed of stone, there were also a large number of older wooden-framed thatched cottages in the town, and there was an ever-present risk of fire.

The Accounts of the Hospital of Elgin were examined by the Kirk Session in 1626, but there is no evidence as to where this was situated, although it is possible that some of the buildings at the old Hospital of Maisondieu may have survived. Wherever it was, it had inmates and was a residential establishment

The Hospital of Maisondieu

of some kind. Several of the more wealthy residents of the town are recorded as having made quite substantial donations to the hospital at about this time, which also continued to run the leper hospital, which had a colony and burial ground just to the east of Maisondieu.

The Bow Brig at Oldmills was built in 1630, providing dry-shod access to the north and west of the town, and it is clearly identified in Blaeu's atlas of 1662. Although it lay outside both the burgh and parish of Elgin, the building was financed in no small part by the town's burgesses and magistrates.

THE SHORT-LIVED
REVIVAL OF ELGIN
*

After its decline following the Reformation, Elgin was now beginning to assert itself once more as a centre of industry and commerce, and the first Dean of Guild, George Cuming, was appointed in 1643. From this time onwards the size of the council was increased from 16 to 17 men, probably to allow the new Dean of Guild to take his seat on the council without disturbing the other members. The following year, the town was readying itself for the troubles to come as Civil War raged in England, and Andrew Annand, one of the councillors, was instructed to keep a supply of powder and lead for the town, and the whole town was told to have their 'muscats' and guns ready with ball and powder. The town drummer went through the town proclaiming the need for soldiers to represent Elgin in the army in England, and each volunteer was to be given two dollars and a new pair of shoes, probably essential as they would have had to walk all the way to England.

ELGIN UNDER
ATTACK ONCE MORE
*

The year 1645 was a time of misery for many of the towns in the north. After the Battle of Auldearn, Montrose came to Elgin and burned down many of the relatively new town houses. He chose particularly those of Walter Smith, John Miln, John Douglas of Morristoun and Alexander Douglas, who were obviously on a shortlist of people who had got on the 'wrong side'. Unfortunately the houses of some of their neighbours, including Robert Gibson, George Donaldson and George Sutherland, who were probably, but not certainly, relatively innocent parties, were also destroyed in the conflagration. John Hay, the Provost of Elgin, and also Gavin Douglas had earlier given a 'backhander' to Montrose, and their houses were spared.

There were Royalist and Covenanter troops in the town at various times, and according to contemporary sources 'the whole place was in a state of much confusion'. Other threats later in the year were only prevented by the pleas of the magistrates and the good offices of Robert Gordon of Gordonstoun 'for the saifftie of this poor desolate town . . .', and the hopes of a prosperous future for Elgin, which were so strong just two or three years earlier, were again dashed.

The game of golf was quite popular in Elgin in the late 1640s, although we don't know where the 'golf course' was then. George Watson was identified as a gouffer and burgess of Elgin, so maybe he was Elgin's first professional golfer. He bought a set of clubs from Alexander Geddes, a skinner in the town, but seems to have been a little reluctant to pay him for them, which led to all kinds of arguments.

Cromwell's soldiers were garrisoned in Elgin during the Civil War, and there were many cases of riotous behaviour in the town. The soldiers also, as soldiers do, managed to nearly double the usual number of cases of fornication appearing before the Kirk Session during their stay in the town. As a consequence of this, several women, maybe those who had pursued the oldest profession and had taken advantage of a profitable situation, were banished from the town.

LIFE RETURNS TO NORMAL

✳

In 1657 the magistrates of the town entered into an agreement with the various trades, and the institution of the Trades of Elgin has continued unbroken until the present day.

The last four decades of the seventeenth century saw more public evidence of the cases of witchcraft, real or imagined, which had been festering in communities throughout the country during the time of rule from England. Presbyteries were urging their ministers and kirk sessions to root out the witches and charmers, and Elgin was no exception. One of the first cases to be heard in the town was in 1661, being that against John Rind and his wife Elspet Smith, and Margrat Murray and 'fooll Eppie commonly called'. At least in these possibly slightly more civilised times the culprits were not sentenced to death, but generally, after standing for many Sunday mornings in sackcloth in the kirk, they were put out of the town. It is always interesting to speculate on what actually became of them. What about Elspet Allan, commonly called 'fooll Eppie'? Her appearance before the Kirk Session must have been daunting for this unfortunate woman, who was accused of 'goieng dancing on the night on the streits with aledged witches'. She declared that 'Margrat Murray was there, and ane black dog', but the examination gradually petered out into farce, neither Fooll Eppie nor the black dog seem to have been much use to the prosecution's case.

One building now 'lost' was Calder's House, which stood on the spot where North Street now joins the High Street. It was built in 1669, almost certainly by one Thomas Calder, bailie and sometime provost of the burgh. Donaldson's House stood on land to which the titles had been acquired by his ancestors back in 1591, on the corner of the east side of Lossie Wynd at its junction with the High Street. James Donaldson was a merchant in the town, and the large house which he shared with his wife Jean McKean and their numerous children had lands and gardens which ran the full length of Lossie Wynd right down to the North Back Gait. The couple later built a smaller house, within a courtyard, about halfway down the east side of Lossie Wynd, and the carvings on it suggest it was built in 1689.

The threat of fire in the town was still an ever-present worry, as apart from the wealthy gentlemen with their town houses, most of the smaller properties still used a great deal of timber, and of course, had thatched roofs. The Town Council issued an Act which prevented the inhabitants from keeping peat, heather or firr on shelves above the fire, no doubt the desire to keep the fuel dry was also considered a serious fire risk.

Calder's House in Elgin High Street

On Sunday 22 June 1679, shortly after the congregation had left the church following morning service, the roof of St Giles Church collapsed. The old timber beams, which had not been repaired or probably even examined since the burning of the town nearly 300 years earlier by the Wolf of Badenoch, finally succumbed to the great weight of the heavy freestone roofing slabs, and the nave was totally destroyed. Although the steeple and the choir, and many of the pillars supporting the aisles remained intact, the rebuilding work took several years, and it was not until 1684 that the Church of St Giles was again able to welcome worshippers to their morning service.

The building work had been carried out under the supervision of John Ross, and the final cost of the work was in the region of £4,000. This was raised by means of a cess or tax on the townspeople, and also from the many donations and contributions made by the merchants and tradesmen of the burgh. The walls around both the cathedral and the St Giles churchyard were also rebuilt, and the people of Elgin were asked not to erect any more tombstones without the consent of the magistrates. The new gallows which

The Old Church of St Giles and the Tolbooth

The interior of Old St Giles Church

was erected at about the same time never seems to have been used, the authorities, both religious and secular, seeming to find it more profitable to impose large fines. Maybe there were many repeat offenders.

CROP FAILURES AND FAMINE
✳

The later years of the seventeenth century were marked by the 'seven ill years', a time of climatic deterioration which some sources suggest was due to volcanic eruptions on Iceland. The crops failed totally for four out of the seven years, and many of the poor and starving from the surrounding areas came to Elgin in search of whatever food was available. Mr Dunbar of Burgie, who lived at North College, was a very charitable man and gave aid to these people, but as the word got around the corpses of many of those poor starving people who did not quite make it were found lying in the lane leading to North College. As a final act of charity Mr Dunbar paid for the interment of the victims.

In spite of the shortages, however, there were no fewer than 80 breweries operating in Elgin at the end of this century, being supplied from the 32 malt kilns or malt barns in the burgh. These barns were described as good buildings, about 100 feet long, with slated roofs. Between March and June of 1697 one of the principal hoteliers in the burgh, William Douglas, brewed and sold some 4,000 gallons of ale and 400 gallons of aqua vitae, a good indication that the drinking water in the town was not of the highest quality. It was perhaps also symbolic of the social divide at this time, with the better-off people enjoying their beer and whisky in the hotels while only a few streets away near to the cathedral the starving poor were dying in the streets.

ELGIN IN THE
EIGHTEENTH CENTURY

By 1700 the population of Elgin was estimated to be about 3,000 people. The gradual rebuilding of the town had meant that the High Street was now lined with stone buildings, many of them designed in what some sources have described as an 'Elgin School' of building within the Scottish architectural tradition. They were generally of three storeys, with the ground floor frontage to the street often, especially at the eastern end of the High Street, consisting of an open arcade of low round arches carried on sturdy pillars, and the topmost storey being formed of a line of often richly ornamented dormer windows. The gables were invariably 'crow-stepped' and frequently they displayed the initials of the owners, a date, and in some cases a coat of arms.

The tolbooth was burned down in 1700 due to the actions of Robert Gibson of Linkwood. Due to the consequences of his marital problems he was declared to be a lunatic and was imprisoned in the tolbooth, but one night in October, during one of his insane rages, he set fire to the building, which was razed to the ground. He was lucky to escape with his life. Just two years later his wife Lady Linkwood was also imprisoned for her adultery, but managed to escape with the assistance of Ludovick Gordon, the couple then fleeing the town.

Building material became much more freely available in the town following the collapse of the great steeple of the cathedral in 1711, which demolished much of what was left of the old structure and scattered material all across the old burial ground. The local masons quickly made use of the remains, and several pieces of the quite ornate masonry which they were able to salvage soon decorated the frontages of the new houses being built at that time. By 1718 the face of the High Street was changing, the square tower and steeple of the Church of St Giles were built, as were the new courthouse and council chambers, buildings which stood until 1843. The closes were also beginning to acquire names, often from the business or hostelry which stood at the mouth of the close. Forteath's Close, Shepherd's Close, Red Lion Close and Old Seceder's Close all have names originating from this time. Glover's Close (now Glover Street), Raggs Wynd (later to be called Murdoch's Wynd) and the larger wynds such as Lazarus Wynd (now Lazarus Lane), Wiseman's Wynd (Cathedral Road), Shuttle Ra' (named for the weavers who occupied what is now Collie Street) and Moss Wynd (later Moss Street) leading down to the town moss can all trace their names back to the early eighteenth century.

The risk of fire in the town was greatly reduced in 1735 when the Town Council imposed a ban on thatching roofs with heather, and gradually more and more of the dwellings in the town had slate roofs. The High Street had been rebuilt as 'a causy of pebble stones 40ft broad, besides the cannals . . . for carrying away the watter'.

The poor harvests of the middle years of the eighteenth century led to some hardship in the town, but although Elgin had diminished in importance since the Act of Union in 1707, the economy was still strong enough for most people to be able to survive this downturn. At the time of the Jacobite Rebellion of 1745 the town, like many others, was divided, some, mainly those with Episcopalian and even Catholic sympathies, supporting the Jacobites, and others, those following the Presbyterian cause, being more favourably inclined

Red Lion Close, Elgin, c.1930, a typical Elgin close

Old shop and pend entrance in Elgin High Street

to the Government side. Families were even divided among themselves over the rights and wrongs of the dispute. There are no records of the Town Council or the Presbytery during the time of the Rebellion; either they were too afraid to meet, or they did not want to commit anything to paper. The presence of some 2,000 Rebels in the town from February until April of 1746 may have been an important factor in this decision. The story of the visit of Charles Edward Stuart to the town, and his stay at Thunderton House, is well known.

In 1746 John Duff Snr, merchant in Elgin, was elected provost, replacing James Stephen. This was a move which was to see the start of a gradual rise to power of the Duff family in local politics and in the governance of the town, a power which was to last for many decades. Although there was a regiment of troops stationed in Elgin for at least five years after the Rebellion, they did not seemed to create any great disturbance, and generally the town settled down well under Provost Duff. He was not too popular, however, when he was forced to increase taxes to attempt to recover some of the money which had previously been appropriated by the Rebel forces.

The routine of the town drummer had changed little over the years. William Edward still walked the town with his drum at 4 a.m. to wake the population, and again at 9 p.m. to sound the evening curfew. By 1769, however, when William's son George took over his father's job, the 4 a.m. call did not always have the desired effect, and he was obliged to go round the town again an hour later in an attempt to wake the townsfolk.

Elgin Becomes a Neat and Tidy Town
*

Between 1776 and 1778 a major tidy-up of the town seems to have taken place. Twenty-eight oil lamps were set in place along the High Street, Carseman's Wynd (now Lossie Wynd), School Wynd, College Street, East Street and Greyfriars Wynd. Due to the cost of the oil, the lamps were only used during the winter months, basically from October until about March, the long evenings and the 9 p.m. curfew no doubt making them unnecessary during the summer. Fortunately some aspects of life in Elgin from this time are now well and truly 'lost', the threshing and winnowing of corn in the streets was forbidden, as was the penning of sheep. The dung-heaps at the entrance to each close, and also those of the horse market, were cleared away, and the making of new dung-heaps was forbidden. The throwing of waste and refuse from the upstairs windows into the High Street was also forbidden, as it was damaging to the clothes of the passers-by. Elgin must have quickly become a brighter and sweeter place to live and work.

New Buildings and New Businesses

✳

The new hall of the Trinity Lodge of Masons was built in 1781 on the north side of the High Street at the Little Cross, and two years later Mr Francis Russell, who lived at West Park, adjacent to the West Port, decided that he needed a new garden wall, so he demolished the town's West Port to use the stone. This was done without the permission of the council, and he was instructed to rebuild it, an instruction which he, being a powerful landowner, totally ignored. He was probably not very popular with the workers, however, as the poor masons he had employed to demolish it, Robert McCraw and James Nicol, were fined £3 and £2 respectively for their destruction of the West Port, and were both imprisoned for 14 days.

In 1784 the Elgin Brewery was established at the east end of the cathedral lands, on an area which had been formerly occupied by the Petty Manse. The partners in this enterprise were Peter Rose Watson of Westerton, George Brown, the Provost of Elgin, William Robertson, John Ritchie Jnr and

Trinity Lodge Assembly Rooms at the top of North Street, Elgin

Malt kilns in Elgin in 1937

Alexander Brander, all merchants, and William Young of Oldmills. With an initial working capital of £1,000, they were able to build up a profitable business, and large quantities of beer, ale and porter were brewed, which was not only sold in the town but was transported by sea to other towns across the north of Scotland.

The 'Plainstanes' at the west side of St Giles Church were laid out in the same year to form a market place on the site of the old churchyard, and have remained in existence until the present day.

One of the most popular inns in Elgin was taken into new ownership in May 1786 when Mr Andrew Pearie took over the Duke of Gordon's Arms. According to the *Aberdeen Journal*, he then expanded the business to include Elgin's first taxi service, having 'brought from Edinburgh neat fashionable post-chaises with able horses, and has engaged careful drivers, so that the public may at all times depend on good and ready service'. His son was later to become a prominent farmer in Miltonduff, and was one of the founders of the Miltonduff Distillery.

The *Survey of the Province of Moray*, which appeared in print in the same decade as the *First Statistical Account of Scotland*, or the *Old Statistical Account* as it was more commonly known, contains a good description of Elgin as the eighteenth century came to a close:

> The town . . . consists of one principal street, in a winding course, for little more than a mile from east to west, widening to such breadth towards the middle of the town as to have the church awkwardly placed upon it, and a little distance farther on the town house, a mean building, adjoined to a clumsy square tower, almost without windows, which contains the hall where the courts and the county meetings are held, and the common goal. Behind the houses which front the street, buildings are carried back on either side, in narrow lanes, for the length of eight or ten dwellings, in some cases separate properties, and containing for the most part distinct families. Many of these lanes terminate in the gardens, affording a more immediate access to the country than the few public avenues offer. The water of the pit-wells in the town is a little brackish, a considerable quantity of this commodity must therefore be carried from the river, although distant from the town.

Dr Robert Young, in his *Annals of the Parish and Burgh of Elgin*, attempted to summarise the fortunes of Elgin through the past century:

> The eighteenth century was not generally one of much progress in Scotland, and like the preceeding century it closed with a season of severe scarcity, almost approaching to a famine. In the Burgh of Elgin the trade, which had been so brisk and prosperous before the Union with England, gradually declined and by the middle of the century the foreign trade, which consisted of exports of corn, malt, cured meat, salmon, and other home articles, and the imports of wines, spirits, silk, hardware etc, had entirely ceased, the fiscal laws of England having been extended to Scotland. . This was succeeded by a demoralising contraband trade, which long prevailed on the coast, and in which many persons were largely engaged. There were few good homes erected in the burgh during this century. Many of the old families left the town, and for the last fifty years the population seriously declined. In short, it was a time of inactivity and depression.

So we come to the end of a century by which time William Leslie, in his *Survey*, thought little of the layout of the town, the town house or the jail, and Robert Young took the opportunity to look back on a burgh which, in his opinion, had from an economic view, been in serious decline.

ELGIN IN THE
NINETEENTH CENTURY

The Little Kirk of Elgin, which although it formed the chancel of St Giles Church, had been served by its own ministers since the Revolution, was now thought to be beyond repair. The congregation built a new church on Moss Street, but the Presbytery refused permission for them to take their own minister with them. The congregation then had no alternative but to separate from the Established Church of Scotland, and they eventually linked with the Anti-Burgher Presbytery of Elgin. This move took away many of the church-going body of the Established Church, and resulted in a considerable increase in the followers of the Secession Churches in the town.

INCREASING EMPLOYMENT IN ELGIN
*

Alexander Johnston, already an established manufacturer in the town, had recently built a factory on the banks of the River Lossie at New Mills, and this was now becoming a major employer in the area. As a consequence of such

Elgin Tanworks in Lossie Wynd in 1855

rapid expansion, he petitioned the council for some financial aid to defray part of his original expenditure, a request which was approved by the council, obviously not wishing to put obstacles in the way of such an enterprising businessman.

The tannery on the east side of Lossie Wynd was opened by Andrew Culbard, a glover in Elgin, at about this time. It had tanning pits and also buildings for the dressings of the skins, and not long after the business opened his son James entered into partnership with him which allowed the business to expand even further. In 1839 the tannery owners purchased land from Isaac Forsyth and Thomas Miln, on the other side of Lossie Wynd, and by 1841 the tannery became the largest concern of its type in the north of Scotland, sending its products to Edinburgh, Glasgow and London. By the middle of the century it was employing almost 50 men and boys.

The new school was completed by 1801, and the old Grammar School building was sold for the princely sum of £74, while the sale of the English School raised £54. The new establishment taught all the subjects which would be expected in this now more prosperous burgh, including Latin, English, grammar, arithmetic, mathematics, writing and church music. Within a short time the school was designated the Elgin Academy, and the final bill for the building came to £791 8s 6d. An additional crossing point over the River Lossie was established in 1803 with the opening of the Brewery Bridge, adjacent to the now very profitable Elgin Brewery. This also gave easier access to the New Mills, which had been opened by Alexander Johnston just a few years earlier. The roads were being improved at this time, but the idea of extending the Edinburgh to Aberdeen Mail Coach as far as Elgin, and eventually on to Inverness, was rejected by the Burgh Council who declared that they were 'not materially interested' in the plan.

The North Port, which straddled what is now Lossie Wynd, was damaged by a cart with a load of hay, which eventually prompted its demolition, but it is now rebuilt, as mentioned earlier, on a nearby site.

Helen Duff resigned as the teacher of the Female School in Elgin in 1810 and was replaced by the Misses Elizabeth and Mary Shand, who received an annual salary of £50 from the magistrates of the town. The sisters ran the school for about 30 years and built it up into not only a large public day school but also a well-respected boarding establishment which catered for young ladies from all parts of the country and some from abroad. The boarding school was usually home to between 20 and 30 girls at any one time. When they retired in about 1840 it is said that this had been the last female school at which the salaries of the teachers were paid by the town.

EXPANSION INTO THE SUBURBS

✳

Many of the houses in the town had stood since the late seventeenth and early eighteenth centuries and there had been little new house building in the town for many years. In 1811, however, Robert Young built Ladyhill House, and this seemed to generate an interest in the development of properties in the town. Colonel Alexander Hay of Westerton built his new mansion house at the north end of the street which was named after him, and Calder's House, which had stood since 1669, was now demolished to make way for North Street. Many other old buildings were also demolished to make way for the new developments.

The western entrance to the town came in through the Snuff Croft, an area now long gone, which was occupied by a few small and quite run-down cottages. This part of the town was transformed in 1815 with the building of Dr Gray's Hospital, to a design by James Gillespie Graham, at a total cost of about £6,000. The new hospital, with its graceful dome, was opened the following year, but the building works were not completed until three years after the opening. The coming of the hospital tempted several people to build new houses at the west end of the town, among whom were Miss Agnes Ross, who built 'The Cottage' on the north side of the Forres Turnpike Road, and William

Laurel Bank House in 1855

Newmill House in 1855

Young who feued the lands of Maryhill from the magistrates of the town and built his new 'Maryhill House'. In about 1820 Sir Archibald Dunbar built 'Northfield', now Highfield House, on the lands of Cherry Gardens to the south of the west end of the High Street. There was also a lot of building going on around the new Academy, leading to the formation of Academy Street. Embankments were made along the southern bank of the River Lossie to prevent flooding, and also to provide a pleasant pathway alongside the river for the inhabitants of the town.

In these early years of the nineteenth century the style of living had changed little over the years, as the end of the Napoleonic Wars had brought economic problems from which no part of the country was immune. There was a collapse of trade and commerce, and many of the men returning from the wars found little hope of gainful employment. The way of life had changed little over the years, and for most people the daily routine was still probably quite monotonous, especially when it came to meal times. Their main meals were of soup, fish and meat, and little was served in the way of desserts. Wine was used infrequently, except by the wealthy, and French and German wines were almost unheard of now in Elgin. Dinner was usually served quite early in comparison with towns further south, usually between three and four o'clock, and what parties there were broke up early, probably due to the state of the streets and the lack of lighting as the town was now unable to afford the oil for the lights which they had so proudly introduced 25 years earlier. The activities of the gangs of unemployed who loitered in the streets may also have deterred many people from being out late, and quite often a day's socialising was finished by the early evening.

Money was scarce and an annual income of £200–300 would have been considered enough to provide a very comfortable way of life for a middle-class family. The shops were small and poorly lit, and in general the merchants had a quite low turnover of stock. Despite this, the low rentals of the shops enabled the merchants of Elgin to maintain a secure and comfortable lifestyle. The lower classes did not fare so well, a cook could earn maybe £5 a year, and she would have been one of the better-paid servants in a household. The poorer people had a very simple diet: porridge for breakfast, fish and potatoes for the main meal, and meat when it was available at a price they could afford, which was not all that often. The roads were full of potholes, but the council felt that they could afford to do little apart from some very temporary repairs. In 1819 the Poet Laureate, Robert Southey, visited Elgin and was disconcerted by the 'appearance of decay . . . and an abominable drum . . . beaten at nine'. Obviously the town drummer, George Edward, was still doing a good job.

POLITICAL STRIFE IN ELGIN
*

The Parliamentary elections of 1820 created considerable argument and disturbance in the town. The two parties, the Fife faction with their candidate General Duff, and the Grant party with their candidate Archibald Farquharson of Finzean, were very finely balanced in the pre-election polls, and the whole election became a very contentious issue. The Earl of Fife gave a stirring public address in Elgin, giving away dresses to the ladies and gowns, bonnets, shawls and rings to the wives and daughters of the tradesmen. He also scattered money among the lower classes, and, 'acting courteously towards all', he soon became a very popular figure in the town. Feelings were running high and, although few men at that time had the right to vote, the progress of the election was followed by everybody, rich and poor alike.

With the election being so finely balanced each party was trying to remove some of their opponents, and although the main protagonists may not, at least openly, have endorsed it, some of their followers decided to resort to the abduction of some of the council members. It seems that there had been unsuccessful attempts to abduct two of the Duff supporters, which enraged the Fife faction to the extent that on a Saturday morning before the election they seized Robert Dick from his own shop doorway and spirited him away by boat from Burghead across the Moray Firth to Sutherland. A similar fate befell Bailie Francis Taylor, who was seized during his morning walk and suffered an enforced cruise across the water to Brora in an open boat, which due to the stormy weather took all of 17 hours. Although they were treated well, they had to make their way back to Elgin by land, but they arrived home too late for the election of the delegate to go to the meeting in Cullen, where the main election was to take place.

The next morning, although it was the Sabbath, was a scene of great turmoil in Elgin. A body of Highlanders was sent from Cromdale to guard Grant Lodge, but a messenger sent by a tenant of the Earl of Fife was able to get to Elgin before them and warn the Earl of Fife and the Duff supporters. By the next morning, the townspeople watched in amazement as some 700 men eventually arrived at Grant Lodge, but as the morning progressed the Earl of Fife's tenantry arrived in the town from the surrounding countryside, and by the afternoon there was a well-armed force of men on both sides.

Elgin was on the verge of its own civil war. By the evening the drink was already flowing quite freely through the troops on both sides, and the townspeople feared the worst. Sir George Abercrombie, the Sheriff of Moray, was in Elgin at the time, and he eventually persuaded Lady Ann Grant to send the Highlanders home by assuring her that a force of special constables would be appointed to keep the peace in the town. The constables and the inhabitants kept watch all night, in case the Grant men returned, but the night passed peacefully. With all the arguments and disputes, the appointment of the delegate to go to Cullen had to be postponed, but when the election eventually took place on 31 March, despite serious concerns about the validity of the commission sent from Elgin, Archibald Farquharson of Finzean, the candidate of the Grant party, was duly elected as Member of Parliament.

Although the Grants were victorious in the Parliamentary elections, it was a hollow victory, and by the autumn of the year the Duff party had a 12 to 5 majority on the Town Council. These elections had created great divisions in the town, relatives not speaking to each other for long periods, and the differences in some families lingering for several decades, probably long after the original reasons for the disagreements had been forgotten.

Patrick Duff, the Town Clerk, died in the spring of that year, vexed and weakened, it is said, by the conflicts and trials the town had recently suffered. He was succeeded by one of his sons, Arthur, as Sheriff-Clerk and another son, Patrick, as Town Clerk and Commissary Clerk. By the next year, the whole council was made up of supporters of the Duff party.

THE REBIRTH OF
THE TOWN OF ELGIN

*

The opening up of North Street and the spate of building of new houses was to see the beginning of two decades of transformation for Elgin. The stinking open sewers and gutters were to become a thing of the past, and the whole place was being transformed into a stately neoclassical town. It was to have all those public institutions that were already found in other towns of a similar size and status, and soon became surrounded by elegant villas dotted among the trees. Provost Alexander Innes took action to remedy the deplorable state of the streets, raising funds to level the High Street by removing the line of flat stones from the centre of the road, laying pavements along each side and placing the gutters in drains below the ground. This instantly transformed the street into a thoroughfare which would be recognisable by the present-day inhabitants of the town. The improvements in the High Street were soon continued into many of the smaller streets in the town. The first suburb of Elgin was beginning to be built on the south-facing slope between Moss Street to the east and the new Gray's Hospital to the west, and Moray Street, Academy Street, Reidhaven Street and South Guildry Street were all becoming lined with attractive stone-built villas.

In 1825, the Trustees of General Anderson applied to the council for a site to build an Institution, for which the General had left provision in his will. They had already chosen a site at the east end of the town, on the south side of the road to Fochabers, and near to the site of the old Hospital of Maisondieu. The council accepted their offer of £12 per acre per year for 6 acres of the old lands of Maisondieu, and by 1830 a new road was laid, running from the chosen site along the Maisondieu lands and Greyfriars to meet with Moss Street. This was to be named Institution Road. Work on the new Institution was started in the same year. Meanwhile the new Episcopal Church had been built at the foot of North Street to a design by the late William Robertson. The Duke of Gordon donated £100 towards the building costs, and there were many other handsome donations from people of all religious denominations within the town.

On Monday 2 October 1826 the final sermon was preached in the old St Giles Parish Church by the Reverend Dr Richard Rose, Minister of Drainie. No sooner was the service over than the contractors began removing the roof, and by the end of the year the whole site was cleared. The whole centre of the town must have been a macabre sight during the building work, and according to Robert Young 'the building itself and the whole street around were filled

Elgin Episcopal Church

with the remains of the dead, this having been the cemetery of the Burgh from the twelfth till the seventeenth century. Large quantities of bones were carried away, showing the extent of interment here must have been very great'. Remember all of this when you next stand chatting on the plainstones. The council later donated £50 towards the cost of the clock for the new church; in August of that year the last stone was placed on the tower of the new St Giles Church, and it was opened to the public on 28 October 1828.

The Great Moray Flood of August 1829, so ably documented by Sir Thomas Dick Lauder, struck Elgin on 4 August. Although there had been heavy rain in the town on the previous evening, with some of the roads being ankle deep in water, nothing could have prepared the inhabitants for what they awoke to the following morning. The River Lossie, in what must have been the greatest spate ever seen in the town, was one enormous expanse of flowing water, a wide river stretching from Maryhill to the Morriston Braes, and almost all of the cultivated land around the town was under water. The bridges at Palmerscross and the Bow Brig at Oldmills suffered serious damage, and the bridge at Bishopmill washed away. The after-effects of the flood continued for several years in the lower-lying parts of the town, and the flood defences and embankments along the Tyock Burn and along the river itself were raised even higher.

The building of Anderson's Institution at the eastern end of the town had greatly enhanced the appearance of this part of Elgin. This handsome building in the Grecian style bears an inscription above its main frontage, on the north side of the building, which tells us that it is 'The Elgin Institution for the Support of Old Age and Education of Youth'. When it was first built it could accommodate 50 children and 10 old people, but it would appear that the most useful part of the Institution in its early days was the Free School, which educated a large number of boys and girls. Although there was some discussion at the time as to whether such an institution, effectively isolating its residents from the general population, was of value to the town, it soon became clear that the Anderson's Institution was of great value to both old and young alike.

King Street, leading from the cathedral to South College Street, was opened as part of these improvements to the eastern part of the town, and many good new houses and villas were built along it. Unfortunately in the progress of this frenzy of building activity much of what remained of the old buildings and walls of the College of Elgin was destroyed, and this totally changed the atmosphere of what had been thought of as a rather holy and dignified part of Elgin. The West Brewery was opened at Gallowscrook in 1831,

Elgin Jail and Police Office

but never really reached the prominence of the Elgin Brewery near to the cathedral, and soon went out of business. Gas lights came to Elgin at this time, the new gas works being built by the Elgin Gas-Light Company near to the Lossiemouth Road at Borough Briggs. Street lights were installed in Elgin, and many of the private houses and shops were also connected to the gas supply.

What was probably the last execution to be conducted in Elgin was carried out on 7 June 1834, very likely on the Gallows Hill between Maryhill and the Ladyhill. William Noble, a young man, had murdered William Ritchie on the road between Elgin and Lhanbryde, and he was the first person in Elgin to suffer such a fate for nearly 70 years. Plans were also made to build a new jail in the town at about this time.

The Victorian Age

*

The Victorian age started on 26 June 1837 when Her Majesty was duly proclaimed, and many of the gentlemen of Elgin met afterwards in the new Assembly Rooms to drink a toast to her health. McKean comments that 'by 1838, "society", particularly Nabobs from India, had returned'. The town had become upwardly mobile and was 'resorted to by families in easy and affluent circumstances who find in Elgin most of those rational pleasures and advantages which attend a residence in the Capital. Its new buildings reflected its aspirations, and included an excellent Academy, extensive Public Library, a well conducted weekly print, and a richly endowed institution for the support of old people'. The Assembly Rooms were a target for the mobs, however, in 1840, and when a public ball was held to celebrate the marriage of Queen Victoria, tar barrels were placed around the building and set alight, resulting in serious damage, but fortunately no loss of life.

A new courthouse was built during 1837 and 1838, and included the town jail, but this was only to last for about a quarter of a century before the present courthouse was built on the site of the old house of the Knights Templars in 1864.

The Museum was founded in 1842 by the 26 gentlemen members of the Elgin and Morayshire Literary and Scientific Association. It was built to a design by Thomas Mackenzie on a site near to the Little Cross at the east end of the High Street. The building of the Caledonian Bank in the same street was completed in 1845.

The Disruption in the Church of Scotland in 1843 led to Revd Alexander Topp leaving the Established Church and taking with him a large and influential part of the congregation. In the summer and autumn of that year a large church was built on land acquired from the Elgin Guildry Fund Society, at the top of Batchen Street. The new 'Free Church' was capable of holding 1,200 people, and contemporary reports suggest that it was frequently crowded to the doors. The demolition of the old jail, courthouse, meal house and weigh house, all of which had stood in the centre of the High Street, considerably changed the appearance of the town centre. A water fountain was erected on the site of the old jail, and stands there to this day.

The 'New' Market, opened in 1851, was in its day an institution in the town; the lower floor, approached from the double arched entrances at 130 High Street, held the town's butchers and greengrocers shops, while the upper level, approached through an archway from South Street, was the fish market. The fish market especially was a very welcome venue, as previously the fisher-women had had to stand near the Muckle Cross, exposed to all the elements which the Moray climate could throw at them. Gradually, as the economic life of the town changed towards the end of the nineteenth century, and the butchers and greengrocers opened new shops elsewhere in the town, the lower market became less popular. Above the first floor was the concert hall, a valued addition to the life of the town, with its side galleries and balconies, and well patronised by local and touring companies alike. Over the lower market was the Corn Market Hall, for many years used as the drill hall for the local Volunteer Companies. All that now remains of the market is the name, continued in the Newmarket Bar, at the top end of one of the original arched entrances to the market hall.

The home of General Anderson, the donor of Anderson's Institution, had been built after his return from India. After his death, the house was bought by the Commercial Bank of Scotland, and during 1852 and 1853 they took down the front of the house and replaced it with a highly ornamental frontage, including the elaborate carved stone capitols which graced the parapet of the roof. The building, at what is now 209 High Street, was demolished in 1971 and replaced by the anonymous grey cube which is now the Royal Bank of Scotland.

Almost opposite this on the High Street lies the building which formerly housed the Caledonian Bank, latterly the Bank of Scotland. This had been built on the site of Auchry's fine mansion, later known as Elchies House. This had been built in about 1670 by the Cummings of Lochtervandich, from whom it passed by marriage to the Kings of Newmill. The fine architectural features of the old house, including its palisaded piazza, were a sad loss to the appearance of the High Street when the new bank building was erected in about 1845.

Next door to the bank is the hostelry of the White Horse Inn. Mrs

The Caledonian Bank, High Street, Elgin

Elizabeth Innes, who reigned as landlady of the inn for 51 years, is immortalised in verse by William Hay, a local poet:

Her name is Mrs Innes and the 'White Horse' is her sign
And happy is the man or beast that chances there to dine;
For all her provender is good, her whisky, ale and wine;
An' each an' a' hae often turned this weak, weak head o' mine;
O! she's a jewel o' a gudewife, the pride o' Elgin Toon'.

The White Horse Inn is still there, probably having stood on the High Street of Elgin for about 400 years. The pend to the close alongside it now provides shelter for those who come out of the inn for a quick cigarette, and despite some renovations the inn has probably changed little over the years.

Nearby Thunderton House must have been a handsome building, surrounded by its large gardens which extended all the way from the High Street back to include land on the other side of what is now South Street. The mansion was the royal residence after the castle on Ladyhill fell into disrepair, and it was known in earlier times by the name of the 'Great Lodging', the

'King's House' or sometimes the 'Sheriff's House'. Probably the manor house referred to in a charter granted by Robert the Bruce to his nephew Thomas Randolph, Earl of Moray, in the first years of the fourteenth century, it was the residence of the earls of Moray when in Elgin, mainly to administer justice there. In 1455 the house passed by forfeiture to the Dunbars of Westfield, and after several changes by 1650 it was in the possession of the Sutherlands of Duffus. Lord Duffus built the tower, surrounded by a bartizan having a peculiarly shaped balustrade which it was said represented the name Sutherland and various astrological figures. All of these stones have now vanished except for one which remains in a low wall on the east side of Thunderton Place, a sad reminder of former glories.

Following the bankruptcy of the family, the house, now having been given its modern name of Thunderton House, had several tenants, and in 1746 it was occupied by a Mrs Anderson of Arradoul, the self-styled Lady Arradoul, who entertained, and even nursed Prince Charles Edward Stuart on his visit to Elgin prior to the Battle of Culloden.

In 1800 Thunderton House was purchased from the Dunbar family by John Batchen, 'a rough but kindly auctioneer' in Elgin, 'to make a Kirk and a Mill of if he liked'. He accomplished this by leasing out the lower part of the house as a preaching station, and a windmill was erected on the bartizan. He feued off the eastern part of his lands to allow the building of what is now Batchen Street, and the land on the other side of South Street was Mr Haldane's Church. The land fronting the south side of the High Street was sold to various people in the town. In 1822 the tower, the most picturesque part of the building, was removed, and Batchen Lane, now Thunderton Place, was formed. By the end of the nineteenth century, the house had become Gordon's Temperance Hotel and is now the Thunderton House Hotel.

The buildings surrounding the house, almost all of them erected at the instigation of John Batchen, really mask what an impressive building it must once have been, but close examination will still reveal much evidence of its architecturally chequered history. Batchen Street itself was to become home to numerous establishments, including the Commercial Hotel on the corner with the High Street and the Moray Tweed House, a shop which was opened in about 1870.

RAILWAYS AND COMMERCE

✳

The Morayshire Railway, linking Elgin to Lossiemouth, was opened on 10 August 1853 with great ceremony, and within five years Elgin was connected to both Aberdeen and Inverness by this new and exciting mode of travel, and the line southwards to Rothes also came into use. The Laich Moray Hotel was built near the railway station for the benefit of all of these new travellers. The newly formed Elgin Fire Brigade got its first fire engine in 1855, and the Police Commissioners were put in charge of training the firemen and running the Fire Service. On 23 January 1858 the council enacted and declared that from this date forward, and in all time henceforth, the title of 'The City of Elgin' should be strictly observed.

In 1856 the Stag Hotel in Commerce Street was opened, and in 1858 the Duchess of Atholl stayed there. The town Post Office moved into Commerce Street in 1860, into what were to become known as the Post Office Buildings.

Weston House School, at the corner of Hay Street and South Street, was the result of a dispute between the Established Church and the Free Church over the Academy in Elgin. Mr Morrison, the classics master at the Academy, resigned his post and, taking some of his boarding pupils with him, set up a boarding school at Weston House in 1859 with ten resident boarders. Alexander Graham Bell, the inventor of the telephone, was a pupil at Weston House and for a short time was an assistant master there. The school

Greyfriars Chapel

Elgin Roman Catholic Church

Elgin Constabulary, 1890s

concentrated on getting its pupils through the Civil Service Examinations, and at its peak had about 40 boarders. In 1870 it was taken over by a Mr Turner, but closed a year later. In 1882 it was reopened as a boarding and day school 'to promote the mental and moral culture of young ladies', and by the end of the century was run by the Misses Watson in association with Mrs Macdonald.

Elgin seems to have reached a peak of development at about this time, and in 1872 Queen Victoria paid a fleeting visit to the town, alighting from her royal train for about 15 minutes to meet with the civic dignitaries on the station platform. This was the first time a sovereign had visited Elgin since the unfortunate Mary Queen of Scots in 1562.

By the 1880s the academy, which had stood for many years in Academy Street, near to the head of School Wynd (later Commerce Street), was proving to be inadequate for the needs of its scholars, and in 1886 a new academy was opened on Moray Street not far from the new town hall which had only been opened the previous year. The Victoria School of Science and Art was opened on Moray Street just a year after the opening of the new academy.

Although the centre of the town changed little, throughout the later years of the nineteenth century, there was a large amount of building all around the outskirts of the town, and the population continued to increase right into the next century.

ELGIN IN THE TWENTIETH CENTURY

The developments of the nineteenth century continued apace into the new century. Carseman's Wynd, leading down to the river, had by now gone through two changes of name. By the nineteenth century, it had been renamed the Shambles Wynd, no doubt due to the slaughterhouses and fleshers businesses situated there, convenient for supplying skins to the nearby tannery. As the blood and gore of the slaughterhouses was moved further away from the centre of the town, however, for a short time in the early twentieth century it bore the more respectable title of Union Street. By 1919 the decision had been taken to rename it Lossie Wynd, a name which has remained to this day.

In Batchen Street the house occupied by Robert Gow became the George Restaurant in 1922, and was a popular eating place for the townspeople until the 1960s.

Weston House on Hay Street continued as a girls' school into the early twentieth century, but was subsequently closed, and Weston House became a private dwelling. Sometime in the 1930s, Weston House was demolished, and

The Elgin Laundry in 1903

The Playhouse Cinema on the High Street

OVERLEAF. *Fife Arms Close, Elgin, c.1925*

new flats were built on the southern part of the land facing Hay Street. The frontage on to the junction of Hay Street and South Street became a garage and car showroom in the 1950s, later to be taken over by the electrical retailers, Comet.

Lossie Wynd in the twentieth century was home to various business establishments: at No. 41 was the Elgin Aerated Water Manufactory, which operated from 1906 until 1983. Also on Lossie Wynd was the 'Hole in the Wa' public house, a drinking place which had a chequered and sometimes

The old Elgin Town Hall

notorious career, which was at various times to become the centre of entertainment for many of the townspeople. In 1929, the new bus station was built at the foot of Lossie Wynd; the increasing use of public transport and the expansion of the network of routes out into the surrounding countryside was already creating congestion on the High Street. The cold and windy bus station, with its lack of shelter and even greater lack of seats, served the town until a new one was built as part of the St Giles Centre in 1992.

The building of the St Giles Centre, on the north side of the High Street at the Plainstones, was a contentious issue. The nineteenth-century shops lining this side of the High Street were popular with the people of Elgin, and the closes between them led to some quite interesting properties. Originally this had been the site of Craigellachie Place, which from the eighteenth century onwards had been occupied primarily by families who had connections with Clan Grant. By 1901 only 15 families were living in the close, almost half of its

Yeadon's corner on Commerce Street, Elgin, before it became the shop

earlier residents having left. No doubt due to its very central location, it was considered to be one of the more prosperous closes in the town.

The shops along the High Street, Arnott's and Fraser's, were threatened with closure from as early as 1985, but delays in the project meant that it was not until 1990 that work really got under way on the new centre, which eventually opened in November 1991, but with none of the shops yet occupied. The first tenants were the Hydro-Electric Board, and with the opening of their shop in February 1992 a steady flow of other retailers moved into the centre, with a café opening just a month later.

Grant Lodge, the mansion house of the family of Grant, in the Cooper Park, was taken over by the Moray Council in 1961 as the town library, and later also housed the local studies centre. A fire in the building in 2003 caused considerable internal structural damage, and also damage to some of the material archived there, and the house has stood derelict ever since.

The town hall on Moray Street was destroyed by fire in 1939. As the academy expanded during the second part of the twentieth century, a new one was built on Morriston Road in 1969, and the old Moray Street Academy eventually became part of Moray College.

CHAPTER 10
THE CATHEDRAL CITY
AND COLLEGE OF ELGIN

ELGIN CATHEDRAL

As was mentioned in an earlier chapter, the bishops of Moray had at various times used the churches of Birnie, Spynie and Kinneddar as their cathedral. At the succession of Bishop Bricius in 1203, however, it was agreed that the Cathedral of Moray would be fixed at Spynie, but afterwards Bishop Bricius applied to Rome for permission to build a new cathedral on the lands of the Holy Trinity at Elgin. It was only during the time of his successor Andrew that the See was finally transferred in 1224, and building work commenced.

Since then the magnificent Cathedral of Elgin, the 'Lantern of the North', has stood as a symbol of the Christian faith in the north of Scotland. It was, along with the neighbouring abbeys and priories of Pluscarden, Urquhart and Kinloss, one of the main centres of the Roman Church in the north, and endowed the fledgling Royal Burgh of Elgin with a status which was the envy of many other towns in Scotland.

A fire in 1270 caused some damage, but in 1390, during the incumbency of Bishop Burr, Alexander Stewart, the 'Wolf of Badenoch', attacked and burned the cathedral, the College and much of the neighbouring town. Bishop Burr, however, immediately commenced the rebuilding of the cathedral, work which was later continued by his successor William de Spyny. Bishop John Innes was consecrated as Bishop of Moray in 1406, and it was he who began the building of the great central steeple, which was the final phase of the completion of this glorious building. How well this work was done is a matter for conjecture, because just a century later the steeple collapsed. Despite this, the cathedral remained a place of worship throughout, and the damage caused in 1506 was fully repaired by 1538.

The cathedral stood as a place of worship and learning right up to the time of the Reformation, an event which in the north of Scotland was not a sudden collapse of the Roman Church, but a more gradual decline over the decade

Elgin Cathedral, 1538

following 1560. After the expulsion of the Catholic Bishop of Moray, the cathedral fell into disuse, although some of the more staunch Episcopalians, and doubtless also some of those who had resolutely clung to the Catholic faith, continued to use part of it as a place of worship. This was in spite of the inevitable anger this aroused among the new presbyteries and kirk sessions of the Established Church of Scotland.

At various times, however, the building suffered depredations at the hands of both the establishment and the local population. The lead was removed from the roof by an Act of Privy Council of 14 February 1567, 'Seeing provision must be made for maintaining the men of war, whose services cannot be spared, until the rebellious and disobedient be reduced, therefore appoint that the lead be taken from the Cathedral Churches of Aberdeen and Elgin, and sold for sustenation of said men of war . . .' The ship carrying the lead was sunk in a storm in the North Sea shortly afterwards. The removal of lead accelerated the decay of the building, allowing the weather to exert its destructive force on the now exposed roof and beams. On 14 December 1637, severe gales demolished the rafters of the cathedral and exposed more of the building, hastening its eventual ruin.

There were further acts of despoliation against the cathedral, such as when on Monday 28 December 1640, Gilbert Ross, minister at Elgin, along with the young Laird of Innes, the Laird of Brodie and several other people, broke down the choir screen which divided the body of the cathedral from the choir. This screen had stood intact since the Reformation some 80 years earlier and had survived the removal of the roof. In his *The Annals of the Burgh and Parish of Elgin*, Robert Young records that 'On the west side was painted, in excellent colours, illuminated with stars of bright gold, the crucifixion of our blessed Lord and Saviour Jesus Christ. This piece was so excellently done that the colours and stars had never faded . . . notwithstanding the fact that the College or Chanonry Kirk wanted a roof since the Reformation, and not a whole window therein to save from storm, snow, sleet or wet . . . On the other side was depicted the day of judgement. All was thrown to the ground.' The minister, taking the wood home to burn, found that it could not be kept alight, and 'forebore to bring in or burn any more of that timber in his house . . .'

The final act of the ruination of the cathedral was on Peace Sunday 1711, when the great central tower of Elgin Cathedral collapsed, taking with it the north transept and the nave arcades. For the following century, the ruins were used as a 'quarry' by the local masons and as a rubbish tip by the general population of the town. During the early nineteenth century, the state of the cathedral ruins was beginning to be a cause of both concern and embarrassment to the town, and in 1809 Joseph King of Newmill, the Provost of Elgin, raised subscriptions to build an enclosure wall around the ruins. This seems to be the first time that any of the residents of the town had any sense of the history and value of the building, or maybe it was just because Joseph King's mansion house of Newmill was almost adjacent to the old ruins.

On February 27 1809 Alexander Cook, a shoemaker, was appointed to be keeper of the cathedral, and a cottage was built for him at the west end of the cathedral churchyard. He seems to have done little to improve the state of the buildings, but was doubtless able to prevent any further deterioration and damage until his death in 1823.

In 1816 the Town Council had petitioned the Barons of Exchequer to repair the cathedral, but with little effect until 1820, when Mr Isaac Forsyth took the matter in hand. Through his relative Adam Longmore, the Barons of Exchequer were persuaded to look again at the state of the ruins, which was not before time, as one of the two western towers was deteriorating rapidly and in danger of falling. The Exchequer were persuaded to make grants for the repairs, and the western tower was strengthened, but the cathedral ruins and graveyard were still in a very untidy state. In 1824, it was decided to give a cottage and a salary to the keeper, and in that year John Shanks, another shoemaker, was appointed as Keeper of the Cathedral. He was at this time already an elderly man, 66 years of age, and contemporary records suggest that he was quite frail and weak.

'When the Grants and the Duffs fought for the parliamentary influence of the Elgin burghs' wrote the Revd Dr Gordon of Birnie, 'John was a drouthy cobbler, living on the north side of the High Street opposite the Muckle Cross'. He had been of some service to the winning party in these hotly and sometimes quite criminally contested elections, and he was seemingly rewarded by being given this appointment as Keeper following the death of Alexander Cook. Apparently John Shanks was well known in the town as being somewhat idle, a gossip, and some of the more influential residents of Elgin maybe looked on this job as a means of getting him out of their way. He had not long been in the post, however, when he began to prove what spirit he had, and that he was the right man for the job.

On taking over the position, he found that, despite the fact that there had already been a keeper of the Cathedral for several years previously, the interior was a mass of ruins and rubbish. Although the cathedral burial ground had been used for all of the burials in Elgin following the closure of the St Giles churchyard in the High Street of Elgin in 1605, only the exterior area bore any resemblance to the original outline of the building. He took great pleasure in labouring among the ruins, and was always at work clearing away the accumulated rubbish. With his pickaxe and shovel he is reputed to have removed some 2,866 barrows-full of litter and debris. Isaac Forsyth was the Secretary of the Morayshire Farmers Club at the time, and on hearing of his good work some of the members of the club sent horses and carts to help clear away the rubbish.

One day John's spade made contact with something hard just in front of the main West Entrance. On clearing away the debris, the main entrance steps were revealed, and it became obvious that the general floor level of the cathedral was lower than had been at first thought. Public interest in the old ruin was now aroused, and the Crown authorities came up with funding which made it possible to reveal the full western approach to the cathedral. As the debris was removed and the original floor level was reached, many of the previously buried tombstones saw the light of day again for the first time in over a century.

His work revealed the bases of the pillars of the cathedral, which had once supported the massive roof, and also the entrance steps, and gradually began to define the outlines of the original building. He removed many thousands of cubic yards of rubbish, and gathered up the remains of the carved stones. A new lead roof was put on the chapter house, and a new cottage was built for John Shanks on the site of the old one, a cottage which now serves as the cathedral shop. Some of the fragments of sculpture which he recovered were put on display around the walls of the chapter house, but have since been removed elsewhere.

Although the cathedral gradually fell into ruin, one can judge from the number of gardeners mentioned in the records that some of the more substantial houses which had survived were put to good use as private dwellings. The isolation from the Burgh of Elgin, which had so dominated life prior to the Reformation, was now ended, and the people of the burgh were free to live and work in the College surrounding the cathedral. The narrow lanes of Lazarus Wynd and Weavers Close now became home to all manner of artisans and tradesmen.

There are many old prints and photographs of the cathedral and its churchyard, but many of the old drawings have taken a considerable amount of artistic licence in regard to the positions of the tombstones. The market cross, in particular, seems to have stood in several locations within the churchyard. It is not until the late nineteenth and early twentieth century that a good photographic archive is available. Some of the earlier photographs indicate that there were other enclosures and burial aisles around the inside of the perimeter wall, many of which are now identifiable only as foundation lines or lower courses of masonry.

The tombstones, other than those in the south choir aisle, have received little protection from the elements, and there is considerable evidence of delamination and surface decay on many stones, especially those carved from the softer local sandstones or freestones. There are several examples of fragmentary recumbent stones, and in some cases entire tombstones, being used as bases for later table stones. There is also some evidence of the recycling of tombstones, where inscriptions are visible on the underside of a table stone with a later inscription on it. Although there are suggestions in some antiquarian sources that tombstones may have been removed from the old churchyard of St Giles in the centre of Elgin into the cathedral churchyard, there is no documentary evidence for this except from secondary sources. It is likely, however, that fragments of tombstones used to reconstruct the staircase in the south-west tower may have come from this source, as well as some of those used for the seats in the chapter house. A full recording of all of the visible tombstones in the cathedral has recently been completed and published by the Moray Burial Ground Research Group, a task which has taken over three years to complete.

Elgin Brewery at the back of the cathedral

The Pictish Stone, which at present stands in Elgin Cathedral, was found during work on the improvements to the High Street in the nineteenth century, in a position just to the north-east of St Giles Church. It was removed to the cathedral and stood in various places within the building until being set in its present location.

Sometime about the beginning of the twentieth century, the cathedral came under the guardianship of the Ministry of Works and was later placed under the care of Historic Scotland, who retain guardianship of the site to the present day. Although the main fabric of the building and its surrounds has altered little since the site was cleared by John Shanks, a gradual process of tidying and conservation has been ongoing. The main changes have been to the boundary walls and railings, which were realigned when the roads surrounding the cathedral were improved. The Elgin Brewery, which stood to the east of the cathedral adjacent to the Brewery Bridge, produced beer and other alcoholic beverages from the late eighteenth century until the early twentieth century, but was eventually demolished. Sixty feet of the land formerly occupied by the brewery was made into an extension to the churchyard, and a sunken ha-ha was constructed to replace the eastern boundary wall, but a new wall was built at a later date.

THE COLLEGE OF ELGIN

Surrounding the cathedral was the College of Elgin, or the Chanonry. To quote McKean, 'The Bishop of Moray was king in his own city, and, being one of the most powerful prelates in Scotland, had the Chanonry enclosed with a wall. . . . over half a mile in circuit.' This, rather than the Burgh to the west, may have been the original 'City of Elgin'.

The College, containing the cathedral, chapter house and the manses and dwellings of many of the church dignitaries, was enclosed by a curtain wall, now 'lost', except for a small section at the Pans Port, which was generally about 12 feet (3.7 metres) high and some 6½ feet (2 metres) thick. It extended from the River Lossie at the Pans Port to the main road between Elgin and Fochabers. The wall then turned westward along the northern side of the road, broken by the South Gate at the end of what is now King Street. It continued from this gate to the Little Cross, where the West Gate was situated. The wall turned northwards until it reached the North Back Passage of the town, at which point it then turned eastwards, broken by the North Gate, until it again reached the River Lossie some 300 yards north of Pans Port. The North Gate gave access to the track to the ford and footbridge at Deans Haugh, leading eventually to the Bishop's Palace and the harbour at Spynie.

This walled 'city' met with the Burgh of Elgin at the Little Cross, the finial of which may date from an earlier 1402 cross erected by Alexander MacDonald

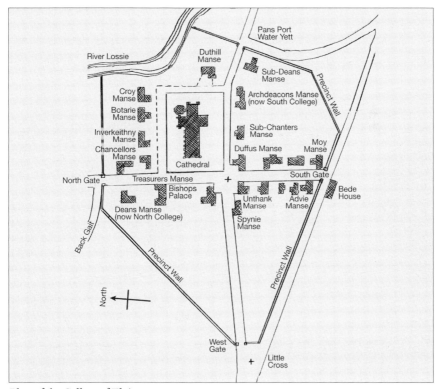

Plan of the College of Elgin

of the Isles in expiation of his desecration of the cathedral. The pillar of the present cross dates from a rebuilding in 1733. The walls enclosed much of what are now Cooper Park, North and South College Streets, King Street and Cathedral Road. Within it lived the officers and dignitaries of the cathedral, comprising 8 dignitaries such as the dean, precentor, chancellor, etc., 16 canons, 22 vicars choral and a similar number of chaplains, many of whom had livings elsewhere in the Diocese, such as at Duffus and Unthank. Within this curtain wall lay the cathedral itself, together with the chapter house, both enclosed by a smaller stone wall, outside which ran a cobbled roadway for the full length of the perimeter of this central area. It is, however, the other buildings within the College, and their inhabitants, which are less well-documented.

Only one of the ports or gates into the College of Elgin has survived, this being the Pans Port, also known as the East Gate or the Water Yett. The port itself is in a fair state of preservation, having been restored in 1857. The groove or *chase* for the lifting of the portcullis is still visible in the wall of the broad, pointed Gothic arch flanked by arrow loops. The structure, in its original form, must have been at least one storey higher, to house the mechanism for raising and lowering the portcullis.

Outside the walls lay the crofts, generally of about 2 acres each in extent, although some may have been larger, covering about 50 acres in total, and

The Little Cross at the east end of Elgin High Street

providing lands for the occupants of the manses within the walls, hence the names Deans Haugh, Moy Croft, Subchanters Croft, etc.

The Bishop's House is immediately opposite the west end of Elgin Cathedral and was supposedly built by Bishop John Innes in about 1406 or 1407. It is also variously known as the Precentor's Manse, the Chantor's Manse or the Alves Manse, possibly showing changes of use and occupation over the centuries. Judging from its size, and also by the presence of the nearby Bishop's Palace at Spynie, the Bishop's House was probably only used by him when he was required to be at the cathedral in connection with the business of the Diocese or at the great festivals of the Church. Alexander Seton, Commendator of Pluscarden after the Reformation, and sometime Provost of Elgin, lived at the Bishop's House, and, according to Rampini, on being granted the title Earl of Dunfermline he renamed it Dunfermline House. The property fell into the hands of the Seafield family and, although much of the building was demolished in 1851, the decorative ruins were gifted to the Burgh of Elgin by Caroline, Countess-Dowager of Seafield in 1885. All that remains now is the ground floor of the south wing and a tall narrow tower, with many heraldic panels and ornamented crow-steps. To the north of the Bishop's House is the Dean's Manse, now North College, built to an L-shaped plan in 1520. It is a substantial building which was modernised in 1858.

To the south of the cathedral itself lay the Archdeacon's Manse (now

North College (The Old Deanery)

South College), and part of the vaulted under-storey of this building is incorporated into what is otherwise a relatively modern house. Next door to this was the Sub-Chanter's Manse, also known at times as the Rafford or the Ardclach Manse. Duffus Manse, which survived into the nineteenth century, lay on the corner of the road leading from the cathedral to the South Gate. Across the road from the Duffus Manse lay the Unthank Manse, which also survived into the mid nineteenth century, with another manse next door to the south-west. This was probably Spynie Manse, which was set back from the street with a cobbled courtyard in front of it. There are indications that there were various other manses along either side of the road to the South Gate, which was flanked by the Advie and Moy Manses. Immediately opposite, on the other side of the road to Fochabers, lay the now vanished Bede Houses.

Each of the dignitaries had a deputy, and no doubt a fairly large staff to conduct the daily routine of the work. They were well rewarded for their efforts with the revenues they enjoyed from the lands in which they were invested by virtue of their offices (their temporality), and from the income they received from the church for the discharge of their duties (their spirituality).

The churches of the diocese provided income to the other canons, vicars and chaplains. Each had his own tithes, his 'maills and duties', his payments in kind and his dues for conducting services in his own church. Certain churches, the common churches, were assigned to provide a general table allowance for the chapter. These are identified as Artendol, Ferneway, Aberihacyn, Logykenny, Kyncardin, Abirnethy, Altre, Ewain and Brennath. The identity of some of these can only now be guessed at. The manses of the canons or vicars are identified as Kinnoir, Advie and Cromdale, Rhynie, Kingussie, Dipple, Spynie, Inverkeithny, Botarie, Croy, Duthill, Dallas, Auldearn, Rafford, Ardclach, Duffus, Moy, Unthank and, of course, Elgin. These lists show the wide geographical power which the chapter of the Cathedral of Elgin exerted.

There must have been many other smaller dwellings in the College to house the servants of these men of the cloth, and the tradesmen and artisans who serviced them. Many of these people, especially in pre-Reformation times, were never identified by name, only the more prominent ones being mentioned in the records. After the Reformation, from 1560 onwards, things were to change. The Protestant Church wiped away much of the hierarchy of the Catholic regime, the cathedral was abandoned to the elements and the manses of the vicars and canons gradually became adapted for secular use. The Protestant ministers lived in their manses, in their own parishes and near to their church. The Presbytery became responsible for the running of the church, and the status of the College of Elgin declined rapidly.

CHAPTER 11
THE COASTAL SETTLEMENTS

The main coastal towns and villages of the Moray and Nairn coast, from west to east, can be identified as Nairn, Findhorn, Burghead, Hopeman, Lossiemouth, and Garmouth and Kingston. Each of these has its own history, whether as a trading harbour, a fishing port, a centre for shipbuilding or in more recent times as a holiday resort, especially during the Glasgow Trades Weeks. Nairn has been covered more fully in its history as a royal burgh, as it is the only one of the three royal burghs that is actually situated on the coast. There were also several other smaller fishing villages, in most cases just a few cottages near the beach, such as Delnies and Mavistoun.

DELNIES

Just a couple of miles to the west of Nairn, the settlement of Delnies was a fishing village until the late nineteenth century. It had no harbour, the boats being launched from the beach, but as boats became larger and the fishing business became more competitive, most of the fishermen moved eastwards to take advantage of the harbour of Nairn.

MAVISTOUN

Now long vanished as a little fishing village, Mavistoun was, like Delnies, probably never home to more than about half a dozen fishing families, but it was abandoned and fell into disuse during the nineteenth century. The general area, however, continues to go by the name of Mavistoun, and there is a farm of that name there. The Mavistoun Hills, which were formed by the constant westward drift of sand along the coast of the Moray Firth, no doubt eventually overwhelmed parts of the settlement, much as it eventually overwhelmed the estate of Culbin.

FINDHORN

Early names for Findhorn are recorded as Invererne (the mouth of the River Erne) and Finderne, certainly implying that in early times the river was called the Erne and not the Findhorn. In early times the monks from the Abbey of Kinloss set up salmon fishing stations or 'stells' along the shores of Findhorn Bay, and in 1532 the port of Findhorn was established into a burgh of barony by the Abbot of Kinloss. The following century was to see a great expansion of the port, with vessels trading with Europe and the Baltic ports.

The salmon fishings and the export of salmon from the port of Findhorn are well documented in the Exchequer records of the late sixteenth and early seventeenth centuries, which give a good indication of how important this trade was following the Reformation. In August 1558 William Waught paid taxes on the export of 11 lasts of Salmon, and Alexander Acheson for 14 lasts. On 29 January 1587 there is a Sasine of the 'fishings of five stells and yairds' to Mr Edward Bruce, for a period of seven years. This obviously continued as it was restated in a charter of 1598. A 'Charter of Findhorne' dated 1611 makes mentions of James Andersone there, and witnesses include Johnne Steill, William Dunbar and George Duff.

The Merchant Shipping Trade
*

James Calder, later Sir James, a merchant in Elgin, was granted a charter under the Great Seal in 1671, which gave him ownership of the lands and Barony of Muirtown. Sir James Calder, in company with William King of Newmill, Elgin, carried on a most extensive business as export and import merchants. A series of Exchequer documents from the 1670s show that trade was very extensive with Baltic and north German ports such as Bremen, Hamburg and Danzig, as well as with many other ports on the Continent. Findhorn, 'the port of Forres', must have been an amazing sight and a hive of activity at this time, so much so that it was about now that the magistrates of Elgin became determined to build their own harbour at Lossiemouth, to compete with both Findhorn and Garmouth.

By 1690 James Calder and William King exported from Findhorn 'Beaff, tongues, tallow, hydes, bear, malt etc.' to Bordeaux, Drontone (Perugia, in Italy), Rotterdam, etc., and from these ports they imported 'wine, brandy, soap, powder, reassins, ffigs, prunes, green ginger, suggar, pepper, indigo, cloves, nutmuggs, rice, needles, muslen, camel's hair, mourning creapp, hatts of the newest fashion (all black) white Renish wine (Rhine wine or Hock), clear hard seck, tobacco, pypes, ffrench wines etc.'

A bundle of shipping ledgers from the period 1686 to 1695 identifies Andrew Russell as the principal merchant in Findhorn, but there are also mentions of William Jaffray, James Thomson and Jan & Jacob van Rixel. Andrew Russell is also frequently mentioned as being at the ports of Borrowstounness, Leith, London and Rotterdam, and must have been a very influential person in the trade at this time. Just some of the ships using the port of Findhorn during this 10-year period were the *Lyon of Leith, Anoris, Helen of Borrowstounness, Land of Promise of Borrowstounness, William of Leith, Concord of Borrowstounness, Providence, Maria, The Lyon of Queensferry, Lendrie of Leith, Swan of Borrowstounness, Isobel, Boath, Beattie of Burntisland, Friendship of Bristol* and the *Royendermann* of Stockholm. It is interesting to note the number of vessels from the Firth of Forth, from Burntisland, Borrowstounness (now Bo'ness), Leith and Queensferry. Among the given ports of origin or destinations in this one bundle are Leith, Rotterdam, Dundee, Bo'ness, Queensferry, Briel, Amsterdam, Dublin, Waterford, Greenock, Dysart, Kirkcaldy and Stockholm. The average size of the vessels was about 90 tons, thereby carrying a relatively small cargo.

A typical example of the cargo carried by the Findhorn vessels is shown on 2 July 1692, when a contract was made between 'George, Viscount of Tarbet, Lord McLeod and Castlehaven on the one part and William Dawsone, skipper in Findhorn and Master under God of the good ship called the Isobell of Findhorn on the other whereby the latter lets his said ship for freight to the said Viscount to take in at Portmaholmack 440 bolls of bear and transport the same to Leith, for which causes the said Viscount obliges himself to pay £163/10/0 Scots for each chalder of bear he shall deliver at Leith with one boll of meal and one barrel of ale within 48 hours after delivering of said freight . . .'

THE DESTRUCTION
OF OLD FINDHORN
✳

The destruction of the old village of Findhorn took place in autumn 1701, and was caused by a severe storm from the north-east associated with very high tides, which breached the sandbar on which the old village was built. Following this the economy of the port declined rapidly, almost certainly because of the loss of facilities for vessels to moor or beach at the port. It was not until a second, probably temporary village was established in 1705 that the fortunes of the port began to revive. This second village would have been used to keep the economy of the port alive while the existing village was being built, although this was not fully completed until several years later.

REVIVAL AND EXPANSION

*

The revival of Findhorn, however, is clearly shown on 17 November 1708 when the captain of *The Seven Brothers*, William Dawson, who was later to become Provost of Forres, was employed by the lairds of Kilravock, Clava, Thunderton, Kinsterie and Muirtoun to carry a cargo to Lisbon. This cargo comprised '791½ bolls of bear at £3/6/8d per boll, 3 last of hareings at £96 per last, 6,500 dried codd-fish at £14 per 100, 6 barrels salmond at £38 per barrel and 18 barrels of grilses at 1/5th rebate of salmond price', giving a total value of the cargo to Portugal as £4,611 10s 8d Scots.

In 1727 some Findhorn fishermen were moved to Portessie to establish the fishing industry there. The Laird of Rannas provided five houses for them in the village, which was at that time known as Rottenslough.

Eventually the new village, now so popular with tourists, was finally completed, rows of fishermen's cottages built in the typical north-east style with their gable-ends to the water straggling along the arc of the north-east shore of Findhorn Bay. The intervening lanes are known locally as the 'stryplies'. The centre of the village is the square around the Crown and Anchor Inn, a white crow-stepped building dating from 1739.

A letter written on 3 November 1750 by John Grant of Mulben, addressed to the Honourable Sir Ludovick Grant of Grant MP in London gives a good indication of the unreliability of the shipping system of the time, and the value of having several ports around the Moray Firth where vessels could shelter from adverse weather: '. . . none of the shipes are yet arrived at Garmouth tho' they are all at ffindorn or Cromarty, we have had a great fall of snow quh is now mostly off but the sea has been either rough or the wind not for the shipes for some time past . . .'

In 1769 Col. Hector Monro of Novar, the proprietor, was granted rights to 'erect a Corffhouse and Corffhouseyeard upon any part of the contiguous grounds upon the shoar of Findhorn which he shall think most commodiously fit for the purpose of receiving, airing and packing his salmon now that the former corffhouse and . . . are ruinous'. Among other buildings in the village being constructed around this date, it is notable that Quay Cottage has a 1773 date-stone commemorating the building of the cottage by James Rose and Margaret Simpson, and the Kimberley Inn dates from some four years later.

In 1798 Findhorn is recorded as being the most important port in Moray, having four large vessels trading with London, three trading with Leith, two with Aberdeen and also four of its own fishing boats. Other visiting freight vessels would have numbered about 100 during the year, from other parts of

Britain and some also from Continental ports. Cargoes imported from London were sugar, tea, silk, cotton and hardware, while leather, tallow, soap, iron, farm utensils, glass and furniture were brought from Leith, coal from Sunderland, and ropes and flax from Aberdeen. The main exports were grain and salmon, and also haddock dried and cured by the local method and exported as 'Findern Speldings'.

Findhorn was affected by the Great Flood of August 1829, and in places the flood was so deep that several vessels from Findhorn actually sailed inland to take part in the rescues.

In 1841, 12 vessels were registered at Findhorn, in all some 1,000 tons. Foreign vessels also visited the port bringing sometimes two cargoes a year of iron, tar and timber from the Baltic and one of timber from British North America (Canada). 'The coastal trade amounts to 25,000 barrels of Newcastle and Sunderland coal at 1/9d – 2/od per barrel, 7,000 bolls of lime, 4,000 tons of coal from the Firth of Forth, 150,000 slates from Ballachulish, 300 tons of iron from Wales and Staffordshire, 400 tons of salt from Liverpool, and 5,000 – 6,000 barrels of bone dust for manure'. These figures probably relate to the imports for the year 1840. There were regular trading smacks from London, Leith and Liverpool with cargoes for Elgin, Forres and Nairn. Regular steam vessels also plied between Findhorn and Leith, London and Liverpool. The exports from the port, again probably referring to the year 1840, were 2,000 barrels of herring,

Findhorn from the north

Findhorn from the north, with steamer

10,000 quarters of grain, 200 boxes of eggs (each containing 160 dozen) and 200 loads of timber chiefly from the forests of Darnaway and Altyre.

At about this time it was noted that 'Shipbuilding has lately been carried on with considerable spirit under the auspices of Mr Thomas Davidson and other enterprising merchants. They brought up a ship's carpenter from the south, who has now settled in Findhorn and employs about twelve men. In the last five years ten vessels, built of the fine oak and larch of Darnaway, have been sent off the stocks into the watery element.'

The village was served by a turnpike road from Forres to Findhorn 'which strikes off at the Bridge of Kinloss, by a branch eastward to Burghead and Elgin'. There was a daily postal service. The population of the village of Findhorn itself in 1841 was approximately 800, which meant that two-thirds of the population of the parish of Kinloss actually lived in Findhorn. An assembly school had been established at Findhorn, and there was probably also a female school in the village. There was a savings bank, a library and a friendly society. Three fairs were held at Findhorn annually, on the second Wednesday of March, July and October, primarily for the sale of sheep, cattle and horses.

The ice house on the 'Salmon Greenie' was built in 1843, in the same year as the new Free Church was planned. William Robertson, formerly the minister of the Established Church at Kinloss, became minister of the new Free Church at Findhorn, which was initially housed in temporary accommodation.

Back Road in Findhorn

Eventually the Building Committee of the Free Church in Edinburgh granted £162 10s od towards the expense of building the Free Church in Findhorn, while John Dunbar of Seapark donated £5 sterling to the project.

THE FOOD RIOTS

*

In January 1847 the small Moray ports of Burghead and Findhorn were the scene of disturbances which were, over the course of the next few months, to spread to several other places in the north of Scotland. Although the harvest of 1846 in Moray had not been up to the usual expectations, it could by no means have been described as a poor one, and under normal circumstances, although the price of meal may have risen somewhat, the general population would have been content with their lot. Other parts of the country, however, were suffering from much more severe shortages, and the corn-merchants and corn-agents of Moray probably saw this as a good business opportunity. They continued to export grain from the Moray Firth ports in ever-increasing quantities. This angered the working population of the area, especially those living in the ports, which were forced to watch the produce of their local farms being shipped away while they faced possible future hardship.

A branch railway line to Findhorn, from Kinloss, was opened in about 1860, in an effort to boost the trade of the harbour, which was now rapidly being overtaken in importance by the ports of Burghead and Lossiemouth. The railway was not a success, due to the continued silting up of the harbour, and it was abandoned in 1880.

NEWBRUGH

Newbrugh is another small fishing village now long since vanished from the face of the earth. To the west of Burghead, and just to the north of the farms of Hatton and Lower Hempriggs, it possibly stood at the mouth of the Bessie Burn. The only documentary evidence we have that it ever existed is that it is marked on Pont's map. Interestingly, however, following the foundation of the parish of Kinloss, the parish and the landowners of Alves had now lost the use of their harbour at Findhorn, so was this 'Newbrugh' an unsuccessful attempt to form a new harbour for their own use, or was it just a little fishing station on the coast? The sands of Findhorn Bay have long since hidden any evidence of the very existence of Newbrugh.

BURGHEAD

The village of Burghead lies on a promontory which projects into the Moray Firth, at the western end of what was originally an island which stretched from there to the Coulard Hill at the mouth of the River Lossie and Loch Spynie. The origin of the settlement at Burghead has long been a source of dispute among scholars, who seem unable to decide whether the fort there was of Roman origin, the site of Ptoroton; a Pictish settlement, the site of the settlement of Narnia; or a Viking settlement, possibly the Torfness of the Viking Sagas; or was it perhaps an evolutionary development incorporating all three?

It is now generally thought to have been a main centre of the Pictish tribes, the 80-foot-high headland being crowned with the now ruinous remains of an outstanding Pictish fortification, which was mutilated during the construction of the harbour and the new town in the early nineteenth century. Eighteenth-century engravings and plans show a medallion-shaped structure, with a ridge along the centre, protected on the landward side by three 800-foot-long ramparts in almost an arrow-head formation. Excavations show that the walls of the fort were timber-laced and nailed at the joints. Only the central ridge now survives.

An early description of the Pictish site at Burghead notes that 'The northern part of the promontory is divided into two unequal terraces, whose area measures more than four acres. These terraces, the western one being 87 ft above sea level and the eastern one 45 ft, were surrounded by huge ramparts and earthworks varying from 7 to 20 ft high. The upper area was 380 ft by 225 ft, the lower 780 ft by 150 ft. In the western enclosure there were two 8-ft openings, and in the eastern one at the south end (an opening) some 10 ft wide. Immediately to the south were three transverse ramparts, separated by trenches 20 ft wide and 10ft deep, running from sea to sea, with 8-ft openings near the middle.'

The modern consensus of opinion, despite all the writings of the early antiquarians, is that the earliest ramparts at Burghead were probably built around AD 400, and were rough wooden palisades erected by Pictish settlers. Viking raids took place in the late eighth and ninth centuries, and '. . . . in 884 AD Sigurd the powerful captured "Torridun", by which name Burghead was known at that time. We can imagine the dragon ships of the Norseman sailing under the lee of the headland to land their plundering hordes.'

The Burghead well, of unknown origin but of great antiquity, is a rock-hewn chamber reached by descending a flight of 22 stone steps. It was discovered in 1809, and is a chamber cut out of solid rock at a depth of some 20 to 30 feet below the surface. Some sources suggest that it may be of early Christian origin, possibly contemporaneous with St Aethan or Aidan and the early chapel site which is now the graveyard. Wells and springs were often places for worship, but some historical sources suggest that a traditional method of execution among the Picts was by drowning. Christians were repelled by such pagan acts, but often such traditional holy places were rededicated for new purposes, and St Columba himself is recorded as having sanctified such a well for Christian use.

The name 'Chapel-yard' has been applied since time immemorial to the small quadrangular enclosure used as a burying ground. It is likely that a chapel evolved here on the site chosen by some early missionary preacher such as St Aethan. During the later improvements to the town the foundations of a square structure were discovered, possibly an early chapel, the remains of which had, according to local tradition, been carted off to use as part of the building materials for the repair of the mill at Outlet, on the small burn to the south-west now known as the Millie Burn.

One continuing remnant of Pagan times at Burghead is the burning of the Clavie, a festival akin to Up Helly Aa in Shetland. The burning of the Clavie takes place in Burghead on 11 January each year, the New Year's Eve of the old-style calendar. A tarred half-barrel is attached to a 5-foot pole, traditionally by a hand-wrought nail which is hammered in with a stone. The contents of the barrel – wood, burning peats and tar – are lit by a burning peat. In olden times the Clavie was carried around every vessel in the harbour, and a handful of grain was thrown into each vessel to ensure success for the coming year. The blazing Clavie is then marched around the burgh by a relay of carriers before ending up at the freestone pillar on the Doorie Hill, next to the remains of the ramparts of the old fort, the spoke of the Clavie fitting into a hole in the pillar. In earlier times it was allowed to burn there all night, being tended, as a matter of tradition, by the oldest inhabitant of the town. In modern times, however, it only remains there for a short period. It is then rolled, still blazing, down the hill, and the inhabitants attempt to retrieve a piece of the Clavie, however small or hot, to guarantee them good luck for the forthcoming year.

That Burghead was a harbour used for fishing, probably from very early times, is one fact that seems beyond dispute. The coastal waters of the Moray Firth would have provided rich fishing grounds, and the local men were quick to take advantage of this seemingly inexhaustible supply of food, both for themselves and their families and for profit on the markets of nearby Elgin and Forres. In the Kirk Session Minutes of many of the coastal parishes of the Moray Firth, especially in the seventeenth and eighteenth centuries, there are censures of fishermen who, at or near to the date of New Year, would, with their crews, carry flaming 'firrs', not unlike miniature Clavies, around their vessels, thus continuing an age-old tradition which may have been much more widely celebrated. The skipper and his crew invariably received a punishment from the kirk session for their 'heathen' activities!

In November 1729 four whales were stranded on the sands of Burghead, somewhere between Burghead itself and the Mill of Outlet. The three principal local landowners, Brodie of Brodie, Sir Robert Gordon of Gordonstoun and Dunbar of Thundertoun all, for a short time, decided to attempt to profit from the misfortune of the whales by becoming dealers in spermaceti and whale's blubber. Five Burghead skippers, together with their crews, were paid £10 for killing and securing the whales, and they employed 200 to turn and tear at the whales, when the tides permitted. They carried 260 horse loads of 'speck' to the Corf House. Barrels and casks were brought in from Cromarty, Chanonry (Ardersier) and Findhorn.

They chartered a ship, the *Susana of Burlingtown* (its master being one Mr. Francis Bulson), a vessel of 40 tons which was at that time lying in the harbour of Lossiemouth. At a cost of 16s per ton, this vessel carried the barrels of blubber and spermaceti to London, where it was processed. Sadly, the unskilful manner with which the whales had been treated meant that the quantity of oil was not all that it was expected to be, and even having sent it to Holland, where the prices were better, the three entrepreneurs made a total loss of £55 13s 11d sterling!

In 1777 a proposal was put forward by John Packman, James Symon and John Morison for the opening of a salmon fishery along the coast between Burghead and Findhorn. The initial trial was to be for three years, and if this proved successful they planned to then take a 10-year lease at a rental of £3 sterling a year. The outcome of these trials was never recorded, but there is evidence that for at least the next 70 years there were stake nets for salmon fishing in the waters around Burghead.

During the later years of the eighteenth century, Sir Archibald Dunbar was already devising plans to build a new harbour, and a planned settlement, to replace the old village of 'Brugh Head'. In 1801 the noted engineer, Thomas Telford, was employed to survey the area, and he drew up plans for a new harbour. Telford's plan is of particular interest in that it shows the layout of the village at the time, and the majority of the fisher cottages had been built with their gable-ends to the sea. This type of building is to this day an obvious feature in many of the other Fishertowns and Seatowns along the Moray Firth coast. Unfortunately war intervened, and 'the late peace being of short duration' the plans were put aside, but the project was not forgotten and just four years later the project was revived by various other parties. In 1805 a group of landowners bought the old fishing village of Brugh, or Burghsea, from Sir Archibald Dunbar, in order to lay out a new 'planned village' of straight, parallel streets, with the harbour on the south-west side of the promontory. The new village was built 'as an inducement to practical fishermen'.

In a document from 1806, the landowners, including His Grace the Duke of Gordon, Sir Archibald Dunbar of Northfield. Joseph King of Newmiln, John Brander of Pitgaveny, George Forteath of Newton, William Young of Inverugie and Thomas Sellar, Writer in Elgin, note that 'A harbour on the southern coast of the Firth of Moray would be of great advantage to the small vessels navigating that coast, and the situation the best calculated for that purpose is at the Promontory called Burghead.'

It would appear that work on the harbour was quite advanced by 1807, as some vessels were able to make use of it at that date. In the vicinity of the harbour large warehouses, many of which still survive as attractive flats, were built for the storage of exports and imports, and accommodation was provided for the curing of herring and white fish. In the early days of the port the bulk of the catch had to be cured, and substantial smoke houses were built adjacent to the harbour.

The other developers soon dropped out of the venture and by 1818 William Young of Inverugie had become the sole proprietor. He gradually developed Burghead into one of Moray's principal fishing stations, and a major port for import and exports, this in no small way contributing to the final decline of Findhorn as the most important port on the south coast of the Moray Firth.

As originally built, the harbour was an unqualified success, and met the requirements of the users of the port for many years. With a short horseback breakwater, over which the sea rolled at high water, there was little surge or silting and vessels could be safely moored in the stormiest of weather. In bad weather it was frequently filled with vessels from other harbours along the coast, especially Hopeman and Lossiemouth. On at least one occasion it was so full that the larger vessels had to seek shelter at Cromarty, while, with night falling, other vessels had to be run ashore on the Burghead sands. As the harbour became more popular, however, the original breakwater was replaced by a larger one, the design of which subsequently created problems with the silting up of the harbour.

After the opening of the new harbour the net fishing for herring invariably commenced on 20 July and closed about the middle of September, while line fishing, chiefly for haddock, was carried out during the other months of the

Burghead Harbour entrance

year, providing steady employment not only for the fishermen but for a large number of both male and female workers on shore, including, no doubt, some of the former agricultural workers who had been displaced from their lands by the recent 'Improvements'. Other kinds of fish, such as cod, were also caught on a regular basis. From 1808 onwards both the net and the line fisheries made rapid progress, the first to show signs of failure being the herring fishing in the middle years of the nineteenth century.

With the expansion of the village of Burghead in the early nineteenth century, despite the availability of the 'fisher's loft', the fact that the kirk was located at Duffus was inconvenient for a large number of the parishioners. In about 1823 Burghead was raised to the status of a *quoad sacra* parish, with its own church or 'chapel of ease'. The first minister was David Symson, who served from 2 July 1823 until being succeeded by David Waters in July 1826. Mr Waters or Walters left the Established Church at the time of the Disruption in 1843, and became minister of the Free Church at Burghead from that time until 1887.

As the general trade of the port increased, so the population expanded. In addition to the fishing there were exports of grain, potatoes, timber, freestone, cured herring and oatmeal, and imports of coal, slates, ore and various kinds

Burghead Harbour, clearing up floating timber

of fertilisers such as guano from Callao and bones from Prussia. The shipping in the early nineteenth century consisted chiefly of fast schooner-rigged vessels with a registered tonnage of 99 tons. By staying below a registered tonnage of 100 tons, various concessions were available as regards the qualifications of the skippers, who were able to sail to the Baltic and Russian ports, to Hamburg or to the home ports, without obtaining additional certification. The best round of voyages was thought to be to take a cargo to the Baltic ports, then one back to the coal ports, followed by a return voyage laden with coal for the home port. There is some evidence that shipbuilding was carried out on a small scale at Burghead during the late eighteenth and early nineteenth centuries.

By 1835 Burghead was not only a major port on the coast, but was well on its way to becoming a popular sea-bathing resort. Many 'respectable families' from Elgin and Forres arrived each summer attracted by 'its advantages as a watering place'. These advantages by this time included a suite of saltwater baths, comfortable lodgings and pleasant seaside walks. Sailing ships, and later steam ships from London, Leith and other ports called regularly at Burghead, and by now Burghead was accessible by sea with 'Steam Yachts sailing during the summer months on a weekly voyage between Edinburgh and Inverness'. The services of a light gig carrying passengers and mail meant that the village enjoyed a 'daily post and carriers to and from Elgin'.

The year 1847 saw meal and grain riots caused by the failure of the potato crop and the resultant high prices charged for other foodstuffs. Meal, the staple food of the working man, became practically unobtainable. Strenuous efforts were made across the north of Scotland to stop the export of any supplies, meeting, in most places, with indifferent success, except at Burghead where several vessels were seized and their cargoes secured. A mob of about 500 men, residents of Burghead and Hopeman, took part in the plunder, and the sheriff of the county, hearing of this, gathered a body of men from Elgin with the intention of enforcing the law.

When the sheriff's men arrived on the scene a battle with the rioters ensued, not only did the Burghead men use stones but also lug bait spades, a formidable weapon in the right hands. The sheriff's men were quickly routed and driven from the town. Several people were so seriously injured that they never recovered from the riots, and at least one died on reaching his house. In consequence of this a body of regular troops was quartered at Elgin, which had a very calming effect on the local population, and shortly after this prices fell back to the more usual levels. A number of Burghead and Hopemen men were tried at the Circuit Court at Inverness, and several of them were condemned to five or seven years penal servitude.

HOPEMAN AND CUMMINGSTOWN

The village of Hopeman was established in 1805–06 by William Young of Inverugie, at a site formerly known as the Broad Hythe, one of the few usable bays or inlets along the otherwise rocky coastline between Burghead and Lossiemouth. Prior to this date there seems to have been little at the Broad Hythe other than a fishing station comprising a few huts, which was probably used on a seasonal basis by fishermen from Burghead or Lossiemouth, or possibly by one or two boats owned by William Young of Inverugie, and crewed by his tenants.

Once the plans for the development of the village were under way, the site was advertised in 1806, and it attracted craftsmen and seafarers in almost equal numbers, the first house in the village being built in that year. Families were brought into the new village from Campbeltown (Arderseir) in the parish of Petty near Inverness, introducing family names such as McAuley, McPherson and McKenzie, Main, Ralph, Davidson, Young and More. The poor state of the harbour seems to have been an impediment during the early stages, and the construction had not been fully completed even a decade after the start of the building of the village. The families from Campbeltown spoke Gaelic, but when the herring fishing started in about 1818, and the Scots-speaking fishermen and

Hopeman Harbour

fish-curers from Buckie came to settle at Hopeman, the Gaelic language gradually died out. These incomers from the east brought family names such as Bruce, Murray and Slater into the village. The town was designed, like so many of the new planned settlements of the late eighteenth and early nineteenth centuries, on a gridiron pattern on either side of the road leading down to the harbour.

The cottages of Hopeman and Cummingston were built of stone, initially with a thatched roof, but later slated, and in the majority of cases consisted of two rooms, each containing bed recesses, and an outhouse in which to store nets, fishing equipment and other such necessities.

The village of Cummingston, originally known as Port Cumming, was founded in 1808, contemporary with the new town of Burghead. The proprietor, William Gordon-Cumming, saw the fishing industry as a potential money-spinner, and decided to open a fishing station there, even though it had no harbour. Some fishing folk were originally enticed there, but the lack of a harbour meant that it was unable to compete with the neighbouring ports of Burghead, Hopeman and Lossiemouth. It comprised a single street of stone cottages along the road between Hopeman and Burghead, and eventually became primarily a home for the masons and labourers from the nearby quarries at Roseisle and Clashach. In 1831 the population of Cummingstown was 197, the bulk of the inhabitants of this 'straggling and dirty village' being, by this time, quarriers and farm labourers.

It seems that a new proprietor, Admiral Duff of Drummuir, eventually purchased the lands and village of Hopeman, and in 1835 it was being described as 'an extremely dirty but regularly built village'. Admiral Duff provided a new harbour there between 1836 and 1838, primarily for the export of stone from the nearby quarries. The new harbour also proved invaluable in attracting new fishermen to the village, and the fishing industry there was flourishing by the middle of the nineteenth century. In the middle of the nineteenth century a new ice house was built in the village, for the storage of fish, this one being distinguished by its particularly well built and ornamental entrance.

Just along the coast to the east lay the quarries of Clashach, and a small harbour was built there to facilitate the export of stone. Due to its location, the harbour was not a success and was very soon abandoned, and only a few worked stones mark the site of this failed enterprise.

In the first half of the nineteenth century, there was a great demand for lime both for agriculture and for building. Quarried limestone was burnt with coal to produce quicklime for both of these purposes. It was established that there were considerable deposits of limestone at Inverugie, and William Young of Inverugie established the lime quarry and limeworks there, a very profitable undertaking until the advent of the railways in the 1850s meant that much cheaper lime could be brought into the area and the Inverugie limeworks was no longer an economic proposition. Even as late as 1888, however, on a small scale, Inverugie was locally regarded as providing an excellent source of good quality lime. Hopeman Lodge, a harled Italianate seaside pavilion, was built by William Young in 1840, despite the fact that the old Inverugie House was only about one mile further inland on the hill behind Hopeman.

The Disruption of 1843 led to the need for buildings in which the followers of the Free Church could worship, and, in addition to the church already being established at Burghead, the village of Hopeman was decided on as being a good location for a Free Church accessible to the worshippers from the eastern part of the parish. The congregation effectively built this church with their own hands; fishermen brought stones in their boats from nearby quarries, and the men and women of the congregation helped to carry them to the building site. It took some years, but the church, built to a cruciform shape with a Tudor Gothic tower, was completed about a decade after the Disruption, and finally opened for worship in 1854.

COVESEA

The fishing community of Covesea or Coysie is shown on Pont's map of the area drawn in about 1585. In 1641 it is noted that '. . . the fishboats called Stotfauld, Covesea and Annhall, set in tack first to the Bishop, but now possessed by the Earl of Moray, by virtue of a disposition made by Bishop Hepburn to Umquhile James Earl of Moray, that when it shall happen the bishops of Moray to dwell in the castle of Spynie, they to take up the fishes and enjoy them, otherways they belong to the Earl of Moray and his successors'. Annhall is probably Ernhill, a settlement situated where the Covesea light-house now stands. This is shown on sixteenth- and seventeenth-century maps, but then appears to have gone out of existence, another 'lost' little part of the history of Moray and Nairn.

The caves of Covesea had been used for many centuries, as is shown by the wall carvings in some of them, especially in the 'Sculptor's Cave'. The carvings here are probably early Pictish, and include many of the usual symbols associated with such carvings, such as Fish, Crescent and V-rod, pentacles, and Mirror Case. There is evidence of occupation, with various layers revealing Bronze Age and Roman pottery, rings, bracelets, needles and other similar items. Finds in the cave date from the Bronze Age to the fourth century AD, but it is thought that the Roman objects were merely 'lost' items. Maybe the Romans came there at various times to take advantage of the sea air, or perhaps to hide from the local population. Many human bones were found in the caves, and they seemed to be from two different periods. The great majority of them date from the Late Bronze Age, but some others have been placed firmly within the Roman Iron Age. A large proportion of the bones seem to have been those of children.

The year 1644 saw Covesea as the site of the escape of the second Marquis of Huntly in his flight to Caithness, and only five years later he was to be executed by the Covenanters.

At the time of the *Old Statistical Account* of 1791, it is noted that the quarries of Covesea and Lossiemouth provided both white and yellow freestone, and employed, including apprentices, some 20 masons, with approximately twice that number of labourers. The proprietor of Covesea, the Laird of Gordonstoun, was required to provide the fishermen with a new boat every seven years, these normally costing between £18 and £20 sterling. The main fish catches were of cod, skate, halibut, whiting and saith, with herring at times, and plenty of crabs and lobster both for home consumption and for the Elgin markets.

In 1842 there was talk of erecting a lighthouse at Covesea, following at least 40 shipwrecks in the area over the previous half century, and this was completed over the following years. In 1847 the lighthouse keepers are identified as James and Thomas Marchbanks, and William Baird, who lived there with his family.

STOTFIELD

Before the advent of Lossiemouth as a fishing and commercial port, Stotfield was the main harbour for the parish of Kinneddar. The small sandy bay in the shelter of the Hythe of Stotfield, at the mouth of a small creek which ran down from the Coulard Hill, formed an ideal natural harbour for the fishing boats. Although it almost certainly dates from much earlier, it is first mentioned in the documentary records in 1612, when David Anderson, apparently a celebrated engineer of his time, 'was paid 6 shillings and 8 pence by the Magistrates of Elgin to visit the harbere of Stotfauld', possibly to consider plans for improvements. It was never, however, a large settlement, the village being little more than a huddle of cottages set with their backs or their gable-ends to the sea. The survivors of these cottages can be seen in the old Paradise Row.

It would seem that a similar superstition to the burning of the Clavie at Burghead also existed at Stotfield, and in 1699 William Edward, described as a 'Skipper in Stotfold', was censured by the Kirk Session 'for his superstitious custom by binding a blazing torch of firr and carrying it round about his boat on New Years Even'.

When five men from Stotfield were lost at sea in 1715, it took more than a fortnight for the wives and families to realise that their menfolk were never coming back. In those days, it would have taken time for word to get back to the village that they had taken refuge in a harbour elsewhere. Eventually, after they had set sail on 14 June, 'all were lost, for aught we can conjecture, seeing that this July 3rd we had no certain word of them nor from them'. Reports of the loss of a Stotfield boat were a constant feature of the Kirk Session Minutes.

In 1791 it was recorded that Stotfield had 'a creek which admits boats' and there were three fishing boats based there. The proprietors of the village were obliged to provide a new boat every seven years, at a cost of £18–20 sterling, so that the fishermen could catch cod, skate, halibut, haddock, whiting and saith, with plenty of crabs and lobsters.

Disaster struck Stotfield just 15 years later. The morning of Christmas Day, Thursday 25 December 1806 dawned calm and fair, and boats from most of the fishing villages along the Moray Firth put to sea. This included the complete fishing fleet of Stotfield – three boats crewed by twenty-one men – who set to sea early in the morning. This was the whole male population of the village apart from three elderly fishermen who were now too old to go to sea, and three boys who were too young to go to the fishing.

The fishing grounds were just a few miles off the coast, outside the Halliman Skerries, and the boats were quite small undecked open vessels, with only a low rail for the protection of the fishermen. They could easily be pulled up onto a sheltered beach, but provided little protection for the men and were easily swamped in even a moderately rough sea.

In 1806 very few records of the weather were being kept, but from an analysis of the surviving records it would appear that December 1806 was characterised by a series of Atlantic depressions crossing Scotland. This would have made it difficult for the fishermen to put to sea on a regular basis, and they would have been obliged to take advantage of whatever weather window presented itself. Although on the morning of 25 December the wind may have been light, they would almost certainly have been aware that the thickening frontal cloud moving in from the west indicated that a change was on the way, which would have limited the time they were able to spend at the fishing.

This depression, however, seems to have been more intense than the earlier ones, and was probably accelerating and deepening rapidly, the consequences of which caught them unawares. The nearest barometer, albeit several miles from Stotfield, had indicated a fall of 25 millibars in the pressure overnight, which would have indicated the approach of this deepening area of low pressure, but it is unlikely that the fishermen of Stotfield had the benefits of a barometer to give them this advance warning.

By about noon the fishermen were returning to shore, and were in sight of their families waiting on the beach, when, according to contemporary reports 'a violent and tremendous hurricane came from the West and Southwest'. Mountainous seas broke over their boats, and despite the best efforts of the men to row back to the Hythe at Stotfield, the boats were carried down the Firth and into the open sea. Neither boats nor men were ever seen again.

The depression crossed the Moray Firth during the afternoon of Christmas Day, and the temperature, which had previously, despite the time of year, been about 10 °C, suddenly plummeted to 4 °C, and was to fall still further during the evening. By the next morning the wind was north-westerly with snow falling, the temperature stood at 2 °C, and the barometer had risen just as rapidly as it had fallen. In that kind of weather, a small open boat and its crew would have stood almost no chance of survival. The storm affected the whole of the Moray Firth, and boats from Avoch on the Black Isle and from Rottenslough in the parish of Rathven were also lost, and a boat was overturned in Burghead Harbour with the loss of three lives.

In Stotfield 17 widows and 47 children were left unprovided for, and, with two of the wives being pregnant at the time, this made a total of 49 fatherless children, together with numerous aged parents and relatives who were also dependent on the support of the fishermen. Out of the 21 men no fewer than 10 bore the surname Edward, and were all closely related as fathers, sons, brothers, uncles and nephews. Because of the common practice of intermarriage within these fishing villages, many of the womenfolk had lost more than just a husband.

It soon became obvious that a purely local collection would not raise sufficient aid for these families, and the minister of the parish of Drainie sent appeals for subscriptions as far afield as Aberdeen, Edinburgh and London, and a committee was established to manage the fund. The 'Minutes of the Managers of the Stotfield and Burghead Widows Fund' give a very complete list of the victims of the disaster and their dependants.

Agnes Keith, writing in 1975, commented that 'fishing is no longer carried on from the little harbour of Stotfield, and the story of the Stotfield disaster has passed into history. But the echo lingers on. To this day no Lossiemouth fisherman will put to sea on Christmas Day.' In 2009 the fishing industry in Lossiemouth is no more, but the memory of those Stotfield fishermen remains in the haunting words of the song about the disaster, written by Trevor Foster, which was so often performed at the Lossiemouth Folk Club in the Beach Bar overlooking the Hythe of Stotfield, from where the fishermen has sailed to their death so many years before.

Stotfield, however, survived for another 30 years as a fishing harbour, and it was not until the new harbour was built in nearby Lossiemouth in 1837 that the strand at the Hythe became deserted. That was not to last long, though, for the beautiful expanse of the West Beach proved a great attraction. The former fishing cottages in the village of Stotfield began to be taken over as summer holiday homes by the new breed of prosperous merchants and businessmen from nearby Elgin. During Victorian times the old thatched cottages of Paradise Row began to command quite healthy rents during the summer months, the fisherfolk often moving out to live in a shed in the garden, or even going away to find work at the harvest. It wasn't long before the better-off families began to build their own villas along the coast overlooking the beach. With the coming of the railways and the increasing tourist trade, hotels and guest houses began to spring up, and the three open fishing boats drawn up on the Hythe became but a distant memory.

LOSSIEMOUTH
AND BRANDERBURGH

Lossiemouth originated, as its name implies, as a very small harbour at the mouth of the River Lossie. St Gerardine had settled at Lossiemouth in the year 943, and had lived in a small cell or hermitage in the cliffs overlooking the mouth of the river and the East Beach. The cell was still there in 1760, according to the Kirk Session Minutes, at which date it was destroyed by a 'rude shipmaster', and later quarrying along the cliffs eventually destroyed any traces of the hermitage.

The Coulard Hill, to the west of what is now known as Lossiemouth, is now mostly covered by the town of Branderburgh, but in earlier times this was probably the main agricultural land in the area. The southern slope of the hill, draining away towards the Loch of Spynie, would have been ideal for the runrig type of agriculture which was used until the second half of the eighteenth century, and the estate records identify many of the farmers and subtenants who worked the land. The seaward side of the hill was quite intensively quarried, and on the northern side, almost at the beach, there were lead mines.

One of the buildings to the west of the river mouth, now a restaurant, has a lintel stone bearing the date 1629, which provides us with evidence that the harbour was in use at that date, as this was probably originally a small warehouse associated with the trade at the harbour. In later years, as the fishing expanded, it was used as a salt store.

In 1658 the lands passed into the hands of the Brodie family, and in 1698 the part of the river mouth where the esplanade is now was purchased by the Magistrates of Elgin. Some four years earlier they had decided that they should build a better harbour there, to divert trade from the two principal ports of Findhorn and Garmouth. On 19 October 1685, '. . . the Council unanimously condescends that the Harber at Lossiemouth be builtit'. So the council sent John Fyfe, the Dean of Guild of Elgin, south to collect the necessary documents in order to activate the King's Gift of a century earlier, in which it was agreed that there should be a harbour at Holieman Head, as it was then known.

Quarrymen at Lossiemouth

Lossiemouth lead mines at Stotfield, 1904

THE HARBOUR
*

In the eventual agreement to build the harbour it soon became clear that the tenants of Lossiemouth were expected to maintain and operate it, to allow free passage to the landowner's ships, and to expect little or no reward. The Elgin Town Council were really expecting too much of the people, and the fishermen, who already had safe harbourage at Covesea and Stotfield, showed little inclination to move to the new harbour. The limited amount of commercial traffic and the new trade barriers later imposed by the Act of Union meant that, within a few years of opening, the harbour at Lossiemouth was proving to be an almost totally uneconomic venture.

An early description of Lossiemouth following the building of the harbour seems to indicate that there were only two decent houses in the village, and a few huts which were sometimes occupied by visiting fishermen. Following the draining of some of the lands around the Loch of Spynie, and the access to this new and very fertile alluvial farmland, the agriculture on the Coulard Hill had died out, and the hill between Lossiemouth Village and Stotfield produced nothing but whins and stunted grass. By 1722 the harbour was in a ruinous state of decay, and the Burgh of Elgin was unable to pay any of its debts. Hard times indeed.

In 1764 there were ambitious plans for Lossiemouth, and the land adjacent to the harbour was feued off in a series of regular plots along the main street. Thus did what is now Clifton Road come into existence, soon to be followed by the other parallel streets and cross lanes, and Lossiemouth became yet another of the 'planned towns' of this era. The new streets and the feuing lots are clearly shown on a plan dated 1784, which bears little difference to the modern town plan.

Things were beginning to change for Lossiemouth, and by the time of the *Old Statistical Account* of 1791 the minister was able to record that 'besides the irregular street fronting the sea, the town is laid out into four principal streets', now Clifton Road, Church Street, Macduff Street and Moray Street, 'at right angles to the shore, each 42 ft wide, and commodious lanes cutting across the streets, equally to half their breadth, with a handsome square and cross in the middle'. There were 175 feus each 120 feet by 180 feet, on which a number of new houses had already been built and the population of Lossiemouth was up to nearly 200. The harbour, lying within the river mouth, had also been improved and was now 'sufficiently commodious for vessels of about 80 tons burden'. The building of a harbour wall on the east side of the river, at the East Beach, had been started many years earlier, but it was unable to stand up to the forces of nature, and had now become a ruin.

Trade was increasing, however, and although Lossiemouth itself was home to only one sloop and two fishing vessels, there were numerous visitors. During one year 49 vessels visited the harbour, all of them being of between 55 and 60 tons, of which 20 were loaded with English coal, 6 with Scots coal, 10 with London goods, 4 with Leith goods, 3 with tanners bark, 2 with native salt and the others carrying various cargoes. The exports from Lossiemouth were 20 cargoes of barley and oats, and an inconsiderable quantity of 'peltry'. Obviously foreign ships were visiting Lossiemouth as well, and at the end of the eighteenth century Isobel Anderson, a Lossiemouth lady, had a child by the mate of a Dutch ship which was unloading a cargo of flax destined for the 'Linnen Manufactory' in Elgin, doubtless Mr Johnston's New Mills.

THE BUILDING OF BRANDERBURGH

✳

By 1830 the old fishing settlement in the Seatown had become unable to cope with the number of families involved in the herring fishing, and the old harbour at the river mouth was also beginning to creak at the seams. The provision of housing for these new families was one of the main factors which influenced the decision to build the town of Branderburgh. The town was laid out in about 1830 on the top of the Coulard Hill, to the west of the town of Lossiemouth. It was, as its name implies, built on the lands of Colonel Brander of Pitgaveny, to a design by George MacWilliam. It was laid out on the grid pattern so often used for these new settlements, and the main streets, centred on James Square, all ran northwards to the sea, bisected by the east–west High Street.

Proposals and a prospectus for the new harbour of Lossiemouth were published in 1837, and it was noted that Lossiemouth was 'fast advancing in importance'. The new harbour which was being built at an estimated cost of £20,000 would provide a 'safe and commodious haven for shipping', and indeed it did bring trade and prosperity to the town. In 1837 no fewer than 106 loaded vessels came into the port, a total tonnage of 4,816 tons, crewed by a total of 352 men. In 1836/7 the imports are listed as 4,500 tons of English coal, 1,000 tons of Scotch coal, 400 tons of bones, in addition to bark and salt. The expansion of the fishing industry is clearly indicated in the exports that year, 2,000 barrels of herring and 200 barrels of codfish, in addition to large quantities of grain and timber. By now there was also a regular steam vessel from London and Leith, which called at Lossiemouth in the summer season landing goods and passengers.

Lossiemouth Harbour in the early twentieth century

Shipping advert for the steamboat services from Leith to the Moray Firth ports

Steamboat Service between

LEITH, ABERDEEN, BUCKIE, LOSSIEMOUTH, INVERGORDON, CROMARTY and INVERNESS.

The fine Steamer "James Crombie" or other Steamer **Calls** at **Buckie** every Wednesday with Goods and Passengers.

ROUND TOUR TO LEITH
via
INVERNESS and ABERDEEN
CABIN £1 1s. 6d., or with food £2.
Passengers must leave Steamer on arrival at Leith.

A. FRASER, Agent, Buckie.
Passenger Agent for Steamers to CANADA and the UNITED STATES.
37

The Morayshire Railway, linking Lossiemouth to Elgin, was opened on 10 August 1853 with great ceremony, and the rapid expansion of the railway system meant that the fish landed at Lossiemouth could be sent to the major markets much more quickly, another boost to the economy of the town. The railways also brought the tourists, the sweeping sandy beaches to the east and west of the town proving to be a great attraction, especially to the people of Glasgow and the Central Belt of Scotland. The tourist trade reached its climax each summer during the various 'Trades Weeks', especially into the twentieth century when the town became a mecca for the people from Glasgow during their 'Trades'.

The railway, thanks to Dr Beeching, is no more, the station demolished, and the new esplanade along the edge of the river where the railway tracks once ran provides a pleasing view over the wide expanse of the east beach. The twentieth century also brought the 'incomers', first the Navy and later the Royal Air Force, to the large air base which lies just to the west of the town.

GARMOUTH AND KINGSTON

Some of the early mentions of the area refer to events which took place 'near to the mouth of the Spey', and although no specific location is described they must have occurred somewhere in the vicinity of the village of Garmouth, or a little upstream near to the kirk of Essil:

> Near the mouth of the river, the Rebels of Moray, Ross and Caithness, in the year 1078, made a stand to oppose the passage of Malcolm III, but on seeing the resolution of the royal army in fording the river, their submission was offered, and received, at the intercession of the priests.

> In the year 1110 an army of rebels halted at the mouth of the Spey, to dispute the passage, with Alexander I pursuing them. The King, forcing the passage, so terrified the rebels that they were easily defeated by a detachment of the army, under the conduct of Alexander Scrimger.

> In the year 1160 a rebellion, still more formidable, was quelled by Malcolm IV in a battle which must have happened on the moors of this parish, wherin the Moray people were so completely routed that the chief families of this turbulent province were removed to different parts of the kingdom, and others transplanted in their room.

A trading union, probably similar to that maintained by the Hanseatic League, was formed and recognised by King David I in the twelfth century. The ports making up this 'hanse' were Aberdeen, Inverness, Elgin (Garmouth), Forres (Findhorn) and Nairn. It is interesting to consider whether these ports may have later become a small part of the greater 'Hanseatic League' extending from Bergen in Norway, through the Danish ports and into the north of Germany. The older parts of many of these European ports, for example the 'Bryggen' area of Bergen, exhibit a similar town plan to some of the burghs of north-east Scotland, with burgesses or merchants having their own closes. This would have meant that the trading ships from these Scottish ports may well have sailed routes which would have taken them across many parts of the North Sea.

The earliest specific mention of the village of Garmouth is in a deed of 1237, where it appears that the church at Urquhart had 'past memory of man' supplied divine service and the holy sacraments to the inhabitants of 'Meft, Sallelcot, Byn and Garmauch', a state of affairs which continued, at least on paper, until well after the Reformation in 1560.

The earliest record of trade being carried out is a Charter granted in 1393 by Thomas Dunbar, Earl of Murray, which reads: 'Be it knawyn tyl al men thrw this present letters Vs Thomayse of Dunbarr, Eryl of Murreffe, for tyl havr grauntit and gyfin tyl ye aldirman, ye baylis, of wre Burgh of Elgyne, and to ye burges of yt ilke a ye wol, ye calthe and al uthir thyngis, yt gais be schipe owte of wre hafine of Spee (our harbour of Spey).' The earliest specific mention, by name, of any of the inhabitants of Garmouth is that of James Chalmer, described as a merchant in the town in 1573.

Garmouth always seems to have been an established settlement in its own right, as indeed was Slentach in the parish of Urquhart, and these places appear to have constituted the 'Etherurcard' identified in c.1157 in Beroald's Charter to the lands of Innes. Not being part of the Barony of Innes, the port of Garmach was, by a Charter dated 30 June 1587 in favour of Robert, the nineteenth Laird of Innes, erected into a burgh of barony. Much to the anger of the Burghers of Elgin this endowed Garmouth with the powers of creating free burgesses, the erection of a mercat cross and harbour, and initially it was entitled to hold two annual fairs. One of these, the 'Maggie Fair', or the Margaret Fair as it was originally called, held on 30 June, has survived to the present day, but the September fair has long since ceased to exist. The name of the surviving fair is often identified with Lady Margaret Ker, who brought the ducal dignity of the House of Roxburghe into the Innes family at the time of her marriage to Sir James Innes, third Baronet, on 18 July 1666. As it is obvious, however, that the fair considerably pre-dates this event, it is probably more likely that it was originally named after Queen Margaret of Scotland, the lands originally having been in the possession of the Abbey of Dunfermline.

In 1630, a contract which was vital to the future of Garmouth and neigh-bouring Kingston was signed between Sir John Grant of Grant and Captain John Mason. This took the form of a 41-year lease on the woods of Abernethy, for the sum of £1,666 13s 4d sterling, payable at Whitsunday 1631 and Whitsunday 1632. The contract notes that Captain John Mason and his employees were to be allowed safe and free passage 'through and down the River Spey to the sea' and that John Mason and his heirs 'shall procure and obtain liberty to big and uphold an House and Timber Wharf or Cloare, at the Haven or mouth of the Spey, for keeping of their timber and woods unstolen by ill-disposed persons. . . .' Although John Mason died in 1638, his successors continued the lease until its expiry in 1671. This set the precedent for what was to prove to be a major part of the economy of Garmouth, and later also of Kingston, and to place Garmouth in the forefront of timber exports from the British Isles.

The rivalries between various warring factions visited themselves on Garmouth in the mid seventeenth century. In February 1645, a group of Irish mercenaries under the command of Alaistair McColla plundered the village of Garmach and destroyed the salmon fishing boats and nets. Alaistair McColla was second in command to James Graham, Marquis of Montrose. Following his victory at Auldearn in 1645, Montrose arrived at Elgin on 11 May and sent some of his men to burn the part of the village of Garmouth.

In these early days, and in fact throughout the whole of its existence, the harbour of Garmouth consisted merely of a tidal basin, and ships crossed over the bar at the mouth of the River Spey at high tide, and either unloaded onto smaller boats in the main channel, or beached on the shore to unload their cargo and passengers. The port of Garmach or Garmouth, however, was vital not only to the local community, but as a harbour for the merchants of Elgin. 'The tide flows up the river almost to Garmach, and at neap tides the depth of water is 9 feet on the bar. The entrance to the harbour is sometimes shifted a little by the gravel washed down by the stream, but there being always skilful pilots, no detriment ensues. The expense of building a pier is supposed to exceed the value of the trade . . . the shore being smooth gravel or soft sand. . . . several vessels have in necessity been run ashore with little damage.'

A ROYAL VISITOR

✳

On Thursday 23 June 1650 King Charles II landed at Garmouth, on his way from Holland to Scone, where he was to be crowned in defiance of Oliver Cromwell. The Scottish Commissioners who had met with him in Holland had done so on condition that he would subscribe to the Solemn League and Covenant, and his decision to land in the north may have been influenced not only by wind and weather, but by the fact that one of the commissioners was Brodie of Brodie. He had sailed from Holland on a Dutch frigate commanded by the son of Admiral van Troup, and accompanied by the admiral himself. Due to the mist which lay along the coast on that day, the Dutch ship narrowly avoided being captured by four Parliamentary ships which had only a few hours earlier left from the port of Garmouth. As there was no established landing place at that time, the story is that the future king was brought ashore piggy-back on the shoulders of the Garmouth ferryman, a man named Milne, and landed on the Boat Green of Garmouth.

He was entertained by Sir Robert Innes, the twentieth Laird of Innes, in his house on the Brae. One version of the story suggests that it was here on 25 June that the clergy of Moray presented Charles with the Solemn League and Covenant, which he duly signed, probably under a considerable amount of pressure, after which he left for Gordon Castle at Fochabers. Another version of the events suggests that the Presbyterians were so suspicious of Charles that he was made to sign the document on 23 June, even before he left the frigate and set foot on Scottish soil, and that the date of 25 June was added later.

When Charles landed at Garmouth, Cromwell's response was decisive. He crossed the border and at first tried to reason with the General Assembly: 'I beseech you in the bowels of Christ, think it possible that you may be mistaken.' The appeal was rejected, and at the Battle of Dunbar the Scottish army was devastated, 3,000 Scots being killed and 10,000 taken prisoner. This was not quite the end of Royalist resistance; the Scots collected a new army, and Charles made a thrust into England. The following year Cromwell won his 'crowning mercy' at Worcester, and the Cromwellian Union, imposed by force of arms, followed soon after.

In 1652 the Kirk Session of Essil made the decision that the parish school should be built at Garmouth, with a condition that the people of Garmouth, Mathiemiln and Corskie should pay by far the largest proportion of the school-master's salary, as 'they had the greatest ease and commoditie by the school being at ther doores and the rest of the paroch farr distant'. This was agreed by all parties concerned. A 'werie fitt' place for the school was found at the west end of Garmouth, and Mr William Innes was recommended as one who was fit and able to teach such a school, at a salary of 9 bolls victual yearly and 20 merks from the common good, 'if the fund had that amount of money at the time'. He had resigned his post by 1654, and John Dun was appointed on a trial basis. The minister, however, during this trial period 'judged him unfit to be a teacher of young ones, not onlie in regard of his cairlessness in attending upon his charge but also in reguard of his foolishe and unseemly carriage in those places which he frequented . . .' – probably the local alehouses. It was unanimously concluded that he should be dismissed, and Thomas Innes in Garmouth, who was 'exquisit in musick' was appointed.

SHIPBUILDING AND THE TIMBER TRADE

*

It is likely that the construction of small vessels has been carried out at Garmouth for many years, probably since the twelfth or thirteenth centuries. The first documentary evidence of shipbuilding there, however, appears in the second half of the seventeenth century by way of a mention of John Geddes, who is identified as a shipbuilder there in the late 1650s. In 1664 Benjamin Parsons is identified as the master of the sawmill at Garmouth, having bought into John Mason's lease, and Alexander Winster, who died in 1676, is described as a ship's carpenter. Richard Winster, possibly his son, also a ship's carpenter, died in 1696. There is record of a ship being launched there in 1664, and a further vessel was under construction in 1671.

In the early years of the eighteenth century, the Earl of Fife, Duff of Braco, built a small settlement of fisher houses on the beach, and persuaded some fishermen to come to live there. He provided a boat, but after some accident had happened they apparently, as was common at that time, gave way to their superstitious beliefs and abandoned the place. The houses were allowed to fall into ruin, and the boat rotted on the shore.

The York Buildings Company was a London-based business whose main purpose in life was the supply of drinking water to the inhabitants of the English capital city, but they were also ambitious to extend into other areas when they saw the possibility of making a profitable investment. The after-effects of the first Jacobite Rebellion of 1715 meant that many estates were forfeit by the leading rebels, and following the take-over of the company by a speculator in 1719 it was able to purchase several estates throughout Scotland. On 5 January 1727 Sir James Grant of Grant sold some 60,000 fir trees in the parishes of Abernethy and Kincardine to the York Buildings Company for a sum of £7,000 sterling, and this new investment led to a rapid increase in the volume of timber being floated downriver to Garmouth. Only a minimal amount of this timber appears to have been used for shipbuilding, the bulk of it being exported from the harbour of Garmouth.

The Lein Burn, which operated the sawmills at Garmouth and Kingston was an artificial waterway having its origins several miles inland in the Forest of Teindland. A lade was dug to divert the water from Teindland to Kingston, capturing on its way the headwaters of several other streams which originally flowed into the River Spey. The lade passed through Cowfords, where it drove a meal mill until the early twentieth century, and then also drove a further mill at Burniestrype near Garmouth.

The timber-felling operations commenced in 1728, and the men of Garmouth and various other places along the Spey saw this as a great new opportunity, being able to get employment in the loading of the rafts of timber and floating them down the river. This could be a hazardous occupation: if the river was running strongly and the floaters missed their landing point, the rafts could easily be carried right out to sea. It was not an easy job to get them back to the beach, and several men were lost during these operations. The Essil Kirk Session Minutes of 10 August 1730 comment that 'Seventeen Sabbath breakers were cited but they compeared not, they went out to sea with two floats of timber belonging to the York Buildings Company'. The record does not say whether they were rescued to appear before the Session, or were lost at sea.

Like many of the coastal parishes, the gathering of sea-ware, or seaweed, as a fertiliser, was a common part of the life of the agricultural worker. In 1734 John Duff, who was a bailie of the Barony of Garmouth, appointed an act which forbade the taking of sea-ware on the Sabbath, a period extending from Saturday evening until daybreak on Monday morning.

The perils of navigation at the mouth of the Spey were tragically demonstrated on 24 April 1749, at about 11 p.m., when William Gordon, a young man, and third son to James Gordon, merchant in Germach, together with another young man, Charles Gordon, a merchant in Fochabers, and seven fishermen from Buckie were bringing a boat into the mouth of the Spey. The boat struck a shallow in the darkness and was split open, and all on board were lost.

The York Buildings Company never completed their 17-year lease; the business was not profitable, and after four years they wound up their operations in the north of Scotland. Other entrepreneurs, however, ventured into the timber trade, and by 1750 the amount of timber being rafted down the Spey from the Grant estates was large enough to justify the building, making use of the Lein Burn, of two water-driven sawmills at Garmouth, one of which was owned by Sir James Grant, the other by Lord Braco.

On 6 August 1771 there is recorded a

> Disposition and Assignation (by) James, Earl of Fife, to Adam Duff, in liferent all and whole the lands and Barrony of Garmouth and thirty six fewed acres of the same, and haill other fewer houses, lands with acres . . . with the whole right and principles of a Burgh of Barrony and a weekly Mercate upon Thursday in the toun of Garmouth, and a privilidge of two yearly fairs, one upon the (blank) of June and another upon the twentieth day of September yearly to be held in the toun of Garmouth with the whole customs, privilidges and emoluments thereto belonging to the Harbour of Garmouth with the towage, rowage and Petty Pilotage of the same used and wont with the Pilot Boat of the Harbour of Garmouth and privilidges of the same with the Ferry Boat of Garmouth and privilidges of transporting passengers and landing them upon both sides of the Water of Spey . . . etc.

This provides good evidence that in the late eighteenth century Garmouth still had its two annual fairs, a weekly market and a ferry boat across the Spey.

The perils of the harbour entrance at Garmouth were brought into sharp focus yet again when on 3 January 1784 James Leslie with his shipmate James Sellar were attempting to come in with a boat on a wild and stormy night and both of them were lost. Their bodies were later recovered, and they were buried at Essil on 5 January.

By this time the port of Garmach, or Garmouth, had become noted for its timber trade, which by the late eighteenth century was considered to be the largest in Scotland for home-produced timber. In 1783 two timber merchants from Hull, Ralph Dodsworth and William Osbourne, started negotiations for the purchase of the timber of Glenmore Forest from the Duke of Gordon. Under this agreement, all of the marketable timber from the forest was to be felled within a period of 26 years and was to be floated down the Spey, as rafts navigated by two men. Sometimes, however, it was floated as rafts of up to 20,000 logs at a time, conducted by maybe 50 to 80 men going along the river banks, to push the logs off with poles when they stuck to the banks. In 1790 the pay of these men was quoted as ½d per day, with 'a competent allowance for spirituous liquor'.

William Osbourne moved north to Garmouth shortly after the completion of the negotiations and acquired the property known as Corf House as a base for his business. This property was, apart from the 'feal' or turf houses near the harbour, the nearest building to the sea. He made changes to the house, increasing the height to two storeys, thereby making room not only for the offices but also accommodation for his workmen. The river had one of her periodic spates, and the bed of the river shifted eastwards, causing a problem over how to launch the ships which were currently being built in the new shipyard. The company solved the problem by building a canal from the shipyard to the river, launching the ships into the canal and then floating them out into the river. This initiative greatly raised the esteem in which the English Company was held by the local population, and by 1784 Kingston Port had come into being, named after their home town of Kingston-upon-Hull.

The fluctuations in the mouth of the River Spey, especially after about 1750, were to give great concern to those involved with the use of the river, and were a constant source of trouble and expense. Vessels of 350 tons burden were able to enter the Spey at the end of the eighteenth century, and ships continued to be built at Garmouth and Kingston until about 1875. In the early nineteenth century a large amount of money had been spent in stopping up a second mouth of the Spey, which had threatened to carry off the houses at Tugnet, on the eastern bank of the river, and a few years later, in 1815, attempts to protect the western bank at Kingston cost about £300. At this time the mouth of the river had been constricted into a channel little more than 20 yards wide, no doubt leading to very strong currents there. The Great Flood of August 1829, during which the water rose 13 feet 9 inches above normal level at Kingston, created a breach 400 yards wide in the shingle banks at the mouth of the river. It was a very challenging environment for both the shipbuilders and those attempting to operate a profitable harbour at the mouth of the River Spey.

Dodsworth and Osbourne had by now named their business the 'Glenmore Company', and had built a street of houses to the north-east of Corf House in which to accommodate the workforce and their families. There was one sawmill driven by water power from the Lein Burn, and another one driven by a windmill. The channel which had been cut by Osbourne and Company (The Glen More Company or the English Company) was maintained in a navigable condition which enabled vessels to approach Kingston on the high tide, and the loading and unloading took place when they were grounded by the outgoing tide. Some seven or eight years later Revd James Gillan, minister of Speymouth, wrote: '. . . the greatest inconvenience of the harbour is, that the stream, by its strength and rapidity, sometimes brings down in a flood such quantities of gravel as to shift the channel, especially at the entrance of the harbour. But there are always good pilots at the place and many vessels belonging to the English Company, some of them of 350 tons burthen have been coming and going for these seven years. There has never been any attempt to build a pier, and from the above cause it is to be feared it would not succeed, or the expense would exceed the value of the trade.

From this time onwards, it sometimes becomes quite difficult to separate the villages of Garmouth and Kingston as far as the shipbuilding and timber industries are concerned, but in many other aspects of life they remained two separate settlements. In 1792 on average over two large ships each week sailed from the harbour there with cargoes of timber and salmon.

Salmon fishing provided a great part of the industry of Garmouth, and 'the young men about the toun of Garmach are disposed to a seafaring life, and become expert sailors. About 12 of the natives are at present (1793) the masters of vessels. The more wealthy people wear English clothes, in which almost all are dressed on holidays. Most of the smaller tenants keep as many sheep as supply clothing for their families, and almost all raise flax which they also manufacture into linen. Several families make a little both of woollen and linen cloth for sale. Sunderland coal, delivered from the ship at 2 shillings for a barrel of 13 stone, is mostly used about Garmach.'

The Parochial School for Speymouth was situated in the village, and the Garmouth Sabbath School opened its doors in 1822. The quest for knowledge, and the expansion of education, not just in Garmouth, but throughout most of the country, had led to a desire for easier access to books. The literacy of the population was increasing rapidly, and in 1823 a Subscription Library was opened, followed by the Mechanics Library in 1825 and the Sabbath School Library in 1827.

In the Great Flood, or the 'Muckle Spate' as it was known locally, both Garmouth and Kingston suffered severely:

Notwithstanding the breadth of the plain on the right bank of the river, great parts of the lands of Garmouth were under water by seven o'clock on the evening of the 3rd of August, yet none of the inhabitants had any dread of damage, far less of danger. . . . It would be quite hopeless to attempt to give any minute detail of the damage done at Garmouth. Eight dwelling houses and seven other buildings were utterly or nearly destroyed, and there was scarcely a house in the lower quarter of the village which was not injured, or a garden wall which was not swept away. Opposite to the saw-mill of Garmouth, where the width of the invasion was fully a mile, the flood rose 10 feet 2 inches above the ordinary level. . . . The kind and charitable exertions of the inhabitants of such parts of Garmouth as were safe, towards providing for the comforts of their less fortunate neighbours were most exemplary. A party of gentlemen from Gordon Castle were to have dined with Captain Fyfe, but the fall of the bridge of Spey prevented any of them from appearing. The gallant Captain did not lack guests, however, for he went about and indiscriminately invited the families and individuals who had been forced out of their homes, and who now depended for food and shelter on the hospitality of their neighbours, and had the satisfaction of presiding over a numerous and grateful company. As the losses in Garmouth fell chiefly on the wealthy, only eight cases of destitute families were produced here.

In an analysis of the men employed in maritime trades in Speymouth (Kingston and Garmouth) in 1841, probably the peak of the prosperity of the area, there were 6 shipbuilders, 64 shipwrights, 2 square-wrights, 23 sawyers, 7 millwrights, 2 boat-builders, 12 blacksmiths, 2 iron merchants, 4 rope and sail makers, 5 block-makers and 2 coopers. No fewer than 14 ships were launched at Speymouth during that year. In some of the census records it was noted that there were more men at sea than were at home on the day of the census. The *New Statistical Account* of 1843 gives a very in-depth analysis of the 204 vessels which had sailed from Speymouth during that year with cargoes of grain and timber, while there were 40 cargoes of coal, some 3,000 tons, arriving at the port. Twelve vessels actually belonged to the port, a total tonnage of 685 tons, manned by 55 seamen.

By 1850 Kingston, in addition to its shipbuilders and woodyards, was the base for the Spey pilots, and also for the tide-waiter, a kind of joint harbour-master and customs officer. The village also supported a corn agent, two coal merchants, three grocers and spirit dealers, four vintners or ale-house keepers, a baker, two shoemakers, a joiner, three blacksmiths, a carpenter, a rope and sail manufacturer, a turner and block-maker, an ironmonger, a fish-curer and cooper and a general merchant; and all of these only a mile or so from Garmouth, which offered even more services to the local inhabitants.

Garmouth village is now high and dry, the changing nature of the mouth of the River Spey leaving it almost a mile from the sea. Its picturesque, unplanned streets form a pleasant contrast to the nearby planned settlements of Cullen, Fochabers and Lossiemouth. The village of Kingston, according to McKean, 'is an odd place, crouching low against the sea like a whaling station. Two streets of heavy shouldered white cottages shelter beneath the bank of shingle'.

Shipbuilders

CHAPTER 12

PLANNED SETTLEMENTS: THE REPLACEMENT OF THE OLD VILLAGES

The two most prominent landowners in Moray, the Duke of Gordon and the Earl of Fife, together with some of the lesser landowners, got caught up in the eighteenth century fashion for building new villages for their tenants. This was not always done for altruistic reasons, for example the village of New Duffus was built to replace the old Kirktoun of Duffus, which lay around the old Kirk of St Peter. The Laird of Duffus decided that the old village was too untidy and smelly to be so close to Duffus House and that the village school, which was even closer, was too noisy, with all of its unruly boys. So in 1811 he decided to build a new village of New Duffus, about half a mile to the west, and to get rid once and for all of the old settlement.

The Duke of Gordon decided that the old village of Fochabers was too close to his recently rebuilt and remodelled Gordon Castle, and encroached on the area where he wished to extend his gardens. So in 1776 he issued an eviction notice to every tenant in the old town, and within a year or two the new village of Fochabers, with its central square and geometric layout, became home to his tenants.

Taking each new settlement in turn, there is a constant pattern of development across much of Moray, but there is little evidence that the idea of such planned settlements was ever taken up by the landowners of Nairnshire. The three new 'planned' coastal towns of Burghead, Hopeman and Lossiemouth have been covered in the previous chapter.

FOCHABERS

The old 'town' of Fochabers straddled the King's High Way to the south of Gordon Castle, on the main route between Banff and Cullen to the Ferry on the Spey at Boat of Bog. In 1720 the town had a population of around 600, and 'possessed a Grammar School and several good lodgings and inns'. There were also several good mills in the town. It was a focus of life for the lands of the Duke of Gordon, and the Regality Courts of Huntly were often actually held at Gordon Castle. Some 30 years later Fochabers had also acquired its own Court House.

Unlike many such settlements at this time, the town was fortunate that it had a doctor. Francis Gordon, Surgeon Apothecary in Fochabers, was writing 'sick notes' in 1734, when he witnessed an affadavit by Thomas McCulloch, the minister of Bellie, 'that John Gordon, elder of Leitchestoun, John Knight in Coldhouse, Gilbert Knight in Fochabers and also George Simpson and Alexander Brown there are all old and infirm persons and not able to travel the length of Edinburgh' – this was to excuse them from being witnesses at a case at the High Court there.

The town also had its less desirable characters. In the same year, a notorious lady in Fochabers becomes the subject of many pages of the Kirk Session's Minutes, which almost give her whole life story. Katherine Ross, 'a woman of infamous character and practice' was accused of cohabiting with Peter McKay who had recently died, and was now with child by John Grant, a merchant in Fochabers, or possibly by Thomas Dawson in the town of Fochabers, or possibly by some other man. The Kirk Session, as in many such serious cases, felt that this case was outwith their jurisdiction and referred the matter to the Presbytery of Strathbogie. The Presbytery came to the conclusion that 'Katherine Ross is a person of such infamous character that no credit is to be given to her accusation (that John Grant was the father). And in regard this affair has made much noise in the parish of Belly, they appoint this their sentence to be publickly intimat from the pulpit of Belly in hearing of the congregation for removing the scandal raised by this accusation against the said John Grant'. John Grant was off the hook, Thomas Dawson's innocence was not established, but the guilt of Katherine Ross was now decidedly public knowledge. She was banished not only from the parish of Bellie, but from the whole lands of the Presbytery of Strathbogie. It is interesting to contemplate where she went to, almost certainly penniless, after such a scandal.

The Rebellion of 1745 seem to have made little impact on the town, the troops passing through on their way to set up camp on the west side of the River Spey, crossing it at Cumberland's Ford a couple of miles downriver from the ferry crossing. There were, however, troops stationed in Fochabers, as in many other towns, for several years after the Rebellion.

Several of the houses at the east end of Old Fochabers had to be demolished in 1753, to make way for a new eastern avenue leading to the castle. The remainder of the old town of Fochabers was demolished in 1776, on the instructions of the Duke of Gordon, as he had decided that it was situated too near to the castle. A letter or eviction notice, the pro forma of which still exists in the Gordon Castle papers, was written to the tenant or feuar of every property in the old village, which read:

Fochabers, August 1776.

You are all to be paid . . . pounds Stg. in consideration of your disponing to the Duke of Gordon your present tenement ground in Fochabers and agreeing to remove to the New Town besides having right to the materials of your present houses and dykes.

(Signed) J Ross.

At this time a plan of the old village was constructed, showing the names of all of the tenementers in Fochabers, and the lands which they occupied. The tenementers of the old town were paid between £5 and £52 sterling for their agreement to move, and although a rather half-hearted petition against the move was organised by some of the tenementers, it seems to have been ignored by the Duke. The move was not instant, however, and it was not until a quarter of a century later that the last of the feus in the old town was finally surrendered. Some of the earliest applications for feus in the New Town were received from John Barclay, William Logie, James Hay, Alexander Umphray and Robert Anderson, all of whom had been quite prominent businessmen in the old town, and who had probably been encouraged by the Duke to set the trend for this move.

The New Town, to a design by the Edinburgh architect John Baxter, straddled the re-routed main road – the great road from London to Inverness via Aberdeen. The town was laid out as an east–west parallelogram on raised ground, with the Burn of Fochabers lying to the south, and the River Spey to the west. To the north the walled grounds of Gordon Castle were extended right down to the edge of the New Town. At the heart of the town was the Square, with the new Bellie Parish Church being completed some 20 years after the new town, at its southern side, and the Episcopal Church eventually being built at the north side of the square in 1834.

The remainder of the nineteenth century, and almost the entire twentieth century saw little change to Fochabers. New houses were built to replace some of the old cottages and the village expanded to become a home for the workers at the nearby Baxter's factory, and Christie's Garden Centre. The railway came

High Street, Fochabers, looking east

to the village, and then went again, as the branch line from the main Inverness to Aberdeen route did not prove to be very profitable.

ROTHES

By the middle of the seventeenth century the village of Rothes had become well-established along the Burnside, with the kirk and a number of cottages lying mainly along the north bank of the burn. Greens of Rothes lay to the north on the road to Dundurcas. The houses in the village at that time would mostly have been small two-roomed cottages with heather-thatched roofs, and workshops or other outbuildings would have been built in a similar fashion as they were needed by the tradesmen. In the seventeenth century the kirk on the Burnside, although stone-built, would similarly have had a roof of heather thatch. The graveyard around the kirk may have been enclosed by a low turf dyke, and would have been grazed by some of the village beasts to keep the grass short. The main 'road' along the valley of the River Spey crossed the Burn of Rothes at the eastern end of the village, before continuing north to the Glen of Rothes and to Elgin. It would at this time have been little more than an earth track, dry and dusty in the summer and wet and muddy in the winter. The path along the Burnside would have probably been even worse.

The year 1766 was to see the start of the building of the New Town of Rothes. It was one of many new 'planned villages' which were built at around this time, including Fochabers. The plans show that the village at that time extended both ways from the bridge over the burn, and also along what is now Green Street. The new town had stone-built cottages, many with slate roofs rather than the earlier thatch. The tenements each occupied a site of one eighth of an acre, at a rent of 10s 0d yearly, and were on a 38-year lease. Each tenementer also had between a half and two acres of land, without any fixed lease, at the cost of one guinea per acre. The streets were laid out on a more formal grid pattern, but they still had no hard surfaces, with the packed earth proving quite suitable for the relatively light carts of the time.

The people of Rothes had more to worry about than the usual cases of church discipline in the summer of 1829. The Great Flood of that year is ably documented by Sir Thomas Dick Lauder, who seems, within days of the event, to have visited many of the areas which were devastated by the flood. The following extracts from his book give a good idea of the events of that summer.

In the vicinity of Rothes the Spey Valley is about a mile wide, and the 'large and prosperous village' is built along the high ground on the western side of the valley. 'Two burns descend from glens opening directly on the village, cross it, and find their way to the river through the intervening plain, which was entirely occupied by the potato grounds and patches of corn tenanted by the villagers. The village consists of one long street, running NE and SW along the base of the hill, and another crossing it diagonally' [Burnside]. One of these burns ran alongside this street while the other passed at the north-east end of the main street. 'By five o'clock in the afternoon of the 3rd [of August] these rose tremendously, and that at the end of town swept away its bridge. The upper and under divisions of the cross street and the north eastern end of the main thoroughfare were instantly converted into rivers, the water bursting open the doors and rushing into the houses.'

'A large proportion of the inhabitants of these three streets were now in the utmost danger, and those who were themselves in safety flew to succour their friends and neighbours who were in peril. Then were the stout and active of both sexes seen wading in, at the risk of being carried away by the stream, and dragging the young, the aged and the infirm, some of whom had not for years been from under a roof, out of their windows or doors, as best they could . . . and carrying them through the deep and powerful currents.'

The streets were now raging torrents full of floating peats, firewood, poultry and pigs, and the young men of the village were occupied in dashing into the waters to 'haul out huge hogs by their hind legs', and whatever poultry and other items they were able to salvage. As darkness fell the flood levels gradually subsided a little, but this was only a temporary respite, and on the following day, 4 August, the flood rose again to a still greater height, and either partially destroyed or demolished 15 substantial houses which had been built as part of the new town not much more than half a century earlier. The dam for the Carding or Wool Mill at the Dounie Ha' burst during the flood, adding to the general scene of chaos.

The chaos wreaked on Rothes following this flood is unimaginable, and in the aftermath of the flood there were no fewer than 107 destitute families in the parish. The mud and gravel had filled many of the houses to a depth of 5 feet,

New Street in Rothes

The Sawmill at Rothes

and the whole village was actively engaged in the cleaning. The most lamented fact seems to have been the utter loss of all of the stocks of tea and sugar in the village. The only mention of the flood in the Kirk Session Minutes, however, is on 9 August, where it is noted that 'paid for cleaning the church after the flood 4/od'.

So what of Rothes 'after the flood'? Houses and cottages were rebuilt, and the bridges were replaced, but it was the distilleries that really brought business to the town. The Macallan distillery at Elchies, the Glen Grant in Rothes itself and the many nearby establishments all provided a source of employment to the town, and were to put Rothes on the map. The town has never really grown very much in size since the original concept of the planned settlement was first mooted. Many of the buildings along New Street are very typical of the nineteenth century, dominated now by the often quite smelly animal feed plant at the northern end of the main street.

ARCHIESTOWN

In earlier times most of the parish of Knockando had been occupied by small crofts, the two-roomed houses usually built of boulder and clay with roofs of heather thatch. They would almost invariably have been of the but-and-ben design, with one end of the house being occupied by the family and the other end, especially in the winter months, by the beasts. By the middle of the eighteenth century some of the more prosperous crofters may have been able to live in both rooms, with an outside byre being built for the beasts. Only the better-off tenant farmers were able to afford a two-storey house with four rooms, and the more prosperous among them even having slate roofs. There was, however, no real focus for the life of the parish until the village of

The Square in Archiestown

Archiestown was founded by Sir Archibald Grant of Monymusk in 1760, as a way of improving the bleak Moor of Ballintomb, and also of improving the life of the local population.

Archiestown is even now the only real village in the parish, and is typical of the planned villages of the period, with its principal street running through the square, and other lanes running off at right-angles. It was built at a similar date to the New Town of Rothes, and the local masons and thatchers must have had guaranteed employment for many years.

GRANTOWN ON SPEY

The town or village of Grantown was founded in 1766, by Sir James Grant of Grant, 'in the midst of an extensive uncultivated moor'. It was to become the centre of life in the parish, and replaced the old Grantown Village which had stood just a few hundred yards away outside the boundary of Castle Grant. Maybe like other landlords the laird felt that the ordinary people were living just that little bit too close for comfort. The market cross from the old village was moved to the new planned village on 13 June 1776, but was never mentioned again after that date.

Some 15 or 16 years later, in the *Old Statistical Account*, the minister noted that 'Grantown is a village erected under the influence of the Grant family, it being little more than 20 years since the place where it stands was a poor rugged piece of heath. It now contains some 300 to 400 inhabitants, some of whom are as good tradesmen as any in the kingdom. Shoemakers, taylors, weavers of wool, linen and stockings, blacksmiths, wrights, masons and 12 merchants keep regular shops in it.' He goes on to record that there were two established schools in the village of Grantown, one of the teachers receiving a salary of £30 stg with an excellent dwelling house at Sir James Grant's expense. This school was partly funded by the SSPCK. The other school, taught by a woman, was attended by 30 or 40 young people who were not only initiated by her in the first principles of letters but the young girls 'receive under her, a foundation of the various branches of female education'.

A brewery was established in the village right from the start, 'on purpose to keep the people from drinking spirituous liquors'. There were two bakers and a butcher in the town, and two or three public houses. The elegant town house was built above the prison where 'yet few have been confined within its walls'. 'Stone bridges have been erected over almost every rivulet, and of course the roads are in the highest order.' There were two taverns or public houses on the turnpike road, for the benefit of travellers, in addition to those in Grantown. Many of the turf houses had by now been replaced by ones built of stone, with slate roofs, especially in the villages.

By 1829 a branch of the National Bank of Scotland was established in Grantown, with the Caledonian Bank opening a branch some 10 years later. The two principal inns in the town in the 1830s were the Black Bull, under the ownership of James Grant, and the Grant Inn. A church was built in the town in 1835.

In April 1841 James Grant, the minister, wrote his submission to the *New Statistical Account*. He mentions that the sloping hills to the north of the River Spey are 'clothed with deep forests of pine, larch and oak' and that within the past 16 years 1,500 acres have been similarly planted on the south side of the river, 'and it was intended, by the noble and spirited proprietor . . . to plant every acre on which timber will grow and which cannot be added to the culti-vated part of the parish . . .' The great extent of the plantations, especially over the previous 26 years, added another 2,500 acres to the already established forests, which were great benefit to the trade in timber being floated down to Garmouth.

He goes on to comment that while the majority of the common people in the parish continued to speak Gaelic almost the entire population speak and understand the English language. In the lower part of the parish, bordering on to Inveravon and Knockando, the use of English was preferred as the inhabi-tants of these neighbouring parishes did not have the Gaelic. It was probably not a place to get rich, though; the wages of day-labourers were 1s 6d to 2s 0d per day, while carpenters could earn from 12s to 15s a week and masons from 15s to 18s a week. Men servants received £5 to £6 per half year, women servants £1 15s 0d to £2, and boys £2 to £2 10s for the same period.

He tells us that the recently formed Strathspey Farmer's Club 'consisting of gentlemen of the district', was given great credit for the improvements in agriculture throughout the parish. 'Farming is carried on in the parish on the most improved system. The rotations of cropping are the five and six years' shifts. Trenching and draining have been done to a great extent, on almost every farm in the parish. The duration of the leases is nineteen years. The farm buildings and many of the fences, paling and dry stone dykes are substantial.'

The appearance of the town of Grantown had undergone great changes in the 75 years or so since its original conception. Near the centre of the town was a spacious oblong square, 180 feet by 700 feet in length, which, of course, is still a feature of the town. The prison was still situated beneath the town house, but continued to be infrequently used. Four markets were held in Grantown during the year, besides a number of cattle trysts. By now there were six inns or public houses in the parish.

The Speyside Orphan Hospital was by now well-established, under the direction of the Earl of Seafield, Captain Gregory Grant of Burnside, Captain Grant, factor of Strathspey, and by the ministers of the parishes of Cromdale, Abernethy, Duthill, Inveravon and Knockando. The children from these parishes were eligible to apply for places at the Orphan Hospital. In 1841 there were about 30 children there, aged between seven and fourteen years. 'All the children are supplied with clothing, board and education. The boys attend during the day in the Grantown School, and the girls are taught by a matron in the house, who also superintends the establishment.'

'A remarkably neat and commodious schoolhouse, capable of containing 200 scholars, was built by the proprietor two or three years ago, on the north side of the town, at a very considerable expense.' The church could seat about 900 parishioners, and the town also now 'had several handsome shops' where considerable business was transacted. The minister estimated the population of the town of Grantown as about 1,000 people.

Main Street, Grantown on Spey, early twentieth century

By 1841 there was a Post Office in Grantown, 'through which there is a daily communication with Carr Bridge, Forres and Ballindalloch. The roads leading to these places are excellent and kept in thorough repair.' There were also regular weekly carriers from Grantown to Forres, Inverness and Aberdeen. There were at this time six endowed schools in the parish, the large number being necessary on account of the extent and population of the parish. Four of them were parochial schools, the other two being supported by the proprietor. One of these, the Grammar School, had an average of about 150 scholars during any given year, the master receiving a salary of £25 a year plus the school fees, which with that number of students must have provided a very good income. The other school was an infant school, with a female teacher who received a salary of £15 a year. There were also numerous Sabbath schools.

As with many of these planned villages, the basic concept is still very plain to see. The tourist boom of the nineteenth and early twentieth centuries gave rise to some new hotels, mainly at the southern end of the town, and modern housing has replaced some of the old cottages. The railways came to Grantown on Spey, adding greatly to its prominence as a Highland tourist centre, but as the motor car came to prominence the railway was closed in the mindless cuts of the 1960s. At least we still have the Strathspey Steam Railway from Aviemore to Boat of Garten, and plans are, seemingly, in hand to once more bring the sound and the smell of steam trains to Grantown on Spey.

BISHOPMILL

The lands of Frankoklaw, or Bishop's Mill, were supposedly granted to Richard, Bishop of Moray in 1187 by William the Lion. In the records of Bricius, who became Bishop of Moray just 16 years later, it is mentioned that there was a mill called Bischopsmyln. This would have been convenient, if not essential, to serve the bishop's residence and village at Spynie, and also the newly planned Cathedral and College of Elgin, and the River Lossie would have provided a convenient and constant source of power. In 1309 the mill was described as having two wheels and working as a meal and flour mill, and by this time there were a few houses established along the north bank of the river, primarily one supposes to house the millers and their workers.

In 1565 the settlement, in addition to the mill, was based around one small croft, rented at 25s money, 6 capons, 1 fowl, and 8s 8d of smart silver. There were also four small houses bringing in a rent of 12s and 12 capons for the four of them. The rental of the mill itself, with 'knaveship and outsucken' was set at

Slezer's View of Elgin from Bishopmill

£4, 12 capons and 1 pig, 'and the support of the mill'. The following year the croft is identified by names as 'The Acris', and the houses as 'The foure Cott Houses'.

In Slezer's *Prospect of the Town of Elgin* drawn in about the year 1679, the mills of Bishopmill are shown in the left foreground. A small mill, possibly a fulling mill, is also visible just below the main mill, but the whole complex seems to be situated further east than the later eighteenth and nineteenth century mills. Whether this was just artistic licence we will never know. A contemporary description of the mill notes that it was 'a very wretched looking

building . . . and its surroundings are of the most bare and barren description, not a tree or shrub being visible'. This is probably very descriptive of the flood plain of the River Lossie, the 'Borough Briggs' lands, at that time, with the river meandering its way through various muddy channels to the north of Elgin. In 1716 Alexander Black in Bishopmill, by all reports a very enthusiastic 'hunting and fishing man', built a Dye-House near to the fulling mill. He was also known to keep a boat on the Loch of Spynie so that he could enjoy his sporting activities there.

During the eighteenth century the Earl of Findlater improved a lot of the land on the ridge to the north of the village, and parts of the land were made into new 'improved' farms, while the remainder was allocated in lots to the people of Bishopmill village. The village itself at this time lay very close to the north bank of the river, and extended up the hill, but did not venture onto the ridge itself. The Earl of Findlater built a large granary 'of substantial masonry and well slated', almost in the centre of the village, which must have held, for its time, vast quantities of the grain being produced by his new farms. The stone for the building was reputed to have come from the old Castle of Asleisk, near Forres, which had been demolished on the instructions of the Earl's factor.

The Earl of Findlater's improvements benefited not only his agricultural lands but also of the living conditions of his tenants. By 1771 he was feuing out land along the slope of the north bank of the River Lossie for the building of houses. The old timber bridge across the River Lossie had become 'quite ruinous' by 1790. This may have been just a footbridge, as there was also an adjacent ford, but the Town Council of Elgin agreed to give two guineas for the building of a new bridge. This greatly improved communications not only between Elgin and Bishopmill, but also with the harbour at Lossiemouth.

Although Bishopmill was now expanding east and west along the bank of the river, the ridge above the village provided an ideal site for the Earl of Findlater to design another of his 'planned villages'. He proposed his new plan in 1795, and building work commenced the following year, the layout being clearly shown on Woods's Map of Elgin in 1822. The plan provided for a frontage of buildings facing southwards across the River Lossie towards Elgin, with a street running northwards from the bridge which was bisected by two streets running east to west. The layout of the original planned settlement is very easy to trace as you walk around Bishopmill. The majority of the buildings in this new town were stone-walled thatched cottages, with the exception of the houses which had been built by Provost Brown, by the Minister of Spynie Mr Alexander Brown, and the Miller's house, all of which had a slate roof. New meal and flour mills were also included in the plan, and were built during the last four years of the eighteenth century.

At the east end of Bishopmill was the small estate of Deanshaugh. In the late eighteenth century the proprietor John Ritchie, a merchant in Elgin, built a mill on the Lossie for the processing of tobacco, and also built a waulkmill, a flaxmill and erected bleaching machinery. By the second half of the nineteenth century, however, the only mill still in operation at Deanshaugh was the sawmill.

During the nineteenth century the new town of Bishopmill continued to expand. Johnston's Woollen Mill, a valuable source of employment, was opened at nearby Newmills in December 1800, and was expanded in 1836, and

Deanshaugh Sawmill on the River Lossie

by the end of the century it employed some 200 people from Bishopmill and Elgin. Other sources of employment for the people of Bishopmill were the two tanyards in Lossie Wynd, just across the river, a smithy in Bridge Street and there were also several bootmakers and tailors. A brick and tile works at Lochside, just north of the new town, supplied the increasing demand for pipes and drains as the agricultural improvers drained more of the low-lying land in the area. The expanding Burgh of Elgin also provided considerable employment opportunities for this new 'suburb' of Elgin.

A new stone bridge, of two arches, was finally completed over the River Lossie in 1814. Some seven years later the new turnpike road to Lossiemouth was built, which involved a deep cutting right through the heart of the old village of Bishopmill, as the climb from the river would otherwise have been too steep for horse-drawn vehicles. The High Street of Bishopmill, which had been severed by this new cutting, had to be connected by a bridge across the turnpike road, and so the 'Dry Brig' of Bishopmill came into being. It stood until about 1900, by which time it had become too narrow for the amount of traffic using the road to Lossiemouth, and it was subsequently demolished.

New houses were built along the line of the new turnpike road, which according to contemporary report 'greatly improved the appearance of the village'. One of these houses, known as 'The Ark', was down at the bottom of the hill and had an outside stair giving access to the attic. It was built over a mill lade into which, at this point, two other smaller mill lades converged, and the jumping of these mill lades, probably from the outside stair of the house, provided healthy, if not sometimes exciting exercise for the village 'loons'.

Disaster struck the old village of Bishopmill in 1829, in the form of the Great Moray Flood, so ably documented by Sir Thomas Dick Lauder. He comments that 'the bridge of Bishopmill, of two arches, was swept away. The flood was two feet four inches higher on the wall of the house beside the bridge than the record height in 1825. All the houses in the low line of Bishopmill running eastward by the base of the hill on the left bank were filled six or eight feet deep with water.' The new planned settlement, sensibly built on the top of the ridge, escaped any of this devastation. The bridge was replaced by a rather narrow cast-iron bridge on stone abutments, but by 1873 it was deemed too narrow and was replaced by the iron bridge still to be seen to the east of the modern road bridge.

In 1846 a set of handsome villas began to be erected on the brow of the hill overlooking the River Lossie, facing south towards Elgin. At about the same time the eastern end of the granary was possibly used as a schoolhouse, and at the same time there was also 'The Schoolie' in East Back Street, which was kept by two spinsters, Jane and Kirsty Eemins. Their cottage was a thatched butt-and-ben, with a bed closet in between. The school was in the 'ben' end, while from the 'but' end they carried out a business selling oatmeal in stones and half-stones to the 'wifies' of Bishopmill to make their porridge. The new school was built in 1857 and remains in use to this time.

The Morayshire Union Poorhouse, later to be known as 'Craigmoray', was built at the north end of Bishopmill in 1865, and was used for the poor of the parishes of Spynie and Elgin. The first governor was one Peter Grant, formerly Superintendent of the Elgin Burgh Police. It had accommodation for 150 inmates, but was not often more than half full. It was said to have separate drawing rooms for the men and the women, an excellent kitchen and large bedrooms, all enclosed with a good stone wall and approached through an iron gate at the Porter's Lodge. It was eventually demolished to make way for what is now Bishopmill House.

In 1866 Mr Brownlow North, living at 'The Knoll', one of the new villas

The Dry Brig at Bishopmill during demolition

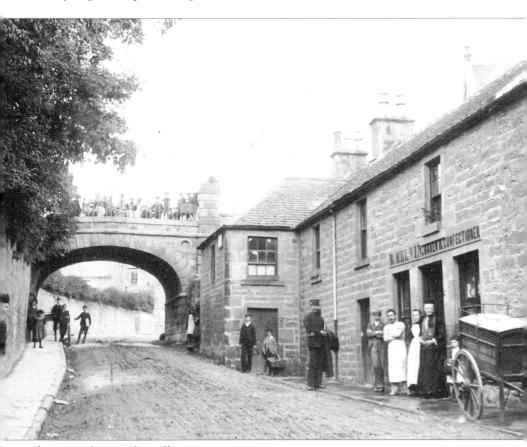

The Dry Bridge at Bishopmill

The Knoll, Bishopmill

Hythehill, Bishopmill

Bishopmill and the private suspension bridge

overlooking the River Lossie, was given permission to build his own personal bridge over the Lossie to give him direct access to Elgin. About three years later he purchased the Granary, which he converted into a mission hall or a church, later passing the ownership on to the trustees of the church. He also made various unsuccessful attempts to dam the River Lossie to provide an ornamental lake, but at every spate the river demolished it. The local newspaper later commented that 'Mr Brownlow North may have damned the loons who broke the windows of his granary, but he was never able to dam the Lossie, which at every spate knocked down the bulwark he erected.'

By the end of the nineteenth century the old thatched houses were fast disappearing, and Bishopmill had begun to merge imperceptibly into its neighbouring Burgh of Elgin.

The mills are now gone, subsumed into a do-it-yourself store, but the mansion houses on the ridge overlooking the River Lossie still remain. The extensive housing schemes built to accommodate the military personnel from Lossiemouth, and the council tenants from the expanding town of Elgin, occupy what was once the agricultural land to the north of the village, and modern housing has expanded westwards across the farm of Morriston towards the old Bow Brig and the 'new' Elgin Academy.

DUFFUS

The original village of Duffus was situated immediately to the north of Duffus House. St Peter's Kirk, which was physically, religiously and economically the focus of village and parish life, lay in the centre of the village. The medieval mercat cross is situated in the churchyard, which would, at that time, and probably continuing well into the eighteenth century, have been the venue for the village markets. The table stones marking the last resting places of many of the better-off parishioners made excellent stalls for the display of the wares. A Gothic porch was added by the rector Alexander Sutherland in 1524, and there is also a medieval vaulted ground floor to the tower at the west end of the church. The churchyard has some exceptional examples of early tombstones. A cobbled roadway, of which there is now no trace, was laid around the outer perimeter of the churchyard by Cromwell's soldiers, who were garrisoned at Duffus in the aftermath of the Civil War.

The houses surrounding the church in the sixteenth century would have been little more than single-storey stone and daub structures with thatched roofs. The interior was divided into two sections, often by a wattle barrier, with the family living in one section, and their animals in the other. The windows would have been small apertures closed by a wooden shutter. Chimneys at this time were almost non-existent, the smoke from the central fire escaping through a hole in the thatch. The hole was not, of course, centred exactly over the hearth, to prevent rain from putting out the fire. Each cottage would have had a small area of garden ground on which to grow vegetables, and to keep a pig, maybe a cow, and some chickens. Each cottager would have also held strips of land in the runrig system, on which to grow bere (an early type of barley), corn or oats.

The kirk, manse and schoolhouse were all in a very decrepit condition by late 1780. Mr Reid, the minister, was maybe a little more forthcoming than his predecessor about the need for action and wrote various letters, which are in the Gordon Castle Muniments, about the building of the new manse, schoolhouse and kirk. All the parties involved came to an agreement, and the new manse was built, much to the delight of the minister. The building of the school was not quite so urgent, and this was delayed for nearly 30 years, but it was going to be another 89 years before the new church was built at the west end of the village of New Duffus.

The proximity of the school and the old village was a constant irritation to the residents of Duffus House, and eventually, in 1811, the planned village of New Duffus was laid out. It consisted of two parallel streets of pleasant cottages running along the southern slope of the ridge, and in fact at the time of the 1811 census it was noted that there were 33 houses in the process of being built. The move from the old Kirktoun of Duffus, adjacent to St Peter's Kirk and Duffus House, was a gradual process over the following two or three years, but eventually all of the inhabitants were moved away from the vicinity of Duffus House, and the last vestiges of the old village were erased by the extension of the Duffus House gardens. Slightly grander houses were built lining the road to the church and to the estate of Gordonstoun, a typical example of which is Well House, which was built in 1815, only four years after the village itself was being laid out.

By 1821 there were 32 houses in New Duffus, and a further two houses were being built. These were occupied by some 47 families, 2 of which were employed in agriculture, 14 families in manufacture or handicrafts and the remainder in other classes of work. The total population of 180 people in New Duffus village consisted of 94 males and 86 females.

During the following 20 years there is little mention of the village of New Duffus, the inhabitants seemingly living sober and industrious lives, giving little trouble to either the landowner or to the Kirk Session. In 1842 Simpson describes the village of New Duffus as being of 'neat, regular and clean appearance', and at this time the village comprised 32 houses, but unlike many of the new settlements, it never seems to have expanded much further until recent times.

CHAPTER 13
AGRICULTURE
AND INDUSTRY

Moray and Nairn are noted for three main sources of economic wealth: fishing, farming and whisky. Much of the old fishing ways are lost for ever. The days when one could walk across Lossiemouth harbour from boat to boat are now long gone; the owners of the expensive-looking pleasure craft would probably take serious exception to the local 'loons' running back and forth across their polished decks in their muddy trainers! The old runrig style of farming lies even further in the past, but the ghosts of the ridges and furrows can still be seen in some places, especially when the low evening sun, with the amazing

Lossiemouth Harbour in 1960

clarity of light that this part of the country is so noted for, casts the shadows of this long-forgotten form of agriculture across the fields. Whisky production is now a highly commercialised occupation, the days of the whisky still up in the hills are not even in the memories of the older folk (or at least, they won't admit to it), and the export trade is vital to the economy of the area. So let us consider each of these once labour-intensive activities in turn.

FISHING

We will never know when the early peoples of Moray and Nairn first fished the waters of the Moray Firth, but the inshore waters, with their wealth of fish and shellfish, must have seemed a very attractive source of food to the people who lived along the coast. Even if they did not venture out to sea in their primitive vessels, the coastal marshlands and lochs would have provided a good source of food, and as they became more specialised, also a source of income.

With the expansion of the towns of Nairn, Forres and Elgin, the need for their harvest of the sea became greater, and the fishermen were able to develop new skills, and larger vessels, and by the fifteenth century the fishing harbours of the Moray Firth were becoming well established. Most of these harbours have been mentioned in an earlier chapter, and the methods of fishing probably varied little along the coast. Some fishermen worked at sea, still probably not venturing too far from the shore, but by now being able to take advantage of the wide range of fish which the Moray Firth had to offer. Others would have set up nets extending from the shore for a distance out to sea, and some would have fished the mouths of the rivers using nets and several other methods of catching their prey, including spears. Yet other fishers would have concentrated on the shellfish harvest, but to very few of these early fishermen would it have been a full-time living. They would have still needed their cottage garden, or even a couple of strips in the runrig, to be able to provide for their families.

By the late eighteenth century things were beginning to change for the fishing industry, and most of the fishermen were now working full time, and all year round. Although the inshore fisherman still owned their own boats, the larger vessels which were needed to go further afield, and even round to the west coast of Scotland, were usually financed by the local laird. These larger boats, with a crew of seven, were about 25 feet in length, still a small vessel when we consider the harsh conditions which would often occur in the Moray

Firth. In most cases, the fishermen were obliged to contract themselves to a boat for seven years, and there are several examples of the local laird forcing the crews to put to sea even when the weather was against them.

The fisher folk were usually a distinct community to the rest of the inhabitants of the coastal towns; Nairn had its Fishertown, and Lossiemouth had its Seatown. It was unusual for a fishing family to marry outside their own community, and a fisherman really needed a wife who could bait his lines and who knew the ways of the fishing. A young girl from a fisher family, though, would sometimes marry outside the community, especially when she had been away 'in service' and had seen the ways of the wider world.

Even into the late eighteenth century it is unlikely that many of the fishermen ventured far from the Moray Firth. True, the vessels had become larger and more seaworthy, but as the Stotfield Disaster of Christmas Day 1806, mentioned in an earlier chapter, shows us, they could still be overwhelmed by wind and sea. The early nineteenth century saw major changes: the expansion of the port of Wick meant that boats and their crews would travel north for the herring season, and it was not long before the harbours and villages along the southern shore of the Moray Firth saw the benefits of this, and a new style of fishing developed, with the fishermen putting to sea to catch the fish, and a new breed of merchants became established at almost every harbour, to handle the commercial side of the venture. By the 1840s and 1850s this had developed into a major industry for Moray and Nairn.

The 1860s saw great improvements in the boats, the open boats were gradually being replaced by half-decked or decked vessels, and the fishermen had the confidence now to venture further from their home ports, and to stay at sea for longer as they chased the shoals of herring. It was not only the fishermen who followed their catches down the east coast, from Orkney to Wick and all the way down to Yarmouth, but the fisher lassies, working in crews, would follow the boats down the coast. Gutters and packers worked on the open quayside until every fish had been prepared and packed into barrels to be sent off to the markets. It must have been a hellish job; one slip of the knife against the brine-soaked fish would have resulted in a cut which took for ever to heal. But it wasn't all bad; these lassies had got away from the restrictions of family life in the fishertowns, and were learning a new independence, and in general finding their feet in the big wide world. The coming of the new Zulu boats in the 1880s and 1890s gave the fishermen even more chance to fish for long spells, and further away from their home port, and the wealth created by the new and expanding industry created a property boom along the coast. The fishermen and their crews were becoming wealthy members of society,

Zulu fishing boats, from a painting by M.B. Fraser

having smart houses built in Nairn and Findhorn, in Burghead and Lossiemouth, and bringing a general air of prosperity to the coastal towns.

The development of the steam drifter in the early twentieth century brought even greater prosperity, but it was not to last. The events of the First World War, and the loss of the continental markets to the fishermen and merchants, resulted in a considerable loss of income and large numbers of unemployed fishermen. Although there was some revival both between the wars and after the Second World War, the developments in the boats and the handling of the catch meant that fewer people were now employed in what was becoming a very specialised industry.

FARMING AND RURAL LIFE

Farming in Moray and Nairn was dependent on several factors, the climate, the altitude of the farm and, above all, the initiative of the landowner. There is now almost no evidence of the primitive types of agriculture which pre-dated the runrig system, and so it is with this form of farming that we must start our journey.

Runrig farming was a means of providing a fair allocation of land among all of the tenants and subtenants of a fermtoun. Usually a fermtoun would be a community of maybe up to 25 cottages, and would come under the control of a principal tenant or tacksman, who held the lands under a 'tack' or lease from the landowner. This tacksman would then have his own sub-tenants, or cottars, in the other cottages, each of them having an allocation of land. Usually each family held three strips of land in the runrig, each strip being maybe 200 yards long and 40 feet in width, often in the form of an open 'S' shape. The cultivated land was the rig, and the ditch between each strip was the run, often just a strip of stagnant water full of weeds, but enough to mark each person's boundary. Generally each strip would be in a different part of the 'infield', as it was known, so that there could be no arguments about who had the best land. The cattle were put to the 'outfield' to graze, invariably tended by the children of the fermtoun. In the hillier areas, the 'outfield' tended to extend up the hill into the less productive lands.

Each cottage also had a garden in which vegetables could be grown to provide a handy source of food for the family, and where they could keep hens, a cow and perhaps even a pig.

This way of farming meant that the land could support a large number of families, with many hands being needed to work the rigs. Even when there were more sons than the runrig could support, it was often possible for the area under cultivation to be extended to accommodate their new families. Many of the landowners were quite happy with this way of life, as they received an income, sometimes in money but more often in victuals, which enabled them to keep a well-stocked granary even in times of hardship. It couldn't last, though, after many centuries of farming like this the land was becoming worn out, and it was difficult to support the increasing population.

By the middle of the eighteenth century some of the more enlightened farmers in the north-east were looking with envy on the 'agricultural improve-ments' which were taking place in the Lothians and other parts of the south. The new farmers there were building prosperous-looking farmhouses, new byres and stables, and were enclosing their land with hedges, fences or dykes, being better able to regulate the new 'fields' in this way. It was not long before the major landowners in the north, the Grants, the Duffs, the Brodies, Dunbars and Inneses were all starting to consider farming their land in this way. The fermtouns were soon to go, to be replaced by a nice slate-roofed farmhouse for the tenant farmer, with the 'offices', the byres, barns and stable blocks all built to the new design suggested by Sinclair. Cottages were built on the new farms for those workers who were still needed, although many fewer than with the

LEFT. The village cobbler

BELOW. Longhill Mill at Lhanbryde

old style of agriculture, and so the 'Lowland Clearances' had begun. Where did all of these displaced agricultural workers go? The countryside had little call for their skills now. The Industrial Revolution was also under way – workers were needed in the industries of Central Scotland and even further south – and the new lands of the Colonies, America, Australia and New Zealand proved to be a tempting destination for many of the younger families keen to start a new life.

So by the nineteenth century the landscape of Moray and Nairn would have been unrecognisable to the country people of just half a century earlier. Gone were the fermtouns and the runrigs, to be replaced with neat new farms, enclosed fields and some crops which would have been unheard of in previous

Alexander Simpson, blacksmith, Nairn

times. Even the less fertile land was being put to use: great plantations of forest were springing up on the hillsides as the need for timber increased, and on the poorer ground at higher levels the white woolly sheep, the new and more profitable breeds imported from the south, were replacing the black cattle and goats of former days. The rural crafts and industries, however, continued well into the twentieth century, the mills, the smithies and the village cobbler were all a constant reminder of a rapidly vanishing way of life.

Such a lot has been lost, the concept of a rural community in the fermtoun is long gone, mechanisation has reduced even further the need for farm workers, but if one looks at the old maps, or searches hard enough on the ground, there are still traces of this now almost forgotten way of life.

Horse and binder working near Nairn

Timber cart somewhere in Nairnshire

A typical croft at Birnie in the 1950s

WHISKY

Somewhere in the distant past of Scotland are the origins of *uisge beatha*, the 'water of life'. Some people say that it was brought to Scotland from Ireland, others that it was always a native drink. It certainly characterises Scotland, and has developed into a major part of the economy. The production of whisky was certainly well under way in Rothes by early 1734 at which time a Mr Waters is identified as the Gauger. Almost all of the other valleys also had many small stills, but the production of whisky on an industrial basis was still almost a century in the future. These numerous local stills were sometimes run as part of a farm, but were more often than not hidden away in the hills somewhere out of reach of the exciseman. We will never know where these early illicit stills were and, although there are many folk tales about them, none of the stories ever seem to reveal exactly where they were. Maybe a sensible precaution!

Although it had been made for centuries for local use, whisky did not become widely popular until the eighteenth century, and legislation and ever-increasing excise duties meant that producing it became in many cases an illegal activity. By the early nineteenth century it was noted that there were about 200 small stills in the Glenlivet area alone, and in many cases the making of whisky became the sole occupation of some of the crofters. Glenlivet was quickly becoming a whisky which found favour with the better-off all across Britain, and the product of these small stills was greatly sought after.

The farmers of lowland Moray and Nairn were only too pleased to have an outlet for their surplus barley, and these upland stills provided a ready market. The easy availability and seemingly endless supply of peat in the upland areas, and the problems encountered by those who were given the task of enforcing the law in these remote uplands, meant that distilling could be a very profitable business for producers and smugglers alike. The smugglers transported the finished product down to the lowlands by little known tracks, but often resorted to the use of force if they were discovered by the exciseman.

In 1822 the government increased the penalties on both illicit distillers and smugglers, and even at times employed the military in their quest to control the whisky trade. The following year, with the reduction of duties and fees for the legal distilleries, and the granting of a large number of licences, whisky production took on a new lease of life. Some of the more enterprising farmers decided to develop this side of their business, and distilleries, on a small scale, were springing up along the valleys of the Nairn, the Lossie and the Spey, and along many of their tributary streams. The Findhorn, by its very nature, did not prove to be such a useful river, but many of its tributaries were harnessed.

Near to Craigellachie, the Macallan Distillery came into production in 1824. Alexander Reid, a local farmer who was well known for his advanced methods of agriculture, took over the lease of a wooden building at Easter Elchies, and leased 8 acres of land from the Earl of Seafield to establish a distillery. He soon became known for the superior quality of his whisky.

In the same year John Cumming, a tenant farmer in Cardow or Cardhu in the parish of Knockando, who together with his wife had for several years been distilling illegally, took out a licence for a small still which was operated as part of the farm. It remained as a small-scale operation for many years, in 'buildings of the most straggling and primitive description', its further expansion being some 60 years in the future.

The 'Glenlivet' was originally produced by John Smith in Upper Drumin in 1824, and he encountered serious hostility from many of the small illicit stills which continued to operate in the area, but overcoming all of these problems he was able to build up a very substantial business, moving the distillery to its new site in 1858. Distilleries were springing up all across Moray and Nairn. Speyside was becoming renowned for its malt whiskies, and all across upland Banffshire, Moray and Nairn the characteristic silhouette of the distillery stood out against the sky.

In the middle of the nineteenth century the spirit merchants started to blend lowland grain whisky with the Highland single malts, and these carefully blended and aggressively marketed brands soon became very popular, and affordable to a much wider cross-section of the people. Despite a falling off of business at the end of the nineteenth century, and the serious decline in exports during the years of prohibition in America, the whisky industry has continued to be a force to be reckoned with in Scotland, and a valuable source of income to the Exchequer in London.

Brackla Distillery

CHAPTER 14
ROADS AND RAILWAYS

THE OLD ROADS OF MORAY AND NAIRN

The modern roads of Moray and Nairn, especially the main roads with their need for an almost direct route and gentle inclines, bear little relationship to the old roads which existed up to the late eighteenth century. Little more than dirt tracks, they were not roads as we would now understand the term, more a skein of tracks across the open moorland, or when they came closer to the inhabited areas they would wend their way around the 'infield' areas of the runrig lands. Dry and dusty in the summer, virtually impassable in the snows of winter, and axle deep in mud for the rest of the year, it was up to the traveller to find the best passage from place to place. Only the King's High Way was a well-defined route, and when it came into the towns of Nairn, Forres and Elgin it could maybe even loosely be classed as a road. All the other routes around the area were of such poor quality that often wheeled vehicles, where they existed, were replaced by sleds dragged along by oxen or a horse.

THE KING'S HIGH WAY

Before the coming of the A96 the one feature which linked the counties of Nairn and Moray for many centuries was the great King's High Way, the route from Inverness to Aberdeen and to Banff. It can only be conjectured as to when this route first came into use, but by the early medieval period it was certainly the main, in many cases the only main 'road' along the southern shore of the Moray Firth.

After leaving Inverness, the King's High Way wandered its way across the moorland to the north of the House of Culloden, through the old settlements of Croy and Cawdor, arriving in Nairn from the south-west where it arrived at its first major obstacle in the River Nairn. Another 'version' of the route almost certainly ran closer to the coast, passing the village of Campbeltown, now Arderseir, and crossing the Muir of Delnies before reaching Nairn from the west.

The River Nairn was originally crossed by a ford, although there was possibly also a footbridge. It was not until 1631 or 1632 that a stone bridge was erected across the river, but this and later bridges have suffered repeatedly at the hands of the frequent floods which swept down the river.

After leaving Auldearn there was not a lot of option for the traveller but to follow the High Way as it climbed gently to the Hardmuir, famed for Shakespeare's witches. A gradual descent then took the traveller down to the House of Brodie, a green oasis in the midst of the moorland, and then onward to the village of Dyke, well to the north of the present main road, before reaching the next and larger obstacle, the River Findhorn. This was crossed at Waterford, where before the building of the bridge at Mundole there was a ferry and an inn for travellers. Crossing the river the King's High Way approached Forres from the north-west, crossing the Burn of Altyre at the Lee Bridge and its ford before climbing the Kirk Vennel to the east of the church before turning eastwards along the High Street.

Forres was at this time typical of many of the smaller Scottish burghs. The

The Toll Cottage at the Findhorn Suspension Bridge

High Street ran through the centre of the town, widening at the tolbooth, and the North and South Back Streets enclosed the town outside the ends of the burgess plots. These were probably protected by a peat or mud wall, which also served in a small way to delineate the boundaries of the burgh.

At the Little Cross at the eastern end of Forres, the High Way turned north towards the port of Findhorn, passing the Abbey of Kinloss from where it swung south-eastwards to the Cairn of Kilbuyack and going to the south of the Crook of Alves. Keeping the Knock of Alves, that prominent hillock and home of the elves and the fairies to the west of Elgin, on its northern side, the road skirted the Mill Dam of Mosstowie, and continued along the edge of the Moss of Mosstowie past Scroggiemill, and reached the River Lossie at the Sheriffs Mill. The Lossie was forded at this point, but with the opening of the bridge at Oldmills in the seventeenth century most travellers were probably persuaded to make a short detour to the north to be able to cross the Lossie dry-shod and reach the west end of the Burgh of Elgin.

The traveller came into the town through the West Port, which was just south of the castle, and then entered the High Street, which widened at its eastern end to accommodate the church of St Giles and its churchyard, and also to provide a market area for the burgh. Being very careful to avoid the

The Toll Cottage at the east end of Forres

dung-heaps which lay at the entrance to each of the closes, and somehow managing to cross the 'common gutter', the open sewer which ran across the High Street to the River Lossie, he would have reached the market cross. This stood within the churchyard, and in addition to the church this area was also home to the town tolbooth, where the Burgh Council met and the taxes were collected, and also the jail. As our traveller had found in Forres, Elgin had no town walls, but protection was provided by the boundary walls at the foot of the riggs, these almost certainly substantial enough to ensure that the only way he could have got into or out of the town was through one of the four town 'Ports' or gates.

Leaving Elgin through the East Port, which was near to the entrance to the College of Elgin and the imposing cathedral to the north of the road, the High Road set its course across the Moss of Barmuckity. This dreary area of peat bog and moorland, originally known, perhaps appropriately, as 'Brownmouldy', the barren waste only broken by the occasional fermtoun with its runrig lands. Through the tiny settlement of Langbride the High Road wound its way past Loch Oire and crossed the Moor of Bauds before reaching the west bank of the River Spey. Some people may have decided, even before they had reached Langbride, to turn their footsteps to the south, towards Dundurcas, to cross the Spey at the Boat o' Brig, it being a somewhat easier route to Keith.

For most people, however, the prospect of a good hotel in Fochabers led them to the Ferry on the Spey at Boat of Bog, which was a long-established regular service, allowing them to cross, for a fee, day and night. The old town of Fochabers straggled along the King's High Way just to the south of Gordon Castle. It was here that the route divided, the coastal road going to Cullen and Banff along the northern flanks of the hills of the Enzie, and the inland road following the east bank of the Spey down to Mulben, or for the more adventurous traveller even passing over the bleak hills of the Dramlachs, not a good route to be on in the winter even to this day.

The whole route was maybe a day's travel on a good fast horse if the ferry crossings were favourable, or for most people some three days' walk, or more if the weather was bad. Such is progress.

THE MANNOCH ROAD

The Mannoch Road, which ran across the hills from Elgin to Knockando was, according to legend, the scene of a tragedy in January 1684. A young couple from Knockando, Sandy Brown and Mary Allen, both aged 20, and in fact both born on the same day, had planned their wedding for their twentieth birthdays. The day before the wedding the couple set off across the Mannoch to collect Mary's wedding gown from Elgin. By midday they had collected the dress, and after chatting to friends in Elgin made their way back through the Shougle and onto the Mannoch Road. They were halfway home when the storm broke; the grey skies suddenly turned black and within minutes the Mannoch moors were shivering beneath a blanket of snow. An icy wind whipped itself up to gale force, and the storm was recorded as the worst in living memory. The barren wasteland offered little shelter and exhausted they snuggled down in a little hollow between some boulders and waited for the storm to pass. It was Mary's father who found the frozen bodies, locked in each others arms, 5 miles from home. Their tombstone, in Knockando churchyard, was barely legible in 1880 and has now vanished.

It was during the first decades of the nineteenth century that the roads in the area were being improved, a process which continued from about 1800 to the late 1820s. Even at this time the Mannoch Road was still considered to be a main route south from Elgin to the River Spey at Knockando, and from Blacksboat the road continued southwards to Tomintoul and onwards to Edinburgh. Only the southward extension of the Rothes road was to lead to the eventual decline of the Mannoch Road, a route which had served travellers well for many centuries.

THE OLD SCOTS ROAD

The Old Scots Road ran from Pluscarden, to the west of Elgin, over the hill to Kellas at which point it was met by another road which branched off the Mannoch Road near to Shougle, in the parish of Birnie. The route of the Scots Road then ran around the northern slopes of Mill Buie, and across the pass between Mill Buie and Meikle Hill to the Oak Hill near the Cross of Knockando, and again ran on into Knockando itself. Another road from Kellas followed the valley of the River Lossie westwards to the ford at Kirktoun of Dallas, with a route then running north-westwards towards Rafford and Forres.

This road from Forres and Dallas was soon, however, to become the main route into Knockando from the north, the Old Scots Road gradually going out of use. In 1828 the road between Fort George and Castleton (Corgarff or Cock Bridge) was being redeveloped, and it is commented that 'If this line was extended the best way would be to take advantage of the turnpike road as far as Forres, and then by going through Rafford to the village of Dallas, which would be on the direct line to Castleton. I would humbly suggest that the road should branch off from Dallas to Burghead, or rather to the Newton Toll Bar on the right and to Forres on the left, were steam boats then established at Nairn and Burghead the communication with all of the northern counties would be complete.' A.J. Cumming of Altyre, writing on 19 December of that year, reinforces the case for the main route south to go through the village of Dallas, this being the shortest route between the Spey crossing near Knockando and the coast at Burghead, a distance of a mere 25 miles. Had these measures been adopted then both Rafford and Dallas would have been on the main route from Inverness and the north down to Edinburgh, a fact which would have dramatically altered the fortunes of both parishes.

THE LOAN ROAD

The Loan Road branched off the Scots Road above Coldburn near Dallas and crossed the river at the 'Highland Ford' near Aultahuish. A branch of this road ran north-west down the valley of the Lossie to Kirktoun of Dallas, while the main Loan Road continued westwards past Ballachraggan, Auchness and north of the Red Craigs where it passed to Dunphail in the parish of Edinkillie. The Loan Road was a cross-country route over the hills and moors, probably best known to those who, for their own purposes, did not want to be seen on the main highway. It was probably also used for the droving of beasts, whether legally or illegally, and seems to have avoided human habitation wherever possible.

After going through the relatively more populous areas of Edinkillie a similar, unnamed road vanishes into the upland areas of Nairnshire. Maybe this was a westward continuation of the Loan Road, making for the valley of the River Nairn. We will never know.

THE ROTHES ROAD

An important route southwards ran from the Cloddach ford near to the Kirk of Birnie, then to the south of the kirk to Castlehill, past Trochail and just east of Burnbank to Gedloch, where it then joined the road south through the Glen of Rothes, which some sources suggest may have been an old military road. On a map dated 1786 the route from Elgin, past Longmorn and Fogwatt to Rothes is identified as the 'New Road'. A road also ran from Cloddach to the west of Hillhead past the Mill of Birnie to join up with the Mannoch Road, the main route south at Easterton.

THE ROADS TO THE EAST

The building of the new turnpike roads in the parish of Bellie feature in the documentary sources of 1807 and 1808, with the improvements of the old King's High Way. The route over the Dramlachs had always been hazardous, and not always very well defined, so in 1807 the Trustees of the Keith Turnpike Road employed John Bruce to oversee the marking out of the best line for the improved road, at a fee of £10 5s 6d, and Peter Gamie and Robert Barclay were paid 1 guinea for planning the bridges on the route. They didn't hang about, and work on this road was completed by the following year. The pile-driving team spent 14 days working at the Dramlachs, for which they were paid £14 1s 6d. Alexander Milne built a toll house, with a toll gate, at the Fochabers end of the road at a cost of £25. Only a few of the farmers received any compensation for the loss of their crops or land while the road was being made.

THE ROADS IN THE WEST

There is little documentary evidence of the building of roads in the western part of Moray and in Nairnshire. The road from Nairn to Grantown on Spey is obviously a long-established route, and the road to Inverness along the valley of the River Nairn was also a possible early route of the King's High Way. The great mass of hills and moorland to the south and south-west of Nairn, and also the Dava Moor to the south of Forres meant that the only feasible routes southward from these towns were along the valleys of the River Nairn and Findhorn.

THE MILITARY ROADS

The only true military road in Moray and Nairn is the one between Grantown on Spey and Forres, over the Dava Moor. The network of military roads was built following the two Jacobite rebellions of 1715 and 1745 to connect the important garrison towns. The road between Blairgowrie and Fort George crossed the River Spey at the Old Spey Bridge at Grantown, and then continued north over the Dava, descending into the valley of the River Findhorn, and then onwards to Forres, Nairn and Fort George. An examination of the larger-scale Ordnance Survey maps will give a good idea of the route taken by this road.

THE COMING OF THE RAILWAYS

The railway age in Moray and Nairn has been well documented by authors who are much more knowledgeable on the subject. Most of these, however, have focused on the buildings and engineering structures, the locomotives and rolling stock, and other more practical aspects of the railways, rather than the social implications of this new form of transport.

Following the completion of the link between Aberdeen and Inverness in 1858, and the opening of the Highland Railway line to the south over the Dava in the 1860s, the lands of Moray and Nairn suddenly became much more accessible. The social isolation and independence which the 'Province of Moray' had enjoyed for many centuries was lost.

People were now able to travel in and out of the area with much more freedom; the mountains were no longer the obstacle which they had been in earlier times. Men were able to travel further afield to find work, and families were able to visit relatives who had gone to work elsewhere in the country. The daunting prospect of a sea journey to Leith or London was a thing of the past. For the merchants, it was now possible to bring in the latest products and fashions at a price which the ordinary person could begin to afford, and they were able to send their own goods to a much wider market.

The fish which were caught by the fleets from the fishing towns along the coast of the Moray Firth could be got to market in a day, rather than spending days in the hold of a coastal schooner, and the fisher lassies who followed the fishermen down to Yarmouth could travel in relative style.

Elgin became an important railway junction, with the lines branching off to Lossiemouth, Burghead and down the glen to Rothes. Forres, until the line over the Slochd was built, was the junction between the Inverness to Aberdeen line and the main route to the south over the Dava. The short-lived and totally unsuccessful Findhorn railway also met up with the main line here. Nairn had its booming tourist trade, the 'Brighton of the North' quickly developing into a major resort, so easy to reach by train, and other seaside towns such as

Lossiemouth were quick to reap the benefit during the Glasgow Trades Weeks.

The whisky distilleries were able to send their products south much more quickly and easily, and their profits increased considerably during the decades following the coming of the railways. Cattle and sheep no longer had to be driven along the drove roads to the great tryst at Falkirk; they were now able to reach the market at the weight they had been fattened up to, much more profitable to the farmers. These same farmers were also able to send their harvest to the markets where the price was best, and could import fertilisers much more cheaply. The salmon fishing flourished not only because of the wider market, but also the easier accessibility to the rich, who would take an estate or a beat on one of the rivers to come and fish the salmon much more frequently, and, knowing they could easily get back to Edinburgh, Glasgow or London should their business require their attention, they would stay for longer periods.

Coal no longer had to come in by sea, which led to a decline in some of the activity in the Moray coast ports, and timber could be more conveniently exported. It is true that some local industries suffered, especially the local

Traction engine waiting for business at Mosstowie Station

breweries, as the imports of beer from the central belt generated a new appetite among the drinkers of Moray and Nairn.

Yes, the railways were a benefit to this beautiful and independent part of the country, but there was also a downside. Moray and Nairn were now firmly fixed as just another part of Scotland, their individuality was diminishing year by year, the sense of local pride and independence was becoming engulfed in a general concept of being Scottish, but even to this day the way of life has a hold on local and incomer alike. How many men and women, and their families, have come to Kinloss or Lossiemouth with the Navy or the Royal Air Force, and have never left the area? I should know – I was one of them.

So we have looked for a 'Lost Moray and Nairn' – maybe found some of what still remains in this proud province, and in the process we have found out about a way of life that seemed once so strange to many of us. We still look up; admire the graceful buildings, the scenery and the hills, and even sometimes the clear blue sky. Feel the wind on our faces, smell the sea and the fields and the heather, and enjoy this beautiful land of Moray and Nairn.

BIBLIOGRAPHY
AND SOURCES

Anon., *A List of those concerned in The Rebellion of 1715* (Moray District Archives).

Anon., *A List of those concerned in The Rebellion of 1745* (Scottish Historical Society, Edinburgh).

Bain, G., *History of Nairnshire* (Nairn, 1893)

Committee for the Society for the Sons and Daughters of the Clergy, *The New Statistical Account* (1843).

Cramond, W., *Extracts from the Minutes of the Synod of Moray* (Elgin, 1906).

Cramond, W., *The Records of Elgin*, Vol. 1 (Aberdeen: New Spalding Club, 1908).

Cramond, W., *The Records of Elgin* Vol. 2 (Aberdeen: New Spalding Club, 1908).

Dunbar-Dunbar, E., *Documents Relating to the Province of Moray* (Edinburgh, 1895).

Dunbar-Dunbar, E., *Social Life in Former Days* (Edinburgh, 1865).

Goldie, F., *A Short History of the Episcopal Church in Scotland* (Edinburgh: St Andrew Press, 1976).

Graham, H.G., *Social Life in Scotland in the 18th Century* (London, 1909).

Innes, C., *Registrum Episcopatus Moraviensis* (Edinburgh, 1837).

Johnson, S., *Journey to the Hebrides* (London: Allan, 1825).

Keith, A., *The Parish of Drainie and Lossiemouth* (Lossiemouth, 1975)

Lauder, T.D. *An Account of the Great Floods of August 1829, in the Province of Moray* (Edinburgh, 1830).

Leslie, W., *Survey of the Province of Moray* (Elgin, 1793).

Leslie, W.A., *General View of the Agriculture of Moray and Nairn* (Elgin, 1838).

MacIntosh, H.B., *Elgin Past and Present* (Elgin, 1914).

MacIntosh, H.B., *Pilgrimages in Moray* (Elgin, 1924).

Matheson, D., *The Place Names of Elginshire* (Stirling, 1905).

McDonnell, F., *Sasines for Banff, Elgin etc.* (St Andrews, 1996).

McFarlane, W., *Geographical Atlas* Vol. 1 (originally 1720s; reprinted Edinburgh, 1906).

McKean. C., *The District of Moray, An Illustrated Architectural Guide* (Edinburgh, 1987).

Murray, J.G., *The Book of Burgie* (Edinburgh, 1930).

Omand, D. (ed.), *The Moray Book* (Edinburgh: Paul Harris, 1976).

Pocock, R., *Tours of Scotland* (Edinburgh, 1887).

Rampini, C., *History of Moray and Nairn* (Edinburgh, 1897).

Sellar, W.D.H., *Moray: Province and People* (Edinburgh: School of Scottish Studies, 1993).

Shaw, L. *The History of the Province of Moray* (3 volumes), ed. J.F.S. Gordon (Glasgow, 1882).

Simpson, E., *Discovering Moray, Banff and Nairn* (Edinburgh: J. Donald, 1992).

Sinclair, J. (ed.), *The Old Statistical Account* (1793).

Skelton, J., *Speybuilt: The Story of a Forgotten Industry* (1994).

Smout, T.C., *A Century of the Scottish People 1830–1950* (London, 1986).

Smout, T.C., *A History of the Scottish People 1560–1830* (London, 1960).

Thomson, D., *Nairn in Darkness and Light* (London, 1987).

Watson, J. & W., *Morayshire Described* (Elgin, 1868).

Newspapers and Magazines

*

The Aberdeen Journal
The Elgin Courant
The Northern Scot

Other Sources

*

Chartulary of Kinloss
Chartulary of Moray
NAS Exchequer Records, E326 series
NAS Gifts and Deposits GD331
NAS Gordon Castle Muniments GD44 various documents
NAS Other Gifts and Deposits GD series
NAS Records of Privy Council
NAS Seafield Muniments GD248 various documents

INDEX